Praise for
Alfred: The Quiet History of a World War II Infantryman

"Many warriors who saw the worst of World War II came home to resume a quiet, peaceful life. Alfred [Endres] was one of those who tried to leave the horrors behind, and as a result, left his family and friends with little knowledge of what he had seen and done. From occasional cracks in his armor, his daughter pieced together the amazing history of a common man who suffered, endured, and survived to say—in his own way—war is a terrible thing. Weeping in reverence and gratitude, you'll be touched by the simple statements of true heroism."

—**Col. Roger T. Aeschliman**, 35th Division (Retired)

"Interviews, massive amounts of research, and in-depth sleuthing give this book its authority. It interweaves the chronological history of Alfred's service with testimonies of others fighting alongside him. The book unfolds with a daughter's love for her father, her discovery of his hidden story, and the attempt to delicately draw it out before the opportunity has passed."

—**Kurt Meyer**, guest columnist for the *Wisconsin State Journal*

This meticulously researched and beautifully written account of Alfred's war is also the war of many others. Like him, quiet and selfless soldiers throughout time have been willing to sacrifice everything for what is right and good. A priceless reminder of what real patriotism looks like." —**Sara Rosenberry**, US Embassy in Luxembourg, Foreign Service (Retired)

"The book *Alfred* made me look at war differently. War is so often discussed in terms of conflict between armies of nameless soldiers from nameless families and towns. This book gave me insight into the life of a single soldier and a completely different perspective of war. I will read it again." —**Alex Ottmer** (age 13)

D1427766

"Alfred called up everything within himself to do and endure the job he was assigned, although the task went completely against his nature. There is no glorification of it. The voice is captivating and carries an essential story for us all. Alfred's character, paired with incredible research, makes this book. I could not put it down.

—**Ray Crary**, Vietnam-era Veteran

Alfred

The Quiet History of a
World War II Infantryman

Louise Endres Moore

Alfred

The Quiet History of a
World War II Infantryman

Louise Endres Moore

HenschelHAUS Publishing, Inc.
Milwaukee, Wisconsin

Published by HenschelHAUS Publishing, Inc.
Milwaukee, Wisconsin
www.henschelHAUSbooks.com

ISBN: 978159598-710-5
E-ISBN: 978159598-732-7
Audio ISBN: 978159598-733-4
LCCN: 2019931982
Publisher's Cataloging-In-Publication Data
(Prepared by The Donohue Group, Inc.)

Names: Moore, Louise Endres, author.
Title: Alfred : the quiet history of a World War II infantryman / Louise Endres Moore.
Description: Milwaukee, Wisconsin : HenschelHAUS Publishing, Inc., [2019] | Includes
bibliographical references and index.
Identifiers: ISBN 9781595987105 | ISBN 9781595987327 (ebook)
Subjects: LCSH: Endres, Alfred (Alfred Nicholaus), 1918-2007. | World War, 1939-1945--
Personal narratives, American. | United States--Armed Forces--Gunners--Biography. |
Farmers--Wisconsin--Biography. | LCGFT: Biographies. | Personal narratives.
Classification: LCC D811.E672 M66 2019 (print) | LCC D811.E672 (ebook) | DDC
940.548173--dc23

Cover photo: (most likely) Vosges Mountains of France, January 1945,
after Battle of the Bulge and after a stop for showers in Metz, France.

Cover design by Meg Moore, Kate Moore, and Jacob Burghart

Printed in the United States of America

DEDICATION

This collection of World War II experiences is dedicated most importantly to my father, Alfred N. Endres. I also dedicate it more generally to the soldiers of the 320th Regiment along with its sister regiments of the 134th and the 137th. These three regiments comprised the 35th Infantry Division, Kansas, Missouri, and Nebraska National Guard.

In particular I acknowledge the nameless machine gunners and riflemen who stood with my father as they protected each other. His heavy weapons company worked most closely with the riflemen, who suffered a casualty rate of almost 400% within this division. A 400% casualty rate means that each rifleman's position was filled an average of four times during ten months of combat because soldiers were killed, wounded, captured, or missing in action.

I respect all veterans who have been forced into a life experience they wish they could have avoided, one in which they personally had nothing to gain in terms of fulfillment or adventure, and one which may have become unrecognizable and unspeakable.

I thank you. I honor you.

~ Louise Endres Moore

War may sometimes be a necessary evil.
But no matter how necessary, it is always evil, never a good.
We will not learn how to live together in peace
by killing each other's children.

President Jimmy Carter
Accepting the Nobel Peace Prize
October 11, 2002

My sister Yvonne Endres Ziegler (1961-2013) included President Carter's quote in a scrapbook she created for our father. In her memory, I include this quote here.

World War II was the most destructive human endeavor in history. Battles were fought on every continent and involved more than 60 countries, affecting roughly three-quarters of the world's population. At least 57 million people were killed, more than half of them civilians.

—Mitchell G. Bard, Ph.D.

TABLE OF CONTENTS

Preface i

Soul of My Father, the Veteran.. vii

1. What We Knew 1
2. Life at the Nursing Home 5
3. Induction and Training 21
4. Normandy Campaign 39
5. Northern France Campaign 59
6. Rhineland Campaign, Part 1 81
7. Ardennes Campaign, Battle of the Bulge/Bastogne 109
8. Rhineland Campaign, Part 2 147
9. Central Europe Campaign 163
10. Waiting to Go Home 179
11. Back in the United States 193
12. Military Medals 207
13. French Legion of Honor Ceremony 221
14. After the Ceremony 231
15. A Discovery 239
16. Albert Simon's Bronze Arrowhead 247
17. A Replacement on D-Day+1 261
18. The Box Unlocked 279
19. There is Nothing Normal about War 293
20. "Some Can Take it and Some Can't." 297

Some World War II Stories 303

Friends and Family Remember Alfred 313

Alfred's General Tour of Duty 337

Some Memorial Sites for the 35th Infantry Division 343

Index of Names 347

Works Cited 351

Acknowledgments 357

About the Author 361

PREFACE

U nable to sleep, I had an epiphany at 2 a.m. after attending a University of Wisconsin—Milwaukee writers' conference, but the sudden insight was not what the organizers would wish. I decided I had to trust myself and just write, almost without regard for anything they had tried to teach me, because no one else can write this story about my father and his involvement in World War II.

At the editing session, I admitted I was clearly out of my element. Unlike the other attendees, I was operating from the opposite side of my brain. An accountant admitted the same, but he did not appear quite as pathetic as me, a math teacher. Have you ever considered the directions given for most math problems? Simplify. So when Kim asked us to look at a quick sample of our own writing and circle words that indicated the heart of our story, my pen was poised but did not move. I felt her eyes on me as my own gaze would stall on an immobile student being directed to make a simple start to solve a math problem. I stared at my page, not exactly certain where one finds the heart of a paragraph among so many prepositions. The group was gracious and supportive, but they did not fully understand. Directions in math never instruct the student to elaborate or embellish. We can occasionally extrapolate, but for math, we typically just simplify.

I had to write this book because average people cannot listen to me for any length of time before their eyes glaze over and they sneak away while mumbling something about a restroom. All this information could be lost if it is not recorded even though someone actually said to me, "It does not matter. Let it go." It matters to me and to my family.

I am writing this book for my daughters and all the grand-children and successors of Alfred N. Endres:

- Meg and Kate Moore
- Aila, Tina, and Nick Waldow
- Nick, Emily, and Matt Endres
- Michael and Tony Endres
- Cyndee, Amy, and Greg Gordon
- Crystal, Deanna, and Danita Ziegler

I want them to understand the reality of war and the background of the soft-spoken, amusing man who relished each one of them as unique individuals.

I already achieved a portion of my goal when my daughter Meg entered our house on a bitterly cold January day, stomped her feet, rubbed her hands, and gasped, "At least I do not have to sleep outside in the snow."

Every time I consider complaining about sub-zero tempera-tures, I remind myself of my father's experiences during the Battle of the Bulge, which was fought during the coldest Europe-an winter of the 20th century.

* * *

After Mom's death, a cemetery marker was designed, and symbols were chosen—praying hands for Mom and an American flag for Dad. My family did not anticipate Dad's reaction. He quietly said, "One is for praying and the other is for killing." He was speaking of his involvement in World War II.

Early in my discoveries I commented at a party about my father's discomfort with war, and the hostess quickly said, "I have a theory. Some can take it, and some can't." That comment struck me then and has driven me since to tell his story. Life is rarely divided into two distinct, mutually exclusive categories such as "taking it" or not. War, in particular, has infinite shades of valor and repulsiveness, and I knew my father's strengths.

This book was difficult for me to write, especially when I identified with my father's pain. It took effort for me to slip into that dreaded frame of mind. It was like diving into cold water; once I acclimated to it, I wanted to remain immersed rather than to be interrupted by so many other aspects of life.

My family was fortunate if good fortune can be measured by our mother's death and our father's broken hip. Without these two occurrences, Dad would most likely have taken the majority of his World War II experiences to his grave. While I studied the path of the 35th Division, we listened carefully to learn the stories of this gentle man we knew as our father, and my siblings relayed Dad's comments about war to me from their exchanges with him.

The eight siblings were Eileen Endres Waldow, Jerry Endres, Bob Endres, Virg Endres, Del Endres, Louise Endres Moore, Bev Endres Gordon, and Yvonne Endres Ziegler. We were raised with more love and support than money on a 110-acre dairy

Alfred

farm south of Lodi, Wisconsin, where our maternal grandmother contentedly lived within our noise for 13 years. When Dad considered the prospect of dairy farming with his four youngest children, all daughters, he sold his cows and chose to work for the Lodi Canning Company while he raised beef, sheep, and crops on the farm.

Mom was the CEO and the CFO of the family, and Dad never thought his kids could do much wrong although there were plenty of fiascos. Even when we did something "wrong," his reaction was minimal.

The phone rings. "Dad, Del is in the ditch. She just drove off the road looking at snow hanging in the trees."

"*Ach*," he said. He stood up from his chair and headed outside for a tractor. That was it, just another inconvenience in a household with eight children.

Ach. What does it mean?

Alana, a third-generation Endres/Kalscheur in California, suggested an online translation of ...Ah! Oh! Alas!

One of her aunts emailed, "Oh and alas are a bit mild."

A cousin suggested "*Ach*" is a bit like the Norwegian "*Uff da!*"

I gave choices:

> A.) For Pete's sake.
> B.) I don't believe it.
> C.) Nonsense!

A friend added another possibility of "That is just not right."

My sister Yvonne suggested, "I imagine Dad saying '*ach*' if he heard we were discussing the use of the word."

* * *

This project has flowed into two decades. I expected the book to be finished when my oldest daughter Meg graduated from high school. Four years later, my daughter Kate graduated. One of her friends commented on the piles of paper on the living room floor before I picked them up for the party. She said, "I don't even see those piles anymore." Another friend who Kate first met in high school added, "I have never seen this room any other way."

Within the length of time it took me to complete this book, I have lost people who supported my project and would have loved to have seen the final product. I regret the loss of so many veterans who contributed to it. However, I write not only for them but for any veteran in any combat situation, who was asked to give the most and potentially lose the most.

My brother Bob learned that a bartender at The Corner Bar in Dane, Wisconsin, served with the Marines in Vietnam. When Bob suggested a particular book to that bartender, he gently let Bob know he was not interested in that book or anything about Vietnam. The bartender served a few customers, returned to Bob and said, "All those guys who died over there … sometimes I think they were the lucky ones."

When the United States was considering entering a war, I stood in the stationery aisle at a Target store with a married couple. The husband enthusiastically supported the war. When I spoke about my father's pain, the husband reassured me, "They don't fight wars like that anymore." Later, an actual veteran disagreed, "Same thing. Different faces."

I intentionally wrote this book without many dates, opting instead to use the age of the veteran or the number of years elapsed since World War II. I wanted to emphasize the longevity of its impact and the toll that can stretch across generations.

I also want my father to be understood as a civilian, so stories from relatives and friends are compiled at the end of the book to describe him from different perspectives.

Dad spoke German as a child before he attended school, and he was never able to say "th" even though I once naively tried to teach him. I have tried to include his language in the manner he spoke. Those who knew him will hear his voice.

Some books are filled with words of bravado like "adventure," "heroics," and "exploits." This book does not include those words. It speaks of a well-humored, slightly quirky, soft-spoken, loving farmer who said of his war, "I tried not to remember."

I wanted to understand why.

ALFRED AND AUTHOR ABOUT 60 YEARS AFTER THE WAR.

Soul of My Father, the Veteran

By Louise Endres Moore

I learned about war from my father's barely audible words,
Clenched jaw, furrowed brow —
A faraway look in his grayed eyes.
He still buried buddies
Five or six decades after the war,
Hung on fences or torn asunder from worthless helmets.
"Dead bodies floating in the water," he recalled.

If God chose to save or chose to abandon,
One must ignore the clovers and bibles
Blown to bits, stained red in death.
Nothing remains sensible when
War becomes incomprehensible.

The naïve fantasize glory,
Confident of their bravery in daring exploits.
"Bring 'em on!" They all agree.
They have no idea.
"Valor of ignorance," Patton regarded it.

Flag-wavers cheer heroics, exploits, adventures,
And press fingers deep into their ears,
Refusing to listen and learn from those who endured the cost.
"Ach," this medaled octogenarian scoffed at heroism.
He knew one's best and worst compete in war.

I witnessed emotions bound by unyielding yokes,
Burdening those who struggle to survive survival.
War revisits in flashbacks, nightmares, and private hauntings.
Survivors are too easily tagged
Either as heroes or those who could not take it.
My greatest respect is for the quiet, soulful, humble warriors.
They "took it" while many did less...little...nothing.

ALFRED AND LOUISE CELEBRATING THEIR 40TH WEDDING ANNIVERSARY.

1. WHAT WE KNEW OF WAR FROM THE 57 YEARS THAT FOLLOWED IT

For Dad's 80th birthday party, I created a 23-question quiz about his life for his grandkids.

In the army Grandpa served as:
a.) barber b.) chauffeur c.) interpreter d.) all of them

I verified all of the answers with him, and I remember him being hesitant about the army question, but he confirmed the correct answer was d.) all of them.

There were so few war stories, and they were all joined by a commonality of what they were not—no stories of bravado or heroism or pride or even patriotism. Never once did Dad brag about, or even mention, being near General Patton or seeing General Eisenhower. His family just knew he did not like war.

One Sunday during the Vietnam War, the kitchen radio was on while Dad and I prepared beverages for visitors. I was not paying attention to the radio, but I clearly remember Dad responding to the newscast in his German accent that converted every "th" to "d" or "t." "I wish dose who got to decide would go fight dere own bitchin' wars."

When I was in my twenties, Mom once said, "War was hard on Dad," and then another time, "Dad came home a different man." Obviously, I never knew my father any other way, and even his siblings did not see him differently when he returned from war.

* * *

When Dad was almost 83, he rose from his recliner, stumbled, fell, and reassured everyone, "I'm fine," but he had suffered a small stroke. At the hospital Dad told his doctor, "Maybe I should start listening to you now."

Within two weeks, something was terribly wrong with Mom because her complexion had become consistently white as a sheet. In another two weeks, on Dad's 83rd birthday, he had carotid surgery for 99-percent blockage, and Mom received the diagnosis of multiple myeloma.

I spoke with her about six months later from the coveted chair next to her hospice bed, and I said, "How can I complain when I have had a mother 40 years longer than two of my friends?" And I reassured her, "We will take care of Dad."

On her final night, Mom said to Dad, "Kiss me good-bye." He left the room, returned, kissed her, and said, "Good night."

Dad became a widower about 57 years after he left for war.

Several weeks later, as I prepared to leave the farm for my class reunion, Dad sat at the kitchen table with a small, blue paperback book called *Story of the 320th Infantry*. We had found the book in his army trunk when family friend Matt Engels had come to the farm to offer condolences after Mom's death.

On that night of my reunion, Dad said to me, "Lots of guys wrote down da cities where we were, but I didn't. I never t'ought I would live t'rough it." I took notice when he mentioned the locations of Saint-Lô and Mortain. In the book, he pointed to a photo of soldiers along a small river and said, "Dat is at da Alb." I walked to our set of encyclopedias to find the Alb River as he continued talking, "Dere was a guy named Lane." I never found the Alb River in the encyclopedia...because the river is the Elbe.

I arrived late to my class reunion and told a classmate, "My dad had 40-some years to talk with me about the war, but he chose tonight." That night I had decided to be late in order to listen to Dad because he was talking more about the war than he ever had, and I knew that situation might not arise again.

After Mom's death, Dad and Bob lived at the farm and were forced to create a new domestic order. Bob told me of Dad's cooking, "We have been eating a lot of meat...all of it black." The meat was all burnt. When there was no milk in the house, Dad poured root beer on his cereal. He said, "Everybody makes fun of it, but it wasn't bad."

Bob casually heard about one of Dad's medical appointments when Dad was taught the proper amounts of food to eat in order to lose weight. After the instruction, he was asked, "Do you have any questions?"

He deadpanned his opinion about the portion size, "Should I eat dat before or after dinner?"

Then, within three months of Mom's death, Dad had another small stroke, and he had to be restrained in physical therapy at the hospital as he proudly tried to show the therapists he could still do push-ups from his toes at the age of 83.

Ironically, we were just "getting him back on his feet" after that second stroke, when he sat where there was no chair in the farm kitchen. The next day was the 60th anniversary of Pearl Harbor. My sister Yvonne had organized a rather ambitious tribute for World War II veterans at St. John's School in Waunakee, Wisconsin, where she taught preschool. All the details were in place and then, within 24 hours of the ceremony, Dad had fallen. Instead of attending the special ceremony, he lay in a hospital bed, awaiting surgery.

He said of his hip hitting the floor, "It sounded like a two-by -four breaking," but he pulled himself up on kitchen drawers, abandoned the idea of shrimp for dinner, and called his neighbors for help. His hip was seriously broken, and he was no stranger to broken bones.

I told a co-worker, "My father has had five broken legs."

She responded, "He must be a very unusual looking man."

ALFRED WITH HIS FIRST BROKEN LEG AND THE FARMERS WHO HARVESTED HIS GRAIN, 12 YEARS AFTER HIS RETURN FROM THE WAR. BACK: ADOLPH ENDRES, ANDY KURT, SYLVAN KURT, BOB KARLS, URBAN WERLA. FRONT: NORMAN SCHMIDT, CLARENCE WIPPERFURTH, BILL WIPPERFURTH, MATT BENZMILLER, ART SCHWARTZ, DAVID MILLER.

2. LIFE AT THE NURSING HOME

J ust a year earlier, both Mom and Dad had been independent and seemingly healthy. Suddenly, Dad had to spend Christmas in a nursing home without her, following a year that included Mom's cancer and death, his own carotid surgery, two small strokes, and a broken hip.

On Christmas morning, my brother Bob called me, excited with a discovery, "I just found ten names in the back of Dad's army book."

I was reluctant to even think about the list, but I realized it would not take much to jot down the names and their rather simple 1945 addresses. Finding one of Dad's buddies after 57 years would be a special gift for him on this thoroughly disrupted Christmas.

Those names were Louis Gogal, Ned D. Johnson Jr., Glen Anderson, W.C. Mitchell, John C. Honeycutt, Benj S. Lane, Fred Hager, Eugene Keller, Ronald Johns, and Johnnie Majerczyk.

The first name revealed no information from peoplefind.com. Upon entering the name Ned D. Johnson and Smithfield, North Carolina, I had a phone number. Rather impulsively, I dialed, explained my connection, and made the woman on the other end cry. She handed the phone to her daughter Sue, who most kindly reassured me, "My mother would have been crying anyway." Ned Johnson had just passed away in October.

Alfred

AUTOGRAPHS FROM FINAL PAGE OF ALFRED'S STORY OF THE 320TH INFANTRY.

Immediately I resolved to write letters after Christmas.

Of the remaining nine men on the list, only one address popped up as being the same as at the end of World War II. I sent a letter to him and also to anyone else I found with the same name and state as someone on the list.

Several days after my mailing, I answered the phone to hear a pleasant, strong voice. "Hello! This is Benjamin Lane calling from Pennsylvania!" My first reaction was similar to receiving a call from a telemarketer, but after a moment, I recognized the name from my recent list. Ben was enthusiastic. "I have been reminiscing about your father for the past couple days. I loved him like a brother. I was with him on Christmas Eve 1944..."

I knew the story.

We continued to chat about health, families, the lost years, and speaking German. Dad could speak German while Ben wanted to learn. Ben added, "I think your father and I got along well because we were both country boys."

Unfortunately, Dad suffered another mini-stroke, and his speech was a bit slurred for the phone conversation that I scheduled for the long-lost friends. Dad had health issues, and Ben had pulmonary fibrosis, but both households marked their calendars for the 35th Division reunion in Springfield, Illinois, hoping these two friends would be healthy enough to see each other in the fall. Dad pondered the last time he saw Ben, and we exchanged photos, wrote letters, and made phone calls, most of them between Ben and me.

After 100 days on the rehab wing, Dad and our family had to make a decision about his staying at the nursing home. He had broken his hip, but it was probably a couple of small strokes that severed the connection between his brain and his feet, because he was never able to walk independently again. I reassured him, "This is just month by month. We can change our minds at any time." But I did not expect anything to change. I told my siblings, "I'll do Saturdays," never expecting a man who was so difficult to restrain would survive five and a half years in a nursing home.

Occasionally on a Sunday, brothers Jerry and Bob picked up Dad and two of his friends, Billy and Leo, for a drive to Culver's Restaurant in Prairie du Sac for custard, that is, if Billy had his way. The stories and banter never stopped. Dad sat in the front seat and winked at Jerry behind the wheel. Then Dad fed comments to Leo that riled him up to the amusement of every-one. On one trip they saw Charlie, a good baseball player back in the day. Leo insisted on backing out of the Culver's drive-thru, so they could talk to Charlie before he got away on them. It was difficult to say "No" to such a group of guys, who all had a way of making people do things with their pure, unrelenting insist-ence.

If Dad ever complained about being in a nursing home, he never did to his kids. He looked like a ruddy old farmer in his recliner taking a respite from chores. One of his neighbors said, "Alfred, we have to get you out of here," but Dad could not walk or get himself to the restroom. His independent nature had taken a hit. Dad once told a family member, "One good t'ing about da war is it makes living in a nursing home seem easy."

Another time, a grandson overheard Dad say to a friend, "I expect to get out of da nursing home more dan I t'ought I would come home from da war."

He was supposed to call for assistance for transfers between his recliner and his wheelchair. When the staff complained that he was attempting to transfer by himself, I said to Dad, "So you have been naughty?"

Unconcerned, he answered, "Dey t'ink so."

He found humor by creating nicknames and clever experiments. He asked his granddaughter Kate to sit in a wheelchair in the hallway and pretend to sleep with her head down while wearing a shawl and a brimmed hat. He wanted to check whether the staff might transfer her to the dining room as if Kate were Annie, one of the residents.

My drive from Cedarburg, Wisconsin, north of Milwaukee, to Lodi was almost two hours. My typical visit was around four hours because I decided that transit time should be less than or equal to the time spent on location. I committed myself to reading about Dad's regiment in my copy of the *Story of the 320th Infantry* that my sister Del had made for each of her siblings. I knew if I did not research Dad's experiences during my time at the nursing home, I would never find the time because I was also working on my master's degree.

The 60-page *Story of the 320th Infantry* booklet was written in a style more familiar to military personnel than to a casual reader. I exclusively wanted to know my father's route and his involvement during the war, but the unfamiliar 134th and 137th regiments, along with the 35th Division, floated throughout the pages. I was confused and could not decipher what applied to him. I repeatedly thought, "Just tell me what my dad did!"

With an encyclopedia, I learned the basic structure and terminology of the army during World War II. Infantry divisions were comprised of regiments which were broken down into battalions made of companies, further broken into platoons that were divided into squads. Casualties include those killed, wounded, captured, or missing in action.

Eventually I learned Dad was in D Company of the 1st Battalion of the 320th Regiment of the 35th Division. To abbreviate these units for my father, I could write D/1/320/35th. Within this book, I most commonly include only two of the designations to identify the placement of a soldier.

During my visits, I told Dad I did not expect anything of him. When he rested, I read. He was far more impressed with my huge 13-by-19 inch *National Geographic Atlas of the World* than he was of my interest in the war. Sometimes, when I asked a question, he responded, "It's all in dat book," or "Read dat book," referring to the *Story of the 320th Infantry*.

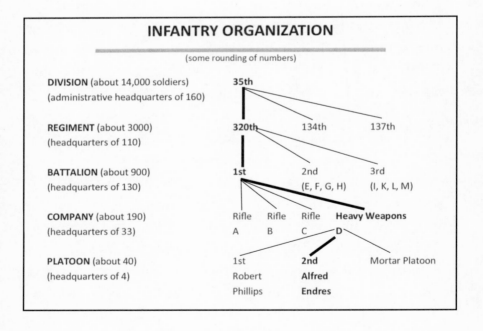

INFANTRY ORGANIZATION

(some rounding of numbers)

DIVISION (about 14,000 soldiers) (administrative headquarters of 160)	**35th**		
REGIMENT (about 3000) (headquarters of 110)	**320th**	134th	137th
BATTALION (about 900) (headquarters of 130)	**1st**	2nd (E, F, G, H)	3rd (I, K, L, M)
COMPANY (about 190) (headquarters of 33)	Rifle A	Rifle B	Rifle C	**Heavy Weapons** D
PLATOON (about 40) (headquarters of 4)	1st Robert Phillips	**2nd Alfred Endres**	Mortar Platoon

Once Dad awakened from a nap, looked at me seated in a chair near the foot of his bed, and sighed, "Do you have any ot'er questions?" He asked purely out of courtesy, and even though he appreciated my presence, I suspect he wished I was reading cartoons.

I circled the names of small French towns in my atlas and tried to make sense of the military descriptions. When I returned home, I looked up various locations and began to understand the scope of Dad's experiences. Within several months, I discovered that his Combat Infantry Badge, or CIB, made him eligible for a Bronze Star Medal for Meritorious Service. In 1947, a new policy had authorized awarding a Bronze Star Medal retroactively because a CIB was awarded only to soldiers who had borne extreme hardship during combat.

I said to Dad, "In my reading, I found that you qualified for a Bronze Star because of your Combat Infantry Badge."

Dad simply replied, "Ya, I heard about dat."

"Would it be okay if I checked into a Bronze Star for you?"

"Ya," he said.

Each week, I had a self-inflicted homework assignment to research, organize materials, or write letters. To apply for the Bronze Star, I contacted Dad's congressional representative, Tammy Baldwin of Madison, and the appropriate person for Ben Lane in Pennsylvania. After the letters were written and mailed, my brother Jerry called me with the fear that the medal could bring publicity, something Dad would never want, so I sent one more letter to be certain the delivery of the medal would be handled simply and privately.

Alfred

The Bronze Star arrived at the farm in July, and my brother Bob quickly took the medal to the nursing home, expecting Dad to have some feeling of accomplishment or satisfaction. Instead Dad did not look at the Bronze Star Medal or touch it. That evening he asked my sister Bev to take it home with her.

My sister Eileen called Dad and began the conversation, "I heard you received a Bronze Star. Congratulations."

He replied, "I really don't want to talk about dat stuff. Why should anybody get a medal for killing someone?"

The next day, one of Dad's childhood classmates visited him at the nursing home while my brother Jerry was also there. Discussion turned to the Bronze Star Medal, and Dad talked more freely than usual. His childhood friend congratulated him and asked, "Do you know what you got the medal for?"

Dad answered, "I suppose for shooting all dose guys in da snow banks."

His Bronze Star Medal was actually not awarded for a particular action, but it seemed Dad had thought about the medal during the night and concluded it was for the Battle of the Bulge. The enemy had hidden in the snowbanks when Dad, a machine gunner, was ordered to blast away at their defenses.

Later, when Dad was alone with Jerry, Dad said, "I've never talked about dat before."

Jerry asked, "Was everyone in the snowbanks German?"

More forcefully that his typical speech, Dad answered, "Nooo, we had to kill dem all."

In addition to the enemy, Dad knew he had killed Americans, who were being held by the Germans as prisoners of war in those snowbanks.

When I relayed Dad's memory on the phone to Robert Phillipps, another member of D Company of the 320th, Robert softly said, almost to himself, "Yes, that could have happened."

Following Dad's receipt of the Bronze Star, it became evident that he thought of the medal in terms of killing. Even I questioned whether the awarding of it had been a good idea. Finally we sent a note to him that all of us hoped he would accept:

> *Your Bronze Star Medal indicates to us that the United States Government recognizes you went through hell with strength and courage during World War II. We are proud of you because you returned from a war you hated, carried on with your life, gently raised eight children, and found humor and goodness in the world for us.*

I did not expect a response from Dad, and I did not get one, but he asked my sister Bev twice to read the note to him, and he kept it on the table next to his recliner.

* * *

Each week, volunteer Don May walked a couple of blocks to the nursing home. He moved with small, deliberate steps from his apartment on Hill Street, noting shadows, cautious of curbs, and acknowledging blurred faces. He said to me, "I know where every piece of furniture is, and I know all my pills even though I am almost totally blind. I line them up like soldiers."

Don May was almost blind in his left eye from glaucoma fogging his world. In addition, he said, "I have not seen anything with my right eye since World War II. A hand grenade blew up during replacement training for the possible invasion of Japan. They gave me a triple typhoid fever shot, and then I had a fever of 105.5 degrees and almost died. The drive to the hospital was so wild, it was worse than the shrapnel." A Purple Heart was never awarded to Don because the blindness occurred in training, during friendly fire, not during combat with the enemy.

When Don offered to volunteer at the nursing home, the activities director sent him to Dad's room. Dad preferred to stay in his room rather than go to activities because he felt bingo was a little boring, the rosary was repetitious, and he did not like cards because too many players could not remember trump.

The activities director said to Don, "You have the gift of gab. You're the type of person he needs. You'll get along great."

Yes, Don May had the gift of gab. He told me, "It can take me five minutes to say hello," and once when I called him on the phone, he said, "This is great. I just used the restroom, and I am good now for about three hours."

Don May stopped in Dad's room one Saturday while I sat with my oversized atlas. I said to Don, "We are fighting World War II."

Don began, "Alfred, I didn't know you were in World War II!" and the conversation continued. Don's animation was contagious as the veterans exchanged humorous anecdotes about George Patton. I enjoyed listening to them talk, and Don had the appropriate knowledge to engage Dad.

As I left Dad's room that day, he peered around the half-opened door and suggested, "Maybe dat guy could come again next week." I was delighted. Don was perfect. Knowledgeable. Supportive. Outgoing. Fun.

When I arrived the following week, Dad was quieter than usual. I assumed he was just tired, but when Don arrived at 2 o'clock, Dad was virtually silent. After a short time, Don excused himself and quietly said to me, "He does not want to talk."

I suspect Dad realized during that week that some memories were painful and dangerous. They had been safely stored away for 57 years, and in his opinion, they needed to stay under lock and key.

Similarly, Ben Lane had admitted to me that he had been interviewed by school children, and he barely got through the interviews without breaking down.

During the war, Don May was part of the Military Police, MP, "Mother's Pet," as some soldiers degraded those dressed in white helmets, belts, and leggings. Don said, "MPs got killed trying to break up fights in England, and the telegram would read, 'We regret to inform you that your son was killed in the line of duty.'"

In the months after D-Day, Don helped to transport wounded soldiers back to England from Utah and Omaha Beaches. These wounded soldiers included German prisoners of war, who wore all their medals. Don said, "Sometimes I held their hands as they died on the hospital ships." One American soldier had been castrated by shrapnel from a German weapon called a Bouncing Betty. He requested of Don, "Kill me because I am no longer a man." Don also described one "tough, crazy sergeant from the 101st Airborne Division." The sergeant took the pin out of a hand grenade and gave the grenade to Don, who further passed it to a naval officer, who threw it overboard where it exploded.

Alfred

Don said of his duties, "I was created to peel potatoes and clean garbage cans." He sang *Chattanooga Choo-Choo* with a blonde, bushy-haired Swede from Minnesota and prayed the rosary with Italians and a Polack from Chicago. With black soldiers, he sang songs by the Mills Brothers and the Ink Spots at a time when many white soldiers preferred complete racial segregation. That was how all units of the United States military were organized during World War II. To the dismay of white soldiers, most English women preferred black men because they were perceived as being less arrogant.

Military police contended with racial fights. Straight-edged razor blades were sewn into the brims of caps. The razors stuck out an eighth of an inch and were capable of cutting a jugular vein with one swipe. Again, Don May said the telegram would read, "We regret to inform you that your son died in the line of duty."

Don studied history, served in World War II, respected and listened to Dad, and drew stories from him even when Dad asked, "Why talk about it?" Don answered, "Your family and their children and their children should know."

Don May's favorite nursing home story involved a monthly Catholic Mass, hosted by a group of parishioners from St. Martin Church in Martinsville, Wisconsin. Dad was not particularly religious, but the Mass had connections to friends from his childhood.

As people gathered in the chapel area before the priest arrived for Mass, Dad motioned for Don May to join him and a couple of his friends. Then Dad directed Don, "Say somet'ing in German. I want dem to hear you."

"How are you, my friend?" Don said in German.

According to Don, Dad's friends "howled," slapped their hands on their thighs in amusement, and responded to Don's unusual accent with humor and a variety of comments.

"That is not German."

"Where did you get this guy?"

"The Germans would know you were a fake."

"Say something again!"

Don good-naturedly defended himself by saying, "I'm going to tell the priest," and "Go to confession." For Don, the banter was pure delight, his most favorite memory of all times at the nursing home, while the following recollection came in a close second.

One day Dad asked for help with a transfer from his wheelchair to his recliner. "Help me into da chair," Dad requested.

"They told me not to," Don said.

"We won't tell dem."

With Don's hands on the back of Dad's belt, ready for a good heave, they counted, "*Eins, zwei, drei....gehen sie!*" Don's hand slipped off the belt and he flew head-first into the back of the recliner, creating such a commotion with their laughter that a nurse entered the room asking, "What are you two doing? What did I tell you about this?"

Like a misbehaving boy, Don admitted to me, "We had a good time doing it."

At other times, they shared Limburger cheese, smelling up the room so badly a staff member asked, "What stinks in here?" She made them open the windows and turn on the fan in the middle of winter.

Alfred

Once when Don needed a restroom, he was reluctant to use the one in Dad's room, but Dad said, "Oh, go ahead. You can use it."

Don was basically blind, and therefore he did not see the alarm attached high on the door to alert the staff of Dad's potentially dangerous independence. Don turned the knob, pulled the door, and set off the alarm. He was convinced Dad was smiling…if only Don could have seen.

Another day as Don pushed Dad in his wheelchair down the hall to an activity, Don commented, "I feel just like Jimmy Stewart pushing General Omar Bradley." There was the usual pause, and then Dad said, "If it is all da same to you, I'd like to be Patton."

"Good choice!" Don replied.

Whenever Don left Dad's room, he would always say in German, "*Alles Gute,*" ("All the best") to which Dad replied, "*Du auch*" ("You too.").

Don admitted to me, "When your father died, I lost all interest in the nursing home."

Just as Don May was never awarded a Purple Heart, the maternal grandfather of my nephews Michael and Tony did not receive a Purple Heart for his injury either. A Jeep driver and a lieutenant were injured at the same time that George Torkelson flew off the back of a Jeep when it hit a mine. George's first memory of the incident was three days later in a hospital in France. At times during his six month recovery, he said, "I did not know whether I was coming or going because of the head injury and my battle fatigue."

He suffered total loss of hearing in his right ear and a significant loss in his left because of that accident. He was never awarded a Purple Heart because, according to the military, there was no evidence of injury.

On the other extreme, I learned from my reading, there was a "million-dollar" wound that allowed soldiers to get out of combat even though it did not disable or cripple them. One soldier was hit in the rump with a small piece of enemy shrapnel when Nature called and his pants were down. He was a lucky man, awarded a Purple Heart, and taken off the lines for a week or two.

Dad said, "Sometimes you would hear da call for da medic and den hear da shot." In such cases, a soldier could not take combat any longer and caused his own injury. There was no honor in a self-inflicted wound (SIW). Yet, Dad did not judge these soldiers, "Dat took guts too."

* * *

On most Mass days, one of Dad's friends, Melvin Ballweg, entered Dad's room to hear him say, "I bought da dinner tickets." After Mass, Melvin and his wife, Alice, would join Dad for lunch at the square table set for three near the kitchen door. Melvin said, "With all the talking, it took forever to eat, and your dad told stories I never grew tired of hearing." Sometimes the three of them spoke German, and no one could understand their conversations.

Prior to Mass one day, as Melvin helped Dad get out of his recliner, Dad fell slowly and softly to the floor. Water dripped onto his face from the straw in his tipped mug. The men missed Mass that day because so many papers had to be filled out for

Dad's fall. Upon entering the room the next month, Melvin held up his hands to stop Dad from moving. "Stay. Don't move. Wait for the nurse."

Dad was difficult to restrain.

Once as I walked toward Dad's room, a nurse commented, "Your father has been getting out of his chair on his own when he is supposed to call us."

"I will mention that to him," I said.

"You think that will make a difference?" the nurse asked.

"So you know the man."

"I like him," she said as she continued down the hall on her duties.

3. INDUCTION AND TRAINING

(March 6, 1942 to May 1944)

Very early on March 6, 1942, Mom, along with Dad's younger siblings, Edward and Celia, drove Dad to Portage, Wisconsin, so he could catch a bus destined for Fort Sheridan, Illinois. The bus stopped frequently along the way to pick up recruits who filled out paperwork before embarking. The existing recruits were supposed to stay on the bus, but some jumped off at each stop to buy alcohol. Neither Dad nor his friend Bonard Leatherberry had any interest in drinking, but Dad

ALFRED (R) WITH BONARD LEATHERBERRY. FORT LEWIS, WASHINGTON, TRAINING WITH THE 44TH INFANTRY DIVISION.

ALFRED (L) WITH BONARD LEATHERBERRY.

HERMAN SIMON WITH HIS FUTURE ENDRES BROTHERS-IN-LAW, EDWARD, ALFRED, AND ADOLPH, ON A HARLEY DAVIDSON MOTORCYCLE IN THE MID-1920S.

recalled a drunken recruit named Barnes wearing dirty, shabby boots. When they arrived at Fort Sheridan, Barnes greeted his future officers, "Here we are! What are you going to do with us?"

While I was doing my research, a museum curator emailed me, "This is your father's enlistment record from the National Archives. I like his civilian job." The curator was amused by Dad's supposed occupation as a MOTORCYCLIST.

With such an occupation, Dad probably had hoped for a more interesting military assignment, and his brother-in-law once owned a 1921 Model F Harley-Davidson. But instead of driving motorcycles in the army, Dad attended a Regimental Driving and Chauffeurs School. He drove Jeeps and half-ton trucks and acquired the nickname of "Cowboy." On one excursion, an officer called to Dad from the backseat of the Jeep, "You watch the front. I will watch the back. Go as fast as you can!"

Dad trained at Fort Lewis, Washington, until January 1943. Then his regiment was assigned to the Western Defense Command in San Fernando, California.

ALFRED WEARING A GAS MASK DURING TRAINING AT FORT LEWIS, WASHINGTON.

ALFRED TRAINING WITH 174TH INFANTRY REGIMENT OF THE 44TH INFANTRY DIVISION.

SISTER LUANA WITH HER BROTHER ALFRED IN MILWAUKEE, WISCONSIN, AT ST. JOSEPH CONVENT OF SCHOOL SISTERS OF ST. FRANCIS.

Alfred

His sibling Sr. Luana wrote a letter to him from Chicago where she taught. She had assigned her students to write letters to soldiers, and she saved her brother's name for her special student, Dolores Engels, who is mentioned in the following letter:

June 6, 1943

Well, out with it! I asked whether I might go home with you when you come home for a furlough. I'll send Reverend Mother's refusal, but please send it back. I might have to prove to dear ones at home that I asked. We can take it, can't we? As long as you come home safe and sound, I'd be glad to do anything. And please wear the St. Benedict medal. I am hoping and praying that I will get to see you. When Dolores Engels showed me your last letter, I said, "Do you know that soldier is my brother?" She smiled and said, "I thought so."

We had a mock air-raid two weeks ago. It was a disappointment. That sounds funny, doesn't it? What I really mean is that we expected a lot of airplanes and much noise. Instead the airplanes were very quiet and flew slowly, dropping papers of different colors. According to the color of the paper, the block captains were supposed to know what kind of bomb it signified and take precautions as if it were real.

There would not be anything I would appreciate more than a letter from you. Correcting tests is such a discouraging thing, you know.

Lovingly yours,

Sister Luana
St. Benedict Convent
3938 North Leavitt Street
Chicago, Illinois

A letter from Dad's mother and sister was also saved for decades in his army trunk:

June 30, 1943

We received your welcomed letter a few days ago. You sure get to see a lot of places.

Last Thursday and Friday we harvested our peas. They were so short of help at the viner and at the canning company, three soldiers from Truax Field were pitching in to help.

I got a letter from Joe Haack today. His family thinks he is somewhere in the South Pacific. It must be kinda awful not to know where a guy really is. You sure can be glad that you are still on this side of the water. It should not be long now anymore until you are home on furlough.

Love,
Celia

(part of a letter to Dad from his mother)

Last night the CYO baseball team had a dance at Springfield to raise money for balls and things, but they are not going to buy much with three dollars. A small crowd. Edward was there. Not Celia. She is going tomorrow night.

Alfred

Pa bought five cases of beer today. A truck from Madison comes around here in this neighborhood and sells beer much cheaper than if you get cases in their taverns. Edward said to Jim it ought to last til over hay season, which I hope they finish this week. My idea is it should last til over thrashing. Anyway I am not drinking any because I do not like it. I like root beer. See you soon.

Close with love, Mother

After repeated cancellations, Dad finally received a 15-day furlough on August 4, 1943, and returned home with the intention of marrying Louise Miller, his girlfriend of almost six years. Priests were not supposed to perform marriage ceremonies on short notice, but Father Waldkirch of St. Norbert Church in Roxbury, Wisconsin, said he knew the couple so well he could make an exception.

Dad's sister Celia felt sorry for Louise because Dad was spending way too much time with his two brothers rather than his girlfriend. He was probably maximizing his time with his brothers before leaving with his new bride. He finally proposed. Decades later, Celia said, "He never rushed into anything."

There were only three full days to plan for the Saturday, August 14 wedding. Mom's family butchered chickens and prepared for 75 guests at a reception on the Miller farm. The next day Grandma Miller cried from exhaustion. On Monday fifteen relatives saw the newlyweds depart from the Madison train station. Dad was due back in California on Thursday.

The new bride used one-cent stamps on her weekly post-cards addressed to "Mother, Dad, and all." Each postcard began

ALFRED AND LOUISE ON THEIR WEDDING DAY, AUGUST 14, 1943, ROXBURY, WISCONSIN, OUTSIDE ST. NORBERT CATHOLIC CHURCH.

THE NEWLYWEDS DEPART MONDAY, AUGUST 16, 1943, FROM TRAIN STATION IN MADISON, WISCONSIN, WITH LUGGAGE CONTAINING ALFRED'S WOOL UNIFORM IN WHICH HE WAS MARRIED AND EVERYTHING LOUISE NEEDED FOR AN UNDETERMINED AMOUNT OF TIME.

with a version of "This is just a line to let you know that we are fine and hope you are too," and each card closed with "Love, Louise" or "Love, Alfred and Louise." These postcards offer a glimpse into the life of a military wife:

> *Sept 17, 1943*
> *Inglewood, California*
>
> *I sure enjoy my work [in a furniture factory], and the days go by fast. Am far away from home, but it does not seem like that to me because I get your nice long letters.*
>
> *We are looking forward to being back with you after this war is over. The people around here think it will be over soon.*
>
> *Alfred still gives lots of haircuts. Good ones too. I saw some.*

In order for soldiers to get a pass to leave base, they needed haircuts. Twenty-five cents per cut. The selection process to become a barber was not elaborate. Captain Bushnell simply asked, "Is anyone a barber?"

Dad answered, "I've cut the tails and manes of horses."

"Good enough!" the captain responded.

> *Oct 1, 1943*
> *Inglewood, California*
>
> *I got a nickel an hour raise today, so now I will get nearly $30 a week. They do not take much out of the checks of soldiers' wives.*
>
> *+ + + + + + +*

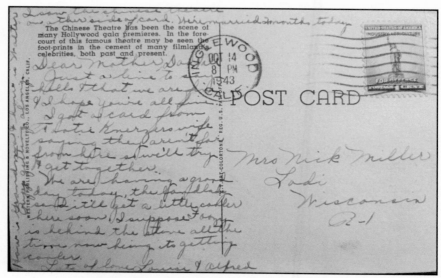

*A **typical** postcard Louise sent to "Mother, Dad, and all."*

Oct 30, 1943
Inglewood, California

Soldiers never know until the day before they move, so send all letters to Alfred's address because then we will be sure to get them.

Pvt. Alfred Endres
Co. H 174 Infantry
San Fernando, California

+ + + + + + +

Nov 4, 1943
Inglewood, California

Alfred was moved to Ojai this morning. That's about 100 miles from here. Several of the soldiers' wives are moving there tomorrow morning. I have a room for $4.50 a week. Am packing my clothes now.

Alfred

*Are we ever happy Alfred can come home every
night while we are at Ojai because the camp is
right in town, and he does not have to go back to
camp until morning. I left my job this noon, and I
hope to go back there again sometime.*

The soldiers and wives moved to Ojai, California, east of Santa Barbara. Mom spoke fondly of Mimi, who rented a boarding house to military wives at 204 Fox Avenue and treated everyone like family. Another landlady charged extra when husbands spent the night.

While in training, some soldiers made extra cash by taking part in boxing matches. Decades later at the nursing home, Dad gazed at a photo of a soldier with a boxing bag suspended from a tree and said, "He looked like Joe Louis. Shot off his mout' a bit but wasn't too dangerous. He seemed like he could have been da way he looked." Another soldier rented a car and raced it up and down a small street in Ojai.

*Dec 3, 1943
Ojai, California*

*We went to a show last night which was good.
The name of it was "Salute to the Marines." It
showed some marines training at San Diego, and
Alfred thinks Simon [her brother] will be at that
place.*

*We are looking forward to seeing Simon, and I am
sure he will like it in California.*

+ + + + + + +

Dec 11, 1943
Ojai, California

This is my lunch hour, and I like clerking very much. Did I tell you that it is a dry goods store? Can't you just see me using the cash register? It is fun. Am so glad I got a job here.

I do not think we'll see Simon until Xmas, but that's only 2 weeks. Alfred cannot get 24-hour passes very often.

+ + + + + + +

Dec 31, 1943
Ojai, California

Alfred's company had a parade yesterday, and we always go to see it. The girls come in the store and tell me when the parade is coming down the street. Then I dash out to see Alfred.

On February 14, 1944, the regiment moved to Medford, Oregon, and the list of military friends coalesced. Jim and Leona Duckett. Rollie and Alice Keegan. Frederick and Louise Irwin. Alfred and Louise Endres. Frank and Margaret Poelluci. Frank and Theresa Ruzek. Eddie and Sophia Grecsek. Jack and Marilyn Jeffalone. Three of these eight military buddies would not return from war. They would never see their first-born children, who became "war orphans" among approximately 183,000 during World War II. Within this group of friends, the rate for those killed in action was 15 times the overall rate for Americans soldiers.

* * *

Alfred

Decades later in the nursing home, Dad looked at photos of his friends from his military training days and sadly commented, "Dere were a lot of plans dat were never to be."

* * *

Sixty years after the war, one of those friends, Leona Duckett, wrote several letters to me about her memories as a military wife. Mom and Dad had spent St. Patrick's Day with the Ducketts at their "dingy apartment." Leona wrote, "It was an enjoyable time but rather sad knowing we all would be parting soon." The men talked about their training exercises, including a time when a dog "did its thing" on Jim's rifle while he stood at attention. When Jim "snapped to," the rifle was damp. He could not laugh then, but "they had plenty of laughs after."

Leona continued, "We had a wood stove that I had difficulty keeping lit. Your mom would come over, and we would chit-chat. Bless her. I had never ironed a shirt, let alone a military one. She showed me how to press the ridges, as I called them, on the back of the shirt."

Soon the Endreses, Ducketts, and Poellucis were sent to Camp Chaffee in Fort Smith, Arkansas. Mom kept her family informed with postcards.

March 29, 1944
Medford, Oregon

This is Wednesday morning, and we just got a telegram from the boys saying we should come to Fort Smith, Arkansas. We are leaving 7:15 tonite and will get there Saturday.

We will enjoy the trip. Alfred and the boys have a place for us to stay already, which is good, so we won't have to look.

Oregon had been fertile ground. Leona remembered that five out of eight of the wives were pregnant by the time they left that state, and she could prove it to me if only she could find the "snaps" or photos of her friends.

As the train passed through Ogden, Utah, on March 31, Mom wrote on a postcard "We are not allowed to take pictures from the train." On that same train *en route* to Arkansas, Leona joked that the mouse they saw was the same one that ran out from behind the stove in the apartment in Medford. The friends stopped in Kansas City where they were able to take baths by paying a quarter, placed into a slot. They finally arrived at Camp Chaffee, Fort Smith, Arkansas, around 6 p.m. on Palm Sunday, April 2, 1944, after several days on the train.

* * *

Sixty years after the war, another military friend Margaret Poelluci recalled shopping for a new hat in Arkansas while she faked a Southern accent to the amusement of her friends Leona and Louise. The price of that hat was well worth it because Dad still smiled as he looked at a photo 60 years later in the nursing home. He agreed with Frank, "It looked like a donut."

The Poellucis and Endreses shared an apartment and feasted on a huge Italian dinner after attending church services on Easter. At the age of 83, Margaret recalled the entire dinner menu: green beans, eggplant with tomato sauce and cheese, roasted chicken, macaroni with tomato sauce and meatballs, potatoes, carrots, and salad.

MARGARET POELLUCI, WEARING THE HAT THAT LOOKED LIKE A DONUT, WITH FRANK, EASTER SUNDAY 1944 AT FORT SMITH, ARKANSAS.

MARGARET POELLUCI AND LOUISE (R), FOUR MONTHS PREGNANT, EASTER SUNDAY 1944 AT FORT SMITH, ARKANSAS.

Margaret wrote with nostalgia, "I was not serving fast enough for my husband, so he said, 'Hurry up. What do I have a wife for?"

"To look at!" Margaret had retorted, and everyone burst out laughing.

Dad wondered who could eat all of the food, but by the end of the day, it was gone, along with dessert, fruit, and the hard-boiled Easter eggs they had colored the previous day.

Less than four weeks after their arrival in Arkansas, Mom wrote another postcard home, just prior to her and Leona following their husbands to the East Coast. Mom's note does not indicate any knowledge that Dad was being sent to Europe:

April 27, 1944
Little Rock, Arkansas

Much to our surprise, we are moving again, so use Alfred's address, and they will forward it. We will be there by the time you get this card.

I'll write a letter Saturday saying where we are. We will have a place to stay when we get there again, so that is grand. We will enjoy the trip, and I feel fine. This move sure surprised us, so I am busy packing and have not written anyone.

+ + + + + + +

April 29, 1944
Washington, D. C.

Excuse my writing as the train is going. We are on our way to Maryland. Alfred will be at Ft. Meade.

Leona's brother is a captain, and he's getting a place for us to live. He is stationed near Ft. Meade, so we did not wait like we did in Medford.

A postcard suggests Leona Duckett and Mom stayed at the Southern Hotel at Redwood and Light Streets in Baltimore, Maryland, after taking a train to Washington D.C. Union Station. Leona's brother, an army captain at the Pentagon, advised his sister to take a cab. If the two women had any trouble getting a ride, they should approach a police officer and "tell him you are pregnant." Leona was amused with her brother's advice because it was obvious Mom was expecting a child, but Leona was also pregnant, even though she had not yet shared the news with her family.

Alfred

Dear Louise —
    Remember the Southern Hotel? We have passed it several times downtown. Am spending a few days with my sister and family who moved from Mass. here. It is hot — Denny is teething and is a bit on the fretful side. You know how that goes. He sits very well on the trains tho, much to my surprise. What do you hear from Alfred? Hope he is on his way home! Will write later after I get settled back home. Love
                    Leona & Denny

POST CARD

Mrs. Alfred Endres
R-1
Lodi, Wisc.

LEONA'S POSTCARD TO LOUISE DATED JULY 10, 1945, AFTER THE WAR.

LEONA'S POSTCARD OF SOUTHERN
HOTEL AT REDWOOD AND LIGHT
STREETS IN BALTIMORE, MARYLAND.

According to Dad's discharge papers, he left for Europe May 21 while Frank Poelluci, who shared the Arkansas apartment, went overseas around Thanksgiving. It took Frank's ship around six weeks, until after the New Year, to get to its destination.

Margaret Poelluci, Leona Duckett, and Mom continued to communicate through Christmas cards and letters for the 57 years until Mom's death. Their life-long bond had been created during less than nine months of shared military life. Leona wrote to me, "Having all the other wives was a godsend for all of us."

Mom wrote to Dad every day during his eventual 17-month absence. She felt he could have written more frequently, but Dad told me he did not always have supplies or even a table to write on.

In addition to Dad's lack of writing supplies, Orval Faubus shared in his journal, *In This Faraway Land*, how he felt about writing home during the war, "Writing makes me think and remember which isn't so good now."

* * *

At the nursing home, I asked Dad, "Do you think Mom understood what you went through in war?"

"Ya," he answered.

"Did you tell her?"

"No."

Alfred

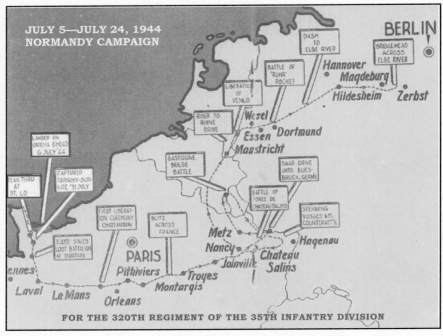

MAP FROM STORY OF 320TH INFANTRY:
OMAHA BEACH ARRIVAL AND SAINT-LÔ

4. NORMANDY CAMPAIGN FOR THE 35TH DIVISION

(July 5 to July 24, 1944)

W hen I first began my research, Dad told me at the nursing home, "I could take a machine gun apart and almost put it back toget'er wit' my eyes closed."

In the First World War, it was generally thought machine gunners were the first to be hit by enemy fire. Some gunners in World War II were told they had three to four minutes to live in combat. Another rumor was that the average life of a machine gunner in combat was 90 seconds.

A platoon sergeant called Dad's serial number and asked, "Are you a gunner?"

He answered, "No." He was 26 years old and wanted to return to his wife and unborn child.

The platoon sergeant said, "Hell you're not. I have your number here. Follow me."

The 35th Infantry Division landed on Omaha Beach about a month after D-Day. It relieved the 29th Infantry Division, and eventually those two units attacked side by side to take Saint-Lô, approximately 20 miles south of the beaches. Dad replaced one of the gunners out of a pair from the 29th Division. Those

gunners had assaulted the beaches and fought continuously for the previous five weeks.

Dad said of the soldier he replaced, "He was buggy...talking nuts."

Some soldiers, who had been under almost constant fire, were dazed with the "thousand-yard stare" of shell shock. Some became paralyzed with fear, babbled incoherently, or rebelled. Others appeared to have seizures. One could not remember how to feed himself. Some of the soldiers held in highest regard during training were the first to fall apart during actual combat.

According to Dad, the second of the two gunners was only half impaired, so Dad asked him, "How can you tell da difference between dere shells and ours?"

The experienced gunner imitated the clear whistle and crack of the superior German weapons, and then he added, "The ones that sound like they are pulling a trailer...those are ours."

* * *

Chester Goralewski (137/35th) wrote in *Santa Fe Express* (July/ August 2005), "We passed some GIs from the 29th Division, and I wish I could describe the look on their faces. I felt like crying as I wondered what they must have gone through during the last 33 days."

* * *

When Dad was in the nursing home, he once talked about preparing for combat. He was ordered to shave with cold water, and then with nicks on his face from shaving, he was further ordered to camouflage his face with dirt.

Almost oblivious to my presence, he softly asked, "How do you get ready for war?"

* * *

As I researched, I discovered the name of Robert E. Phillips (D/320th) among the autobiographies within the book *35th Infantry: Trail of the Santa Fe Division*. I asked a longtime member of the 35th for his address. I received two possibilities and sent a letter to both. I learned Robert had joined Dad's company on July 19, 1944, as a platoon leader for heavy machine guns. I was hoping Robert might remember my father, but he did not. However, by the time Robert passed away nine years later, I was referring to him as "my 94-year-old boyfriend."

Robert was so special to me because he was in the 1st Platoon, and he was confident Dad was in the 2nd Platoon. Robert was the closest to anyone I ever found to explain my

ROBERT PHILLIPS AND AUTHOR AT 35TH DIVISION REUNION IN ST. LOUIS, MISSOURI, ABOUT TWO MONTHS AFTER ALFRED'S DEATH AND 62 YEARS AFTER THEY RETURNED FROM WAR.

father's combat. He told me, "I went to about twenty of our reunions, and that is where I started talking about what happened in war." Robert had come to terms with the war, had knowledge of the war, and wanted to help me learn.

We talked on the phone over the years, but we did not meet until two months after Dad had passed away. My siblings Bob and Bev attended the 35th Division reunion with me in St. Louis. There Robert said of the photo I mailed to him, "I have been looking at the picture of your father so often, he is starting to look familiar."

Of the ten soldiers who signed the last page of Dad's *Story of the 320th Infantry*, Robert knew most of them, including one who told Irish jokes and imitated Hitler in a particularly hilarious way. There was also Ben Lane, who was a runner for Robert. Johnnie Majerczyk, also a runner, had worked "back in the yods" at a freight company in Chicago.

The heavy weapons company had more than the average number of Jeep drivers because they had to transport heavy machine guns, other weapons, and ammunition. Louis Gogal was Robert's Jeep driver. Ned D. Johnson Jr. and Ronald Johns were Jeep drivers. John C. Honeycutt, another Jeep driver, was a nice guy and was only able to sleep three hours, so he volunteered for guard duty. Before the war, he had sung and played guitar at the Grand Ol' Opry. During the war, he sang while Dad played harmonica and another soldier played spoons. Finally, there was W.C. Mitchell. We have a photo of Dad cutting Mitchell's hair while he faked danger and pain just for amusement.

MITCHELL FAKING PAIN FOR A PHOTOGRAPHER WITH ALFRED AS THE BARBER.

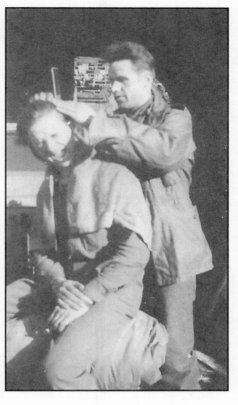

Robert came to the 35th Division as a replacement, a stranger to everyone. He believed, "Soldiers who trained together and fought together were better off." He had studied French in high school, but as he moved through France, absolutely no one could understand him speaking French with his southern accent. He recalled the curved window panes in Germany and how Germany was ahead of us in development while France lagged behind.

Referring to the enemy, Robert said, "They were told to be in the war. I was told to be in the war. I had nothing against the Germans. Mentally, you have to be taught to hate. Germans were more like us than anyone."

In Robert's later years, I gave his phone number to Pat Rowe Cook before she left on a trip to France. She had asked for a 320th Regiment contact within our email group. Later, Pat and I jokingly challenged each other to some sort of fight over our rights to Robert. The only decent thing for me to do was to share him because my father had returned from war whereas Pat's father, Carl E. Rowe, had not. By sheer coincidence, Robert was with her father on the day he received the injuries that eventually took his life. For Pat, Robert was a very important connection to the father she had lost. Within a day of Robert's death, both Pat and I received a box of Mrs. See's Chocolates that he had pre-ordered for those on his Christmas list.

* * *

It was typical for soldiers to carry a blanket, a mess kit, water canteen, cartridge belt, and a canvas shelter half, tied with a rope. Some mentioned carrying a raincoat on the back of their belt, along with their shovel on the side. Most soldiers had discarded their gas masks upon their arrival in France.

The shovel was a high priority item, as important as a weapon, because infantrymen continually dug foxholes as they advanced. Combat Medic Michael Linquata (134/35th) shared on the 134th website, "We almost never had the luxury of using the same foxhole more than a day. Sometimes we thought we were going to hold a position. Then we'd start a foxhole, have it partially done, and have to leave it for another position."

A typical foxhole for two men was about four feet deep, three feet wide, and five feet long. Dad joked of his towering friend, "We would not have to dig such deep foxholes, but Stud was so tall!" At night, one man guarded while the other tried to sleep.

Dad once described, "We were trying to take ground, and dere was shooting in all directions. I jumped into da foxhole, and dere was a rat, snarling at me. I jumped back out." He laughed at himself, "I could have shot it. I had a gun."

Speaking of foxholes, Robert explained, "If you could find a barn … that was heaven, so much better than the ground. Barns were first-class."

Hot meals were rare or non-existent on the front lines. Soldiers routinely raided abandoned farmhouses for food, or they killed chickens. Robert recalled, "Once we found big wooden barrels with eggs in brine in a basement. There were fields of onions in France. Onions everywhere." However, those fields and gardens could be booby-trapped with explosives.

There were different kinds of military food provided on the battlefield. C-Rations were sometimes described as dog food in two small cans, wet and precooked. If the paper labels had fallen off, the soldiers hoped the can was not one of the unpopular entrees of meat hash, mutton stew, or ham and lima beans. The cans were heavy, difficult to carry, and their contents were mushy. Along with cigarettes and other items, C-Rations included several sheets of brown toilet paper.

K-Rations were supplied more frequently. A K-Ration was still referred to as dog food, but it was in a watertight box like *Cracker Jacks* and easier to carry in a large pocket. The waxed cartons could help start a small fire if the fire did not attract the attention of the enemy. These cartons included small cans, about the size of cat food, which could be punched to let the grease drip out of an entrée like fatty pork loaf. K-Rations offered options for breakfast as well as other meals, possibly ground-up ham, powdered eggs, biscuits, cheese…along with cigarettes and sheets of brown toilet paper. Sometimes an entrée was missing because the box had been intentionally slit open. Even worse for the many smokers, cigarettes could be missing.

Occasionally in bombed-out houses, soldiers discovered Calvados or "White Lightning," an apple brandy made by the French farmers. Don May told me, "Everyone has their own hooch." Some soldiers mumbled that Calvados was clear water. They knocked it back and passed out cold. Robert laughed, "Calvados kept me from becoming an alcoholic. I got so sick." Keith Bullock (137/35th) described it as "pure rocket fuel." Calvados was triple distilled from hard apple cider and named for this region in France.

* * *

Several times during Dad's nursing home days, he spoke of a soldier hand-pumping a four-wheeled trolley filled with bottles of wine down a railroad track. American troops called out that Germans were in the area, and he should get out of sight. The over-confident soldier, who obviously had sampled the spirits, shouted back, "They can't shoot!"

Another soldier muttered, "It would be a waste of a bullet."

Speaking of the variety of people among the 16 million men and women who served in the United States military during World War II, Don May told me, "There is every kind of person in the military," while Dad said, "Dere were some real dandies."

Dad recalled how soldiers, with guns loaded, waited for a full group inspection. One of the soldiers shot a duck out of the air as it flew over the troops. The officer shouted, "Who shot?" and repeated the question a couple more times before the culprit grunted, "*Hunh.*"

The officer said, "Don't *hunh* me. I can make you a general, or I can send you home."

The soldier replied, "Either one sounds good to me."

* * *

Dad's heavy machine gun was a water-cooled, recoil-operated, belt-fed .30-caliber Browning M1917. It was left over from the First World War. In his book, *Biography of a Battalion*, James Huston (134/35th) wrote, "Its fire is automatic; that is, it fires continuously as long as the trigger is held back." It weighed 40.75 pounds with seven pints of water surrounding its barrel to prevent it from overheating. The tripod weighed another 51 pounds, but eventually innovative soldiers welded the lighter bipod of a small Browning automatic rifle to the water-cooled machine gun. That eliminated the need for the heavy tripod while still allowing the gun to rest on the ground, on a limb, or on a tree trunk.

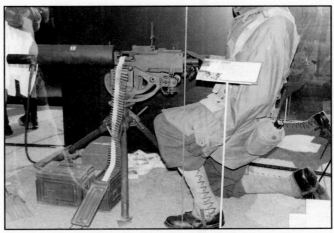

WATER-COOLED .30-CALIBER MACHINE GUN DISPLAYED IN A MUSEUM IN BASTOGNE, BELGIUM.

Alfred

A machine gun squad included six to eight soldiers. Robert explained, "One man fired the machine gun while another fed a belt of 250 bullets into the gun. The other men were ammunition carriers and hauled two large metal containers filled with .30-caliber ammunition, 250 rounds in one hand and 250 in the other. Their only protection was a pistol, and they sort of stuck out." He added, "A machine gun is fired to hit several people, not just one."

* * *

Dad was one of a pair of machine gunners who cross-fired at night. Every fifth round was a red tracer that looked like a ball of fire and allowed the gunner to know whether he was on target or not. The gunners fired over crawling riflemen as they attempted to advance. At a designated time, the gunners stopped firing, and the riflemen stood, ran, and attacked the enemy. In the morning light, the number of American bodies lying on the field indicated the relative success of the advance.

My brother Jerry asked Dad, "Did you shoot three feet over the heads of the riflemen?"

Dad answered, "Not dat high."

I asked Dad, "Do you remember any of the machine gunners?"

"No."

"Did any of them get hurt?"

Dad said, "Dey were always looking for gunners."

Civilians frequently hear of the bond formed among soldiers in combat; however, that bond only exists for those who expect the others to survive. Gunners frequently became casualties.

Robert taught me, "Each battalion commander had his own way to use machine guns, either behind the riflemen or embedded within them." He estimated a 60-40 split in favor of embedding the gunners. The disadvantage was that the gunners could become pinned down on the ground with the riflemen for hours. Then it was difficult for anyone to get out of the predicament because the gunners could not shoot properly on their stomachs nor could they stand up to set up their guns. Thus, no one advanced.

Out of approximately 14,000 soldiers in a division, about 3,000 were riflemen with no one between them and the enemy. Both Dad and Robert said the riflemen were in the worst position, but the machine gunners were frequently with them or immediately behind them, within the range of the enemy's rifle. The heavy weapons and the rifle companies took the vast majority of fatalities, and Robert said more than once, "There are men in the 35th Division who do not know what war is." Those soldiers were too far back from the front lines to experience the reality of combat.

Robert told me his nerves were shot for two to three years after the war. He said, "I had enough of someone trying to kill me 24 hours a day."

I said to him, "I read that combat shows in a person after about two weeks."

He laughed, "One day!"

Robert described to me, "Our machine guns fired about 550 rounds per minute and drew attention with their smoke. German guns fired double our rate at 1,100 rounds per minute. They were smokeless and more difficult to detect." He added, "With our equipment, I am surprised we won the war. The Germans had been fighting for years before us, so their equipment was better."

About three-quarters of a mile behind the machine guns were the mortars that could hit a target about a mile away. Behind them, artillery shells had a range of four or more miles. Robert never met the soldiers who fired mortars and artillery except during reorganization. He said of the mortar section, "They were out of the range of enemy rifles, but not home free. However I would have been tickled to death to have been a mile away."

Robert never saw a company commander on the front lines. The previous lieutenant to Robert would say to his platoon, "I need to go back to direct the artillery." When Robert took over, a couple of guys in the platoon warned him, "If we see you going back, we are going to follow." Therefore, Robert never checked on mortars or artillery. He joked about the false support of having someone's back, "Ya, I have your back, and I will stand behind you until they beat you black and blue in the face."

* * *

Saint-Lô was a major communication center for the Germans and an important hub of roads leading off in all directions. The Allies hoped to take Saint-Lô within the first nine days, but 37 days after D-Day, they still did not have control of the city.

The terrain beyond the beaches was called the French "*bocage*," and our troops had no training for these irregular checkerboard fields about the size of a football field and surrounded by hedgerows.

Hedgerows were made of mounds of dirt and rock, centuries-old, four to ten feet high and about that wide with a twisted growth of trees, bushes, and brush on top of it all. These mounds helped to contain cattle in the fields and mark boundaries. Even Julius Caesar complained almost two thousand years earlier that this type of hedgerow was impossible to penetrate. Narrow sunken lanes between the berms of dirt from one field to the next were canopied by trees and vegetation that made it too narrow for tanks to pass through, so the battle fell to the infantry, the foot soldier. A clipper modification was eventually fit to the front of tanks, initially by using metal from the hedgehogs found on the beaches on D-Day. These clipper modifications allowed the tanks to cut through the hedgerows, but their addition was too late to help the 35th Infantry.

Each field was a fort, and the landscape was an elaborate maze. The Germans had had four years to make themselves at home. They dug into the hedgerows and stole mattresses from French homes to create their relatively safe, buried havens. Some compare these defensive positions to the caves and tunnels of Iwo Jima and Okinawa.

The Germans set up machine guns in the front corners of the fields and waited for the arrival of the Americans, who had always been trained to rush and attack. The Germans also had an excellent vantage point from atop Saint-Lô's Hill 122, so named for its height in meters, and thus about 400 feet tall. From the large, flat hilltop, the enemy could observe the approach of the Allies. Additionally, the Germans had built wooden platforms in the treetops and used flashless gunpowder to avoid detection.

* * *

Video footage of Normandy passed briefly on the television at the nursing home, so I asked Dad, "What do you think of those hedgerows?"

From his recliner, he said, "Dey are not showing da bad ones. Getting t'rough dem was rough. Maybe dey could only get to da easy ones." Then he softly reassured himself, "It does not make much difference. It's over."

* * *

American gains were measured in yards rather than miles, gaining one hedgerow at a time to face another that looked just like the previous one. The darkness at night was so black no one could see the person next to him, even if they were close enough to touch. Surrender messages were broadcast in different languages because Polish and Czech soldiers had been forced to fight with the Germans, or their families would have been killed. At night, some enemy soldiers crawled to the American hedgerows, which was unnerving because they could be surrendering or attacking.

Dad sympathized with the Polish and the Czechs. If they fell back, retreated, or tried to surrender, the Germans shot them. If they advanced, the Allies did.

Tree bursts were common in the hedgerows, sometimes one right after another. When artillery shells exploded within overhanging trees, the hot steel, plus thousands of jagged pieces of the tree, pierced everything below. There was some safety if one's foxhole had been tunneled back into the sides and covered with logs.

Robert Phillips sent me a page about weaponry from *Story of the 320th Infantry*. He had written in the margin of the page, "88's, mortars, and artillery." Mortars and artillery were discharged from a greater distance, but it was the long barrels of the

German 88s that could be hidden within the hedgerows. The 88s were anti-aircraft and anti-tank weapons. Robert highlighted the paragraph about the sound of the 88's. The paragraph said, "The most terrifying of all was the shriek of the incoming freight. Its soundtrack, tapering like a set of rails, started as a small point of noise and roared down the roadbed always expanding, and always heading straight for Joe [the infantryman]."

Robert Phillips spoke of injuries, "You cannot judge anyone for how he reacts...not even yourself." More than once Robert told me about an 18-year-old soldier who was hit with shrapnel in the face and lost his mouth and chin. He was as calm as he could be and spoke with Robert. Another soldier with minor injuries reacted wildly. When Robert was interviewed by the Veterans History Project, he did not give much information about anyone's reaction to injury because he did not know how he would have responded.

* * *

Norman Carey (320/35th) described injuries in his letter cited in *35th Infantry: Trail of the Santa Fe Division:*

> *We fear shell fire more than bullets. They tear*
> *such jagged wounds, cutting like razors...There is*
> *a brilliant flash, a terrific explosion. Then the*
> *shrapnel and steel fragments sing and whine*
> *through the air, ricocheting off of trees and stones.*
> *After you have seen the results of shell fire on*
> *others, you can understand why a man can be*
> *afraid to look at his own injuries.*

* * *

Alfred

As our troops moved through France, carcasses of horses lay bloated and rotting in the fields. Recognizing the "enormous suffering of people in a war zone," Harry Wintemburg (87th Division) shared his perspective of war's impact on animals in *The Bulge Bugle* (November 2015). He explained:

> *Cows would die an agonizing death when there was nobody to milk them...I saw a dog walk by with a human hand in his mouth. He was emaciated and would eat anything he could chew....It was not uncommon that we would have to shoot dogs to protect ourselves and mercifully end their suffering. Cats seemed to just lie down and wait for starvation to end their lives.*

Once, Dad looked out from his foxhole just as six peacefully grazing cows were blown to bits by a blast.

Battalion runner Ben Lane paid attention to charred and rotting animals. He used their stench along with the position of stars to guide his lonely course in the dark as he delivered messages back to battalion headquarters. As the 320th moved forward, there was always a risk that a pocket of German soldiers could have been left behind, making it dangerous for a solitary individual like Ben.

Within the first ten days of battle, the 35th lost more than 2,000 troops. With so many casualties, the upper echelon considered whether it was important for a soldier to have years of extensive training when he was out of action in a half hour. Combat medic Michael Linquata wrote on the 134th Infantry Regiment website, "I don't recall myself or anyone else shedding a tear when a fellow soldier was wounded or killed. We thought the dead were lucky. They were all going to heaven. A merciful God would not send them to hell again." And every soldier recognized the fact he could be next.

During my research, I discovered soldiers and families of soldiers who had never faced combat. It was not uncommon for them to confidently state that soldiers were "so well trained, nothing could happen." The younger the soldiers, the more likely they believed these words, but this is the first delusion to evaporate in actual combat. One veteran said, "I never thought anything could happen to me until I saw it happen to my buddy." Many young soldiers died calling for their mothers. Robert added, "Those who were gung ho in war all died."

* * *

In *This Faraway Land*, Orval Faubus (320/35th) described Saint-Lô to his hometown newspaper:

> *The village lies in ruins, blasted, burned and crumbled...Overwhelming all odors is the awful, horrible stench of hogs, cows, dogs, and men lying dead together, all slain by bursting shells and flying bullets. In addition, hundreds of French civilians had not escaped before the battle, and they lie buried within the buildings that were almost entirely destroyed within their village, now called "The Capital of Ruins."*

Particularly at this point of the war, many acts of heroism went unrecognized because the actions were not written up. Some were only witnessed by soldiers who became casualties themselves.

Alfred

James Huston (134/35th) wrote in *Biography of a Battalion* about burial teams at this time loading bodies into "five quarter-ton trailers. They worked eight to ten hours each day using discarded rifles as staves." Some of the men could only work through the stench by wearing gas masks.

* * *

Shortly after the capture of Saint-Lô, there was an assassination attempt on Hitler at his command post called Wolf's Lair in Rastenburg, Prussia, now Poland. A solid oak table leg blocked the explosion from the bomb that had been placed under the table in a briefcase. Hitler was slightly injured, and none of the veterans I spoke with ever mentioned it. However, Hitler was never quite the same. He became even more paranoid, more frequently in pain, and quicker to anger.

In a radio broadcast on July 20, the day of the assassination attempt, Hitler said of his survival, "I interpret this as a sign from Providence that I must continue my work, and therefore I shall..."

"Naturally, the common people don't like war...but after all, it is the leaders of a country who determine the policy, and it is always a simple matter to drag people along, whether it is a democracy, or a fascist dictatorship, or a parliament, or a communistic dictatorship. Voice or no voice, the people can always be brought to the bidding of the leaders. This is easy. All you have to do is tell them they're being attacked, and denounce the pacifists for lack of patriotism and exposing the country to danger. It works the same in every country."

—Hermann Goering, Nazi Reichsmarshall in Nuremburg jail after World War II, April 18, 1946

Alfred

Map from Story of 320th Infantry:
Mortain, Liberations, and Blitz across France

5. NORTHERN FRANCE CAMPAIGN

July 25 – September 14, 1944

Almost 60 years after the war, on a warm spring day with blue skies, Dad, Bev, another resident, and I watched outside the nursing home as a pilot performed acrobatics with a small plane, cutting its engines, diving, and circling. I was next to Dad and the only one to hear him say so softly, "It reminds me of Bedcheck Charlie." For the first 60 years, did Dad not talk about the war, or did we not hear it?

"Bedcheck Charlie" refers to German airplanes that fired brilliant yellow flares, lighting up the entire countryside around 11 o'clock at night. The flares exposed moving men or larger groups who would then become targets for machine guns as the planes passed over a second time. The first time Dad told me about Bedcheck Charlie, I understood him to say "shraving." I had no idea what he was talking about, and "shrave" is obviously not in the dictionary. With his German accent, he was saying strafing, attacking with machine guns from airplanes.

Dad's reference to Bedcheck Charlie helped me understand his story about running with his machine gun, tripping, and then falling into a foxhole. Two or three other soldiers fell on top of him, and by their sheer presence, their bodies had shielded him. They were either killed or wounded while Dad injured both knees, significantly spraining his right one. Medical records confirm it happened in July.

Dad had hoped for a medical break from combat, but instead, medics just taped both of his knees. He walked with a limp like Chester from the television show *Gunsmoke*. He crawled back and forth on small hills to position himself away from the flares of the oncoming planes. Eventually, his officer noticed Dad crawling and said, "He makes it dangerous for the whole company," so Dad was assigned to burial duty.

When he told me of his knee injury, I asked, "Could you have received more medical attention?"

He said, "We might have been surrounded. Sometimes dere was no way to get out."

"Could you have qualified for a Purple Heart?"

"I suppose."

During the war, the infantry had a superstition about Purple Hearts. If a soldier applied for a Purple Heart for a relatively minor injury, the next one could be fatal.

By the time Dad was assigned to burial duty with Murphy, Nelson, and Stud, many of the dead bodies had been in the sun for three weeks. The corpses, Germans and Americans together, were carried through hordes of flies and lifted overhead into a trailer. Dad described, "Dey stunk so bad it was unbelievable. Maggots fell out as if dey were being poured from a bucket. Den we could not eat for a couple of days."

Initially, the bodies were carried over the top of a hill where Dad could see the occasional movement of a bullet through tall grasses near him. Since it would not be typical for the enemy to be in the area of burial duty, there must have been a couple

German stragglers with a view of the top of the hill. Dad felt a warm stream running down his leg and feared it was blood. Instead his canteen had been hit by a bullet.

Subsequently, the burial team changed their path down to the base of the hill, but a new lieutenant ordered the bodies to again be carried over the top, away from his quarters because of the stench. Dad explained in his later years, "Everybody t'ought he was joking."

Stud had said, "We have to be careful what we say to that guy. He may be shell-shocked."

Then the lieutenant shouted again, "Hey, I thought I told you to go the other way!"

One of the guys on the burial squad hollered back, "Shut up you SOB, or you'll be lying on top with a bullet between your eyes."

Soldiers had little respect for some of these new officers, especially those known as "90-day wonders." Dad was not easily impressed, "Da guy probably went to college, could give directions, and got to take a bat' in a tub."

* * *

On the clear morning of July 25, troops could hear the drone of row upon row of heavy and medium bombers that eventually obliterated the sun.

Dad had recalled this bombing when he spoke of war on one occasion a year before Mom died. He told our family friend Matt Engels, "Planes were coming, and one of da guys said, 'Somebody is going to get it today.' It looked like dey would pass by, but den da planes started bombing closer to us."

Alfred

It was just the beginning of an hour-and-a-half procession of more than 2,500 Allied planes that caused heart-pounding drumming as they dropped bomb after bomb every few seconds, the largest bombing raid in the history of the world. The goal was to cause a breakthrough south of Saint-Lô for Patton's Third Army.

Artillery had marked the front lines with smoke shells, and the Allied bombers were to drop ahead and south of the smoke. A slight breeze from the south caused the red smoke and dust to drift northward, back over some of our own soldiers. There was no communication with or between the bombers because they had left England under radio silence. The larger bombs created craters 20 feet deep and 30 to 40 feet wide. They overturned some German tanks. Even miles away, our troops covered their ears from the deafening and mind-boggling roar of the bombs. Some American soldiers said the concussions were so great that their clothing ballooned out. Soldiers who were closer to the bombardment choked to breathe through the smell of burnt powder as they bounced off the quaking ground. Minutes seemed like hours.

Two-thirds of the German forces became casualties that day, some buried alive, some vaporized with direct hits, some with blood coming out of their eyes and ears. The bombing also caused hundreds of casualties among our own troops, many within the 30th Infantry Division, which included Bob Esser, a native of Dane, Wisconsin. The communication problem was eventually corrected by small planes circling in front of the bombers and directing them to the proper target. At least two soldiers from the 35th Division were killed and three more injured according to the after-action report of the 137th Regiment. General Leslie McNair died during that bombing, on his very first day of combat observation. Bede Irvin, an Associated Press photographer, was also killed.

General Omar Bradley wrote in his memoirs *A General's Life*, "Doughboys were dazed and frightened...A bomb landed squarely on McNair in a slit trench and threw his body 60 feet and mangled it beyond recognition except for the three stars on his collar."

McNair's death was not officially announced for months so as not to give the enemy the satisfaction of knowing that our own Army Air Force had killed one of our highest-ranking officers.

Dad said to me in his later years, "Dey made such a big deal about dat officer being killed." The amount of attention did not seem justified to Dad, an expendable private, like so many killed that day.

Yet it was General McNair in 1943 who had been instrumental in the creation of the Combat Infantry Badge or CIB. The CIB honors the infantry and is to be worn above all service ribbons. The infantry faces the enemy day and night in close-range combat on foot and with so little recognition while suffering the most casualties. Infantrymen are primarily from the rifle companies and also the heavy weapons companies like Dad and Robert. Even General Eisenhower did not have a CIB. All soldiers, except officers, were entitled to an additional $10 per month after receiving it.

* * *

Once, at a pool party, I explained the impact of this Allied carpet bombing on our own ground troops. A woman said, "You mean the Germans dropped the bombs."

I answered, "No, they were American bombers."

"You mean German," she repeated.

I began to explain, "Our own planes accidentally…"

And then while I was still speaking, she walked away because my information did not cognitively fit her image of war. During almost every conversation with Robert, he said, "War is a mad state of confusion." Another veteran called it, "Organized chaos."

* * *

On the second day after the carpet bombing, the 320th began an attack that went on for days and nights. By early August, troops staggered as they walked and were so tired they no longer dodged shell fire. They did not dig foxholes but dropped to the ground, anywhere to sleep. Drivers got out of their Jeeps to move the legs of sleeping soldiers in order to drive past them; the sleeping soldiers never even noticed. More than once in my research, I read quotes by soldiers that were similar to, "It was so bad that after a while, you did not care whether you got hit or not."

Several days later in August, Patton literally flagged the 35th Division off the road because he heard about a possible attack by several German Panzer (tank) divisions near Mortain. He wrote in *War As I Knew It*, "Personally I think it is a bluff to cover a withdrawal, but I stopped the 80th, French 2nd Armored, and the 35th Division in the vicinity of St. Hilaire just in case something might happen."

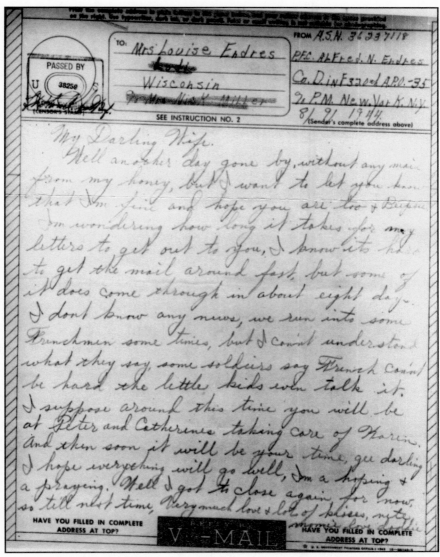

ALFRED'S V-MAIL NOTE TO LOUISE ABOUT A MONTH BEFORE THE BIRTH OF THEIR FIRST CHILD, DATED AUGUST 9, 1944.

Alfred

Patton was called "Ol' Blood and Guts," to which his troops added, "Ya, his guts and our blood."

In Don May's opinion, "Patton thought men were expendable. Patton said he could get more men; he could not get more tanks."

When I passed that comment onto Dad, I thought he might be offended, but he said, "Ya, but Patton was da first to walk across a new bridge." That was a way for Patton to demonstrate his trust in his soldiers.

Patton's grandson, George Patton Waters, spoke at St. Norbert College in DePere, Wisconsin, and his speech was summarized in their alumni magazine (Winter 2008). He described his grandfather as dedicated to America, fond of cigars, and he "could cuss for about twenty minutes without repeating himself."

While Dad was in the nursing home, he spoke of General Patton, "Soldiers did not all like him at dat time. Not too many people cared to be under Patton. He was too rough."

Maybe they knew Patton had been unsympathetic and slapped a soldier who had battle fatigue. Patton had called the soldier yellow-bellied.

Dad further said of Patton and war, "It was as if he t'ought it was fun or some great honor."

* * *

General Patton was called erratic, volatile, unbalanced, and full of contradictions compared to even-handed General Bradley. Some have suggested that Patton's mood swings were caused by the many blows to his head in games of football and polo and from falling off horses. Some say he sacrificed his men for his own glory. General Eisenhower wrote of Patton in *Crusade in Europe,* "His emotional range was very great and he lived at either one end of it or the other." Yet the Germans feared his expertise at warfare, and Patton was generally known to be dauntless, so Eisenhower put up with his personality.

Even Patton underestimated the enemy at this point in the war and wrote to his wife that the Germans were "finished," and "We may end this in ten days."

Then, as the men of the 35th Division approached the city of Mortain, they witnessed more and more civilians hurrying along the hot, dusty roads, urgently pushing carts, or pulling small wagons, piled high with their belongings. Some pointed in the direction they had come, which was the direction the 35th was going, and shouted, *"Boche!" Boche* is offensive slang for a German, especially a soldier.

Mortain was a quaint village with about 1,600 residents, situated at the hinge between the United States First Army and Patton's Third Army. Hitler ordered a counterattack to drive a wedge between the two armies. This would stop the Allied advance and also gain control of the two main roads that could support heavy traffic for a supply line from Mortain to Avranches.

Germany committed a couple hundred tanks to the area around Mortain, along with several of Hitler's elite SS and parachute divisions. Robert said of the Germans, "They wanted to divide and conquer, and they still could have pushed us back into the sea."

The Germans already occupied much of Mortain, but they needed control of more of the area and especially the peak of Hill

314. This hill overlooked the entire area in all directions. Mont St. Michel, on the coast 20 miles away, could be seen from the summit. The 120th Infantry Regiment of the 30th Division was ordered to defend Mortain at all costs. The top priority for its 2nd Battalion was Hill 314.

* * *

The little village of Dane, Wisconsin, created a military memorial decades after the war, and my brother Bob was in charge of ordering the individual bricks. He received an order for:

> *H. Robert Esser PFC WWII Europe 1943-1945*
> *Member of Lost Battalion in Mortain, France*
> *Purple Heart Bronze Star with Oak Leaf Cluster*
> *Forever thankful to have survived and returned home.*

Bob emailed me, "Do you want to contact him? Might be interesting."

I received that email 71 years and one day after Bob Esser's battalion was rescued at Mortain.

I contacted his daughter Jane, and she emailed me the next day, "My dad never spoke to us about the war except a few stories during deer hunting camp. Now he has advanced Alzheimer's."

Jane and I tried to figure out whether our fathers had known each other. They were both connected to the tiny village of Dane, even though Essers eventually moved to Madison. Both veterans knew Doc Bohlman and Kenneth Johnson, Albert Endres, Eva Middleton, and many others. Dad was one of the original members of the Dane Legion, and Bob Esser said in an interview with the Wisconsin Veterans Museum, "I belonged to the Dane

Legion for several years. I think I probably would have even been part of organizing it."

It is almost impossible for the two men not to have known each other, but we are quite certain they never said the word "Mortain" in front of the other. The quiet acknowledgment of each other's involvement at Mortain would have been healing. As Bob Esser said in an interview, "The Mortain thing was a hell of an affair."

On the evening of August 7, Bob Esser's 2nd Battalion was trapped on that rocky, evergreen-covered Hill 314 outside Mortain. They were cut off from the rest of the 120th Regiment, but the battalion refused to surrender even while suffering severe shortages of ammunition, food, and medical supplies. It was very difficult to dig in for the sake of safety because many times solid bedrock was just eight inches below the surface of the ground. As long as this battalion had radio batteries and held onto the highest position on the hill, the rest of the 30th Division would have the ability to direct artillery, mortar, and air attacks on enemy targets.

One day later, the 35th Division entered the battle and improved the situation south of Mortain, but the numbers of German troops and tanks were unknown. German tanks appeared and disappeared with confusing frequency because they had greater maneuverability than American Sherman tanks. Bob Esser and the other soldiers trapped on Hill 314 were suffering from hunger and thirst while surrounded by the nauseating stench of dead bodies quickly decomposing in the hot August sun.

Alfred

On August 9, while the 35th Division simultaneously undertook two major attacks, Dad and Robert's 1st Battalion was ordered to break the siege on Hill 314. They would be reinforced by the 737th Tank Battalion while the rest of the 320th would provide direct support and assistance for the attack.

In Mark Reardon's book *Victory at Mortain*, the division chief of staff ordered, "All tanks will each carry five infantrymen except for the first five. If a tank is knocked out, the remaining tanks will bypass it and carry out the mission. Remainder of the infantry from 1st Battalion will follow on foot and reinforce those who arrive on tanks." When someone questioned the plan, Lieutenant Colonel Hamilton (737th Tank Battalion) said, "We know it's not how tanks fight, but those are our orders from division."

The tanks followed each other up a steep, narrow road, deeply hedged on both sides. The assault, intended to relieve Bob Esser's trapped battalion, began at 3 p.m. on August 10. Air strikes and artillery preparations preceded it.

The riflemen had difficulty finding a place to sit on the tanks, and the leading Sherman tank barely advanced 100 yards before it was knocked out of action by three rounds from a 50mm anti-tank gun. In addition, German machine guns opened fire on the American soldiers that rode on the following tanks.

According to *Story of the 320th Infantry*, "Out of 55 tanks, 31 were knocked out in a few hours." The road became littered with brass cartridges and empty ammunition from thousands of rounds of small arms. In University of Tennessee Special Collections Library 1993, Art Newman (320/35th) described American tanks burning up because their machine guns were so hot they detonated main gun rounds inside the hulls. He also said in his interview, "We did not have food or water with us...I drank water from a creek that night, and during the next day, I noticed dead cows and Germans lying upstream."

By 7 a.m. the next morning, the Germans had shifted all their available forces to counterattack against the 1st Battalion of the 320th Regiment, which included Dad and Robert. The German forces were greatly superior in number. In *Victory at Mortain*, Mark J. Reardon wrote that the enemy opened fire with machine guns, and in a matter of seconds, 14 Americans within Lieutenant Thornblom's C Company were killed, along with six more wounded. Thornblom ran over to a machine gun crew from D Company and ordered the crew to return fire into the hedgerow. The German machine guns suddenly fell silent. However, three German tanks approached undetected under the noise of the American weapons. Those German tanks opened fire, killing or wounding eight more Americans.

Because of the structure of American heavy weapons companies, the machine gun that fired into the hedgerow had to be one of four in either Dad's or Robert's platoon.

* * *

Robert Phillips told me, "It was an awful battle. The Germans could look down and see everything we did. They were looking down our throats."

* * *

The situation was described as "grim," and Bob Esser's unit was still isolated, but by the evening of August 11, the German defenses were weakened. The 1st and 3rd Battalions of the 320th were so depleted, they were reorganized and combined into approximately a battalion-sized unit that night, according to *Story of 320th Infantry.* The attack resumed at first light on August 12. Within 500 yards of what became known as the "Lost Battalion," Dad and Robert's 1st Battalion fought hand to hand while tanks covered their advance.

Finally around noon on August 12, the survivors of Dad and Robert's 1st Battalion linked up with the survivors of Bob Esser's lost battalion. It never actually had been "lost." Instead, it had been isolated and surrounded by the enemy for six days. The survivors were in very bad shape, many wounded, some with gangrene. A 2.5-ton truck delivered food and supplies and evacuated some of the wounded. Bob Esser survived those six days on one K-Ration and a rabbit, but when food arrived, he was not able to eat. Of the 700 men in his battalion on that hill, over 300, almost half, had been killed. Of the 212 men in F Company, Bob Esser was one of the 28 who had not become a casualty.

Up to that point, the city of Mortain had been spared from artillery fire because of the possibility that Americans were hiding there. When that was no longer a risk, Mortain was shelled and transformed into a wasteland overnight. After the war ended, members of the German General Staff said the war was lost when their counterattack failed at Mortain-Avranches.

The Battle of Mortain was Hitler's last chance to turn back the Allied invasion, and it is sometimes compared to the Battle of the Bulge, not in size but in general purpose. Both were German counteroffensives with all available tanks and infantry working to smash through a thinly held American line.

"American estimates for infantry casualties were placed at 70 percent prior to D-Day...raised to 83 percent after the battle of the hedgerows, and raised yet again to 90 percent for the hard fighting during the Mortain counteroffensive," John N. Rickard wrote in *Patton at Bay*.

Dad and Robert's 1st Battalion of the 320th and Bob Esser's 2nd Battalion of the 120th were awarded Presidential Unit Citations for Mortain. Originally named the Distinguished Unit Citation, it is awarded to units, rarely larger than a battalion, that display extraordinary heroism under extremely difficult and hazardous conditions. It is similar to a Distinguished Service Cross for an individual, which is second only to the Medal of Honor. Because of the Presidential Unit Citation, France additionally awarded the French *Croix de Guerre* (War Cross) with Silver Star to those same units for their action at Mortain.

* * *

Forty years after the war, Robert Phillips (1/320th) and his wife visited Mortain on a 35th Division tour. They rode up Hill 314. Robert told me, "I remembered the curves in the road, and I knew the placement of dead bodies at the side of the road, bodies slumped over in certain positions." From his memories, he saw men on top of their tanks, "their burnt bodies, charcoal black."

"Did you tell your wife?" I asked.

"No," he said. "My wife did not know much about the war."

Robert loved her dearly. He told me, "She made me a better person,"

John Cline (106th Infantry Division) wrote in *The Service Diary of a German War Prisoner #315136* that he had a similar experience when he returned to the spot where he had been captured in the Battle of the Bulge 35 years earlier. He described how he stood on the road for about five minutes. "My heart was pounding. I could see the soldiers on the battlefield. I could hear them calling for medics. I was confused, uncertain, and could not understand my emotions. I had to get out of the area."

Jack Brauntuch (320/35th) told me in a phone conversation about his return to Europe, "I did not realize how painful it would be to walk the ground of combat."

* * *

On the morning of August 13, the 35th Division rejoined Patton's Third Army, and the troops were able to liberate towns and move more quickly across France. According to *35th Division: Trail of the Santa Fe Division*, some of the towns liberated by the 320th included Orleans, Chateaudun, Cloyes, Janville, and Pithiviers.

Citizens awakened to suddenly find Americans in their villages and along the roads. The French smiled and laughed and waved, overjoyed and grateful. Bells rang out for the first time in four years, and the troops were offered bread and wine, eggs, butter, and apples.

* * *

At some point, Dad was gifted a harmonica. He said, "It was a very nice one wit' a white button on da side." On occasion he played the harmonica while John Honeycutt sang and a buddy played spoons. Another soldier borrowed the harmonica, and when it was not returned, that soldier said, "I don't know where it is. Somebody else has it." Dad never believed him and never forgave him.

* * *

As American troops moved through France, some problems followed the liberation. Part of Orval Faubus's (320/35th) assignment was to deal with court martials for charges of rape and desertion. He wrote in his published journal, "I am now convinced that a subject much needed to be taught in America is good manners."

Some soldiers entered French homes to take souvenirs. Others forced kisses on the lips of French women when their custom is a kiss on the cheek only. Some French husbands kept loaded guns for those Americans who overstepped boundaries with French wives. It seems one woman resolved her own issue. Dad told me at the nursing home, "I saw a woman shoot a soldier in da back when I was walking down a valley. Den I stopped for a while."

On the other hand, some French women had collaborated with the Germans. These women may have been marched through the streets with their heads shaven, sometimes painted black. At other times, they were stripped naked out of scorn.

The French resistance fighters (French Forces of the Interior or FFI) eagerly helped the Americans. They acted as guides and provided information about the location of Germans. If the resistance fighters had weapons, they tried to clean out snipers ahead of our troops. However, if any of the French were caught helping the Allies, it was considered disloyalty to Hitler, "der

Fuhrer." Their entire family would be executed on the spot, their property confiscated, and their home destroyed.

* * *

According to *35th Division: Trail of the Santa Fe Division*, many Germans were taken prisoners at Montargis. Dad described that once he was told, "Walk these prisoners to camp and be back in five or ten minutes," which meant take them out of sight and gun them down.

Dad replied, "It will take me two or t'ree days."

The officer asked, "You mean you do not want to do it?"

Dad shook his head, "No."

The officer raised his hand and said, "Don't go," and he then looked around for someone else who was willing. Dad did not want to kill if it was not for his own survival. He told us, "Dey had families too."

* * *

Within a small box on the front page of the *Wisconsin State Journal* on August 25, 1944, the United Press mocked Dr. Goebbels, one of Hitler's most devoted followers:

> **Oh, Dr. Goebbels—Have You Heard?**
> **The shortest distance to Berlin from advanced Allied lines today: Northern France—520 miles (gain of 55 miles in a week)**

* * *

The French population had paid a tremendous price during their liberation. As of August 25, between 15,000 and 20,000 French civilians had been killed, mainly as a result of Allied bombing during D-Day and the Normandy Campaign. There were fewer civilian deaths in the following campaigns, while the number of liberated towns increased. The 320th liberated Courtenay,

Troyes, Bar-sur-Seine, and Joinville. The Third Army was advancing so fast that the support services had trouble keeping up with the front lines.

As troops passed through the town of Troyes, there was a funeral procession with 30 tiny caskets. Germans had shot up a children's sanctuary before withdrawing from the town. Dad described the German SS troops, "Dey t'rew babies out of windows as if dey were blocks of wood." He scoffed, "Real tough guys." He could identify with the average German soldier, but most American soldiers considered the SS troops to be fanatics.

* * *

In order to liberate and occupy the city of Nancy, it was necessary for the Allies to cross and control the Moselle and Meurthe rivers. These river crossings were complicated because the Germans had blown up the bridges across the Moselle River, south of Nancy. Following advance combat by the 137th, the 320th eventually crossed the Moselle River to attack north and east on September 13 against German tanks and antitank guns. Additionally, enemy mortars were used against the advance of Dad and Robert's 1st Battalion. On that day, my sister Eileen was born. However, Dad would not receive the news of her arrival for a couple more weeks.

Also on the day of Eileen's birth, General Patton appeared at the headquarters of the 320th Regiment. He continued forward to the command post of Dad and Robert's 1st Battalion and then still further to a forward observation post. According to Orval Faubus's journal, Patton listened with "evident approval" as Germans were driven from their positions.

Alfred

* * *

While visiting Dad at the nursing home, I asked whether he had ever seen Eisenhower or Patton.

Dad answered, "Dey were making plans. Dey did not seem dat important at da time."

Concerning Eisenhower, he said, "You could tell he was a nice guy."

I asked, "You saw Patton?"

"Ya."

"How close?"

Dad replied, "It's hard to remember."

"Within this room?" I asked as we sat in the dining room at the nursing home.

"Oh, ya," and then to clarify any possible misunderstanding, Dad added, "He was not talking to me."

NIECE ANNE GRADY WITH ALFRED ON THE HARMONICA AT ALFRED AND LOUISE'S 40TH ANNIVERSARY PARTY, CHALET ST. MORITZ, MIDDLETON, WISCONSIN.

Alfred

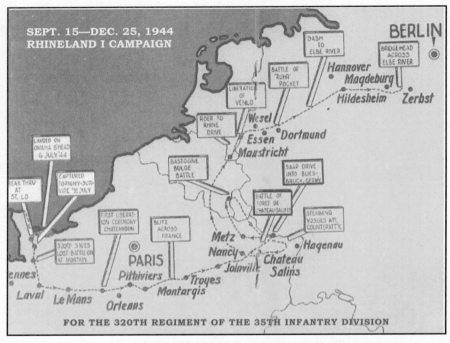

**SEPT. 15—DEC. 25, 1944
RHINELAND I CAMPAIGN**

BERLIN

DASH TO ELBE RIVER

BRIDGE HEAD ACROSS ELBE RIVER

BATTLE OF "RUHR" POCKET

Hannover

LIBERATION OF VENLO

Maqdeburg

Hildesheim

Zerbst

ROER TO RHINE DRIVE

Wesel

Essen

Dortmund

LANDED ON OMAHA B'HEAD 6 JULY '44

BASTOGNE BULGE BATTLE

Maastricht

SAAR DRIVE INTO BLIES-BRUCK, GERM'Y

CAPTURED TORIGNY-SUR-VIRE '31 JULY

REAK THRU AT ST. LO

FIRST LIBERAT-ION CEREMONY CHATEAUDUN

BLITZ ACROSS FRANCE

BATTLE OF FORET DE CHATEAU-SALINS

STEMMING VOSGES MT. COUNTERATT'K

Metz

Haqenau

320TH SAVES LOST BATTL'ON AT MORTAIN

Nancy

ennes

PARIS

Pithiviers

Joinville

Chateau Salins

Laval

Le Mans

Troyes

Montarqis

Orleans

FOR THE 320TH REGIMENT OF THE 35TH INFANTRY DIVISION

MAP FROM STORY OF 320TH INFANTRY:
GREMECEY FOREST AND SAAR DRIVE

6. RHINELAND CAMPAIGN, PART 1

September 15, 1944 to December 25, 1944

After the city of Nancy was freed by the Allies on September 15, 1944, a big sign appeared along one of the roads:

VIVE LA FRANCE
VIVE DE GAULLE
VIVE LA THIRD ARMEE

The front-liners passed by the city and continued on their way to live in foxholes and fight the enemy.

The advances of the Third Army in August had been fast-paced. Patton liked speed, along with surprise and attack. He also liked the use of tanks. General Bradley once said of Patton, "George could not sit still—he wanted movement for his headlines," as recorded by Chester Hansen in *The Bradley Papers*.

Suddenly there was a shortage of gasoline because headquarters had given priority to other groups rather than to the Third Army. Patton made it clear what he wanted, "I will shoot the next man who brings me food. Give us gasoline; we can eat our belts (cartridge)," Carl D'Este wrote in *Eisenhower: A Soldier's Life*.

And then it began to rain. Eventually, combat became a slugfest in the mud. There could be no tanks in the mud and no quick success. With the delays, the enemy reorganized and had time to prepare stronger defensive positions. Patton would find the next months difficult because he had limited experience in static fighting. Many thought the war could have been over if the Third Army had received all the supplies General Patton wanted.

On September 21, Patton wrote in *War as I Knew It,* "The Huns are desperate and are attacking at half a dozen places."

Three days later, it was raining when some soldiers of the 35th Division were entertained by USO's Bing Crosby, an American singer and actor. The setting was an enormous brewery in the village of Vezelise where the American Red Cross made donuts outside in their trailers. Then about a month later, entertainer Don Rice performed twice for soldiers, some of them from the 35th Division. He shared with Orval Faubus his observations about the differences between rear-echelon troops and front-liners. The troops who had not seen combat were noisy, shouting, laughing, and back-slapping as they waited for his show. War seemed to them to be a great adventure. In contrast, Don Rice told Faubus the front-liners trudged in and sat silently without regard to dirt or mud. There was no joking or horseplay, maybe some low voices, similar to being at a funeral. It appeared the front-line troops did not fully comprehend what they were seeing, and yet, the entertainment was a welcomed break from combat.

* * *

I asked Robert Phillips, "Did you ever see Bing Crosby?"

"No. No one," he answered

Dad never saw an entertainer either.

* * *

Before I found Mom's actual letter informing Dad of the birth of their first child, I asked him, "Did you find out about Eileen a couple months after her birth?"

"Not dat long."

"A couple of weeks?"

"Ya."

"What were you doing at the time?"

He responded far too quickly, "I don't know."

My brother Jerry, a father of three children, had no doubt, "He knows what he was doing."

"I t'ought I would never see my daughter, and I would never see my wife again," Dad told his nephew Mark Kalscheur.

Mark said to me, "I'm sure he saw so many fellow soldiers die that it was nearly impossible to remain optimistic."

* * *

Around 4:30 p.m. on September 28, two weeks after Eileen's birth, Dad received the letter announcing her arrival, and he acquired the nickname of "Hot Papa" from his friends.

On that day, Dad's 1st Battalion had been surrounded on three sides by attacking Germans. They were Field Marshall Rundstedt's best troops. There was even a fear that the 35th Division would collapse. It was initially fighting without an attached armored division when it was ordered to seize the Gremecey Forest and to occupy a 12-mile front, about 15 miles northeast of Nancy.

Alfred

On the previous day, Dad's 1st Battalion had been attached to the 137th Regiment. There had been intense fighting back and forth through the wooded terrain as decimated Allied units refused to be driven out of the Gremecey Forest. The 35th Division website provides statistics for the 3rd Battalion of the 137th Regiment. The 3rd Battalion had entered the Gremecey Forest with over 900 men. Four days later, the unit had lost almost half of them.

Receiving Eileen's birth announcement after such intense combat, I can imagine Dad emotionally breaking down in sadness, or maybe even in anger, something that would never make sense in a normal environment when a man becomes a father for the first time. Early on, he told me of war, "I never t'ought I would live tr'ough it."

Dad wrote to Mom sometime the next day:

> *My Darling Wife and Eileen,*
>
> *I was so glad today to get the letter you wrote on Sept 13 when Joe took you to the hospital and then to see your handwriting on the letter you wrote the 14th after Eileen was born. The two were together. Darling, it meant so much to me to know that you both were feeling fine. I still did not get the telegram, but the letters were better…I also got the letter you wrote the 12th when you were still home… I bet I will get a lot of mail, and I will be glad to get it. I hope I will have time and enough stationery to answer the letters.*
>
> *Darling, how are you and Eileen now? I hope fine. I'm a really proud daddy and hope that we can be together soon. That's what I'm looking toward so much now…*

Some of the married men here think I was better off here than waiting in the hospital because they said they smoked one cigarette after the other, walking the floor. I maybe would have done the same, but I still would have liked to be there. Sometime Darling, the three of us will be together, happy as we should be, and that's what I'm looking forward to.

Darling, I got the envelope in your letter but I think I will use another envelope as the stamp was a little loose on it, and I want to be sure that it doesn't come off, but thanks very much for the envelope and all the news. Your letters mean so much to me, and now I'm waiting for the picture you are going to send me of you and Eileen. Boy I will be glad to see it. I am wondering when I am going to get the letters I have coming yet, those you wrote in August, but I do not care too much. I got the main letter now. I'm glad that I got the news from you first and even in your own writing. I did not expect that.

But be sure and do not work too hard and be careful that you won't get a cold, Darling. I suppose you are thinking now, I know how to take care of myself and the baby. Well I know you do, but take good care of both of you anyhow.

And now Darling, I will close…so til next time, Louise and Eileen, here's all the love that Daddy can send and all kinds of kisses. Give Eileen a kiss. So til next time, I love you very very much and always will and pray and hope that we can be

*together soon. Say hello to all the rest of them and
tell them I will treat them when I get home.*

To Mommie and Baby,
Daddy

On Eileen's 61st birthday, Dad said to her in a phone conversation, "I did not t'ink it would be so long before I saw you."
Eileen, living in Colorado, initially thought he was talking about
the current time. Instead, he was talking about six decades earlier
when there had been a 13-month gap before he finally held her.

A first-time father may be celebrating, but the situation was
much different for Dad. Author Faubus lamented at this time,
"The last day of September has slipped away…the worst for our
unit. They have been shelled heavily and continuously in their wood positions." It was the most concentrated artillery fire the 320th ever received, even including Saint-Lô and Mortain.

***Griffiths stacks Alfred's arms
with K-rations in Pettencourt,
France, Fall of 1944.***

MY FIRST GLANCE AT THIS PHOTO WENT FROM THE DRIVER TO THE SOLDIER BEHIND HIM. I THOUGHT, "THAT'S GRIFFITHS." MY EYES DARTED LEFT. "THAT'S DAD." ANN HELMER MALTA, DAUGHTER OF THE DRIVER, CLELAON ARTHUR "ART" HELMER, SHARED THIS PHOTO ON THE 35TH DIVISION WEBSITE.

On October 1, Orval Faubus also described artillery striking the command post:

> *The dust and flying glass, the heart-rending cries of some of the wounded, the red stains and the sickening smell of blood, all form an awful picture not easily forgotten. The flesh and blood of the guard, who was standing by the gate, was splashed all over the steps and walls by the door. The leg of another man was blown clear up into the hallway, and there was also a finger lying there. Another man's leg was almost severed and dangled when someone attempted to drag him to*

cover....I was the last to speak to the guard at the door. He suffered almost a direct hit and his flesh and blood were splattered over the front of the gray-walled building.

Dad could never put such an experience into words, so I include Orval Faubus's description to understand Dad's reality, not on one occasion, but with frequency as an infantryman. Orval Faubus wrote, "...my soul has become sick of the sight, the smell, and the memory."

On October 11, the 320th was ordered to guard and secure the bridges in the area of Pettencourt, northeast of Nancy, France. We found a photo within Dad's army trunk that had been taken in Pettencourt where Griffiths, one of Dad's buddies, stacked Dad's arms with boxed K-Rations in front of a muddy trailer. I was never able to find "Griff" or his family with such a common last name, but Dad appreciated him. Dad recalled that as they slogged through Europe, Griff had reminisced about his basketball skills, "Man, I was hot."

Front-line troops occasionally slept in houses during the war, most of them bombed out. In Pettencourt, Robert Phillips spent a night in a basement rather than in a foxhole. That night, a fellow soldier fell the last two steps into the basement and died without any visible sign of injury. He probably died from a severe brain concussion following a series of explosions. Orval Faubus wrote about a similar occurrence, "The terrific stunning detonation of the missile had simply wrecked his internal organs and blown the life from his body." That soldier bled from his eyes, nose, mouth, and ears, but there was not a mark on him.

* * *

Finally, after more than three months of combat, Dad was given an 8-hour pass. It started at noon on October 16 when he was transported by truck to Nancy, France. Some soldiers said their clothing almost stood up; it was so coated in sweat and dirt. Others said the only clean part of their body was their fingertips where grime was constantly rubbed off as they worked and fought.

Somewhere along the 15-mile drive to Nancy, General Patton stopped a Jeep as it transported a small group of soldiers. Patton had a list of rules and regulations about appropriate dress in public. The lieutenant, who was the driver, listened politely as Patton complained about the messy, dirty appearance of the passengers in the Jeep. Orval Faubus wrote in *This Far Away Land* that General Patton finally asked, "What is your outfit?"

The lieutenant identified his men as part of the 320th Regiment of the 35th Division.

General Patton softened immediately. "That's a damned good outfit. All right, son, go ahead. But the next time you come in, try to fix up a little better."

Dad seemed to have pleasant memories of Nancy. He would have been able to shower for the first time in three months, eat a hot meal, change into clean clothing, and most importantly, walk around without being shot at. The city had been minimally impacted by the war, and Robert Phillips told me, "People in Nancy did not understand war."

Two to three days after being in Nancy, author Faubus was still greatly distressed by the difference between rear-echelon troops and front-liners. He wrote, "The contrast was so sharp, no

Alfred

ALFRED'S 8-HOUR PASS TO NANCY, FRANCE, FOR HIS FIRST SHOWER IN OVER THREE MONTHS.

one could ever clearly express the difference. I was so greatly depressed that I have not yet fully recovered."

About this same time, Orval Faubus wrote about three P-51 pilots, who "gave up a leave in Paris to come and see how we live…a very kind gesture on their part." Faubus continued, "Then they remarked that they had heard stories how the infantry lived, but none of the stories were as bad as they found."

Some rear-echelon troops in the area of Nancy, who were not used to German shelling, said, "They threw everything at us but the kitchen sink." Orval Faubus more objectively wrote, "…

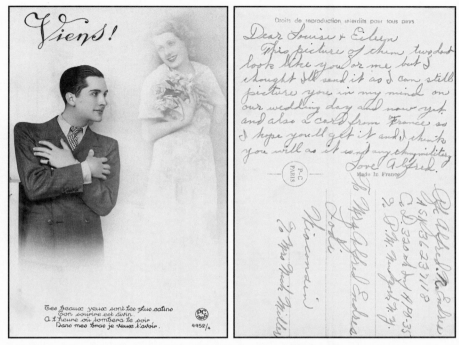

POSTCARD LIKELY PURCHASED WHILE ON PASS IN NANCY, FRANCE, WHEN EILEEN WAS ONE MONTH OLD.

the Germans used their railway guns and threw 17 shells over us into Nancy about 12 to 15 miles back."

In contrast, just four days later, a German barrage woke the front-line troops in the Gremecey Forest. One of Captain Stone's men counted 596 shells until he grew tired and stopped counting.

At the end of October, Colonel Byrne wrote in the after-action report for the 320th, "Perhaps no more unfavorable and uncomfortable living conditions or fighting positions could be found than those they endured in the wet forest during the past period when rain and mud was almost always the rule rather than the exception, and every round of artillery resulted in a tree burst...."

* * *

I asked Dad, "So it rained a lot in the Gremecey Forest?"

"Jeeesus Christ. We'd dig a hole and den it would just fill up wit water," he answered.

Some described the mud like pea soup. Others said it could be a foot deep. Some troops were able to stay in deserted houses near the front, sleep in beds, and use China dishes, but according to the *Story of the 320th Infantry*, "...most of the company riflemen were confined to their foxholes 23 hours a day by the rain and the shells."

* * *

Murray Leff (137/35th) wrote about himself as one of four soldiers with four blankets, all of them soaking wet. At this time, foxholes were filling with water, so the soldiers decided to place two blankets on the ground and cover themselves with the other two. He described, "All four of us slept together facing the same direction. Turning was impossible. We all did a lot more shivering than sleeping." (*Santa Fe Express,* September/October 2010)

* * *

Under the same muddy conditions, General Eisenhower spoke to several hundred men from a battalion of the 29th Division. He wrote in his memoirs:

> *We were all standing on a muddy, slippery*
> *hillside. After a few minutes' visit, I turned to go*
> *and fell flat on my back. From the shout of*

*laughter that went up, I am quite sure that no
other meeting I had with soldiers during the war
was a greater success than that one.*

The rains were unprecedented. Some said they were the heaviest in at least 100 years. Overshoes were rare and actually made movement difficult. *Story of the 320th Infantry* described, "Water seeped in the tops [of the overshoes] because of the streams and knee-deep puddles which had to be forded."

If soldiers wore wet socks and wet shoes for long periods of time, trench foot developed. Dad said, "Guys' feet would swell up like balloons when dey took off dere shoes." The troops were forced to live in constant rain and mud and had to be ready to move at any time, so it was quite difficult to avoid trench foot from the wetness or frostbite from the cold.

* * *

About a year after Dad's death, I received a link to a collection of silent black-and-white National Archive videos. The videos were from wwiireels.com, and I received the link through the group email of the 35th Division. I casually looked over the list and clicked on "MUD" because I was familiar with the conditions in the Gremecey Forest. Just over a minute into the footage, after watching a Jeep and a truck slide and slosh through mud, two soldiers approached a foxhole and then dropped into it.

The facial features, hand position, posture, and height of one of the soldiers caught my attention. I replayed those 15 seconds of video over and over. With 16 million Americans involved in World War II, it was unlikely I would ever find Dad, but the shorter of the two men looked like him. His hand rested on his knuckles, and his wrist was raised above his knuckles with a slight but unusual forward rotation. As crazy as it seems, I

Alfred

***LOUIS GOGAL IS ON THE RIGHT, ACCORDING TO ROBERT PHILLIPS.
IT IS LIKELY THEN ALFRED IS ON LEFT. NOTE THE HOLE IN ALFRED'S HELMET.
NATIONAL ARCHIVE VIDEO CALLED "MUD" FROM WWIIREELS.COM.***

remembered that hand placement from a photo of my parents, sitting at our kitchen table on their 35th anniversary.

I sent the video to Dad's relatives and friends and asked for their input. My niece's husband may have been most definitive with his response, "There is no question." One of my neighbors commented that the soldiers looked clean, which made me realize the video was probably taken shortly after Dad's trip to Nancy.

A colleague of mine captured a still-frame from the video of the two soldiers in their foxhole. I wanted the soldier on the right to be Ben Lane, but his daughter said he had worn glasses ever since he was seven years old and would never have been without them. If the soldier was not Ben Lane, maybe it was Stud, but I had not yet found his family.

Eventually, I sent the photo to Robert and asked him during a phone conversation about the soldier on the right. His answer was without hesitation, "Louis Gogal."

How I wish I had had that National Archive video before Dad passed away. He may have had an interesting story as to how they found the dashboard of a car to serve as a roof to keep the rain out of their foxhole. How did his helmet acquire a hole directly through the top center of it?

* * *

The 320th was held in reserve until November 7, the day of the presidential election in the United States. According to James Huston (134/35th), *The Public Opinion Quarterly* indicated 55% of those polled during the summer would vote for President Roosevelt if the war continued, whereas 58% would vote for Dewey if the war ended.

Whether by coincidence or not, the entire Third Army began an attack toward Sarreguemines the day after Roosevelt's victory. The temperature wavered around the freezing point in the cold mud of the early morning darkness.

Prior to this offensive, General Patton spoke to a group of assembled officers about the difficult tasks ahead. Orval Faubus wrote of Patton, "It was then he wept as he spoke."

Orval Faubus continued, "In the brief period in reserve, we had quickly grown accustomed to the relative quiet and a little more comfort. Now we must go back to the hell of fierce combat, back into attack after attack with the attendant casualties and heartbreak." He added that the drive across Alsace-Lorraine

would be their worst campaign because the Germans had been given time to dig in.

On November 11, Armistice Day, the 35th Division was almost at the same place it had been 26 years earlier at the end of the First World War, which had been called "the war to end all wars." Armistice Day was also Patton's 59th birthday, and he wrote to his wife, "I celebrated my birthday by getting up where the dead were still warm."

During this time, Hitler was being fed reports of false German victories. A headline in the *Wisconsin State Journal,* November 18, 1944, was "Hitler Failing, Stockholm Says," followed by the subtitle, "Kept from Insanity by 'Victory' Reports." The final paragraph included, "Any bad news was said to cause a severe nervous reaction in the Fuhrer, varying from hallucinations to outbursts of maniacal rage."

Attacks continued while decaying horses and cows were soaked by the rain. Rising waters washed out some bridges. The enemy demolished others, and sometimes the retreating enemy blew up dams, thereby causing our troops to wade through fields of waist-deep water to accomplish their missions.

Patton had hoped to break through to the Rhine River, but the rain hindered combat. He wrote in *War as I Knew It,* "The weather was so bad that I directed all army chaplains to pray for dry weather." In particular, he asked Chaplain James H. O'Neill on the morning of December 8 to publish a prayer. Because Christmas was in several weeks, a Christmas greeting was placed on the backside of the same small card. A quarter of a million copies were distributed to the Third Army from December 12 to 14. The prayer included the words, "…restrain these

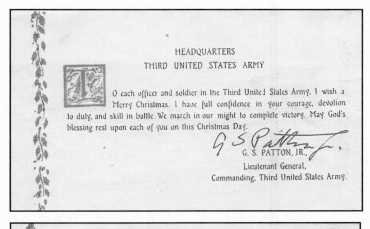

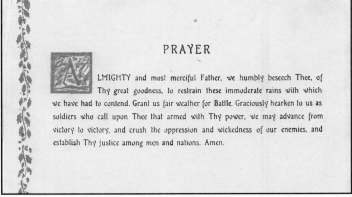

GENERAL PATTON'S CHRISTMAS GREETING AND PRAYER, DISTRIBUTED DECEMBER 12-14, 1944, ACCORDING TO CHAPLAIN JAMES H. O'NEILL. NOTE "IMMODERATE RAINS."

immoderate rains with which we have had to contend. Grant us fair weather for battle."

History frequently associates this prayer with the next campaign which had not even begun when Patton made his request. The Weather Channel features it in its series, "When Weather Changed History," but the prayer about "immoderate rains" relates more directly to the floods of the Saar Offensive

Dear Louise & Eileen.

Here's a card the 35th put out so. I want to have you keep it, as the pack resembles a wagon wheel I think and did you hear that song wagon wheel keep on rolling, well I believe thats us because we are very busy.

Today is Dec 9th the last time I wrote I believe was the 7th and I hope I'll be able to write a letter today, if not I'm fine and hope you & Eileen are too.

If we're not together for Xmas lets make the best of it like we have been, and we got our happy furture to look forward too. so heres wishing you & Eileen a Very Merry Christmas & a Happy New Year Love Daddy

**ALFRED'S CHRISTMAS CARD TO LOUISE AND EILEEN,
DATED DECEMBER 9, 1944.**

than to the fog, clouds, and mist that describes the beginning of the next campaign, particularly around Bastogne.

Chaplain James O'Neill wanted to preserve the true story of his prayer when he wrote in the *Review of the News*, October 6, 1971, that even the footnote in Patton's *War as I Knew It* by the Deputy Chief of Staff Paul D. Harkins "is not the true account of the prayer incident or its sequence."

* * *

The French city of Sarreguemines was on the western side of the Blies River on the border between France and Germany, about 50 miles east of Metz. It was an important rail and industrial center of 15,000 people with many large factory buildings, some that produced iron, coal, and steel for Hitler's war machine. The Germans also had built concrete bomb shelters to fortify the city.

At about 4 a.m. on December 13, the 35th Division began a large-scale offensive to cross the flood-stage Blies River, 60 feet wide and rushing. It was the last barrier to Germany for these troops. Germans were waiting on the hills on the opposite side of the river, looking down on our troops, and ready to fiercely defend the sacred soil of their country.

The 35th Division would have to clear German-filled houses, one by one, in the villages of Bliesbruck, Gersheim, Nieder Gailbach, and Habkirchen. A couple of the cities were in Germany, and a couple were in France. During this advance, nearly a thousand Russian, Polish, and anti-fascist Italian prisoners were freed from a camp on the outskirts of Sarreguemines. A Polish man, who had been a prisoner for over five years, reported that 150 American prisoners captured on D-Day had been moved into Germany two nights earlier. He also said, "I wish the Americans to know their Red Cross parcels saved our lives here. We would have starved without them."

Suddenly on December 16, a new enemy offensive developed, and the 35th Division travelled north for three days on an icy ride from Sarreguemines to Metz to prepare for that battle. Orval Faubus wrote, "Because of the hardships the troops had known for so long, it was by General Patton's personal order that the 35th Division remain a day longer in Metz that we might have our dinner there."

This was the first break from combat for the entire 35th Division, which had been on the line continuously for 162 days. The soldiers received packages from home and a cot to sleep on. Because of all the casualties from the previous campaign, 2,200 replacements were added to bring the division up to full strength before its next assignment. James Huston wrote in *Biography of a Battalion* that some replacements had received only two days of infantry training before joining the ranks for combat.

* * *

At a graduation party several years into my research, I was introduced to a guest by her somewhat distinctive maiden name. I recognized it from my research, and I knew a 35th Division veteran by that name lived in the area.

I curiously asked, "Are you George's daughter?"

"Yes, I am," she answered with surprise.

I explained, "Our fathers both served in the 35th Division. Was your father able to talk about the war?"

"Oh, yes. He talked about it a lot."

The hostess joined in the conversation, laughing, "If anyone could take it, George could!"

On our way home, I sat quietly in thought. Dad and George had both been in the 35th. How could their reactions be so different?

As soon as I got home, I searched for George's biography in my book on the 35th Division. He looked like a friendly, easy-going guy in his photos as a soldier and later in his life. He joined the division from a city unfamiliar to me. I did not figure it all out that night, but I later learned that George was one of the replacements received in Metz.

There were frequent problems within the replacement system, one example being the conditions during the transport of replacements to Metz. Commanding officer Lieutenant Colonel Frank W. Ebey eventually wrote a letter of complaint that was included within appendix 13 of an after-combat report for eight replacement depots, addressed to the Inspector General XX Corps, APO 340:

> **The misery of a long (51-hour) train ride in freezing weather, from Etamps, France, to Metz, France, was intense. It would seem that enough stoves and stove pipes could be obtained and placed in the cars to keep the soldiers of the richest nation in the world from freezing in the crowded box cars...Almost the entire shipment contracted diarrhea as a result of the poor washing facilities set up with two kitchen cars attempting to feed 1500 men.**

One man had pneumonia by the end of the trip, several had frost-bitten feet, and even Lt. Colonel Ebey came down with a fever of 102° the second day after his arrival.

Alfred

The commanding officer's final sentence in his letter of complaint noted there were "...enough examples of indifference and carelessness in the GFRS [Ground Forces Replacement System] to cause an investigation by the Inspector General."

I am certain I would have enjoyed talking to George, and I doubt he would have been flippant about war, but I did not like to hear the comment that "George could take it." I checked the after-action reports for George's 137th Regiment. George missed 80 percent of the men killed in action for his group, even though I gave him combat credit for the entire month of December. It is not a perfect analogy, but missing 80 percent is the difference between working all week versus coming in on Friday. An individual is impacted by the length of exposure to trauma.

* * *

At the 35th Division's reunion in St. Louis 62 years after the war, I observed a veteran glance around the group. From the far side of our large circular table, he said, "I bet none of these guys did the whole thing," meaning they were not involved in the division's entire tour of duty.

Speaking of soldiers who served the full duration of combat, Robert Phillips told me, "We had a few. Scattered. There was a sergeant in the platoon. Very few."

Robert sent me highlighted sentences on copied pages from *Story of the 320th Infantry*. The highlighted section concerned the intensity of a soldier's first experiences and how they burn unforgettably into one's heart and brain. By Christmas, Dad and Robert had already survived six months of combat, so they were in a different mode of operation than Ray Huckaby (134/35th), who remembered so many details from his initial days of war within the 35th Division. He wrote his recollections for the *Santa Fe Express* (January/February 2008), and his descriptions were especially helpful to me to understand what Dad could not talk about. I wrote a note to Ray to thank him, and he called me to answer any questions I might have.

About 50 years after the war, Ray was asked to write about his war experiences. He told the person, "I don't believe I can take it."

About ten years later, he was asked again. Ray tried for an hour and fell apart. He told me on the phone, "I would get too upset and have to quit." However, he persevered and finally wrote two to three pages in a notebook, even though he found that he could not spell correctly as he wrote. It took him three weeks to write his memories as he walked with his dog through his 76 acres of cattle pasture. There were tears on his pages, and he promised himself never again to read what he had written. I suspect he may have been crying as he spoke to me on the phone.

Ray Huckaby had joined the 35th Division in Metz as one of those 2,200 new replacements. He remembered a soldier asking, "Is there some way a guy can get out of this outfit?" Sergeant Lewis offered three options. A man could get out of duty by being killed, wounded, or captured.

* * *

Finally in Metz, everyone had a chance after two months to bathe again. When Dad and Ben Lane learned the manager of the bathhouse had nothing to give his children for Christmas, they delivered army rations of fruit and chocolate to the manager's home on Christmas Eve. They left quickly so they would not be

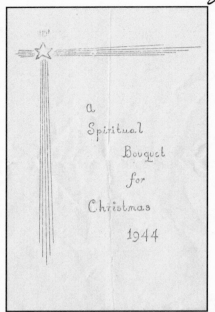

Somewhere in Germany
with the
320th Inf Regiment

Remembering you in my prayers-
attended Mass and received Holy
Communion today with the
sincere wish that you are
enjoying a very happy Christmas and that the New Year will
bring you its choicest blessings.
Father Bierís, our chaplain,
read the Mass, and sends you
his best wishes. Given to me
to send to you my darling
wife & daughter.
Daddy.

a
Spiritual
Bouquet
for
Christmas
1944

CHRISTMAS CARD CREATED BY A CHAPLAIN "SOMEWHERE IN GERMANY" FOR THE FAMILIES OF SOLDIERS. THE LOCATION WAS INCORRECT BECAUSE OF A NEW ENEMY OFFENSIVE.

LOUISE AND BABY EILEEN IN LATE FALL, 1944.

seen by the children. Ben said, "The manager started to cry and said he would see us when we came back from the fighting."

William Notley (320/35th) celebrated Christmas in Metz by attending religious services in a small chapel. He recalled in *Santa Fe Express* (January/February 2007), "Soldiers of the 320th sat on one side of the aisle and German prisoners of war sat on the other. We all sang identical Christmas hymns; we in English, they in German. What bitter irony that was!"

As for Dad, he sent Mom and Eileen a folded sheet of typing paper with a copied, handwritten message, "A Spiritual Bouquet for Christmas 1944." He had received it at a Catholic Mass, and he signed it, "Given to me to send to you my darling wife and daughter. Daddy." The words on the simple "card" also included, "Somewhere in Germany with the 320th Inf Regiment," but the 320th was actually in France. Patton intended to be in Germany, but the new battle had suddenly developed. Therefore he was forced to leave the muddy battlefields when his primary goal had been to reach the Rhine River still 70 miles away.

As for General Patton's Christmas Day, he was already in combat with other divisions from his Third Army. He wrote in *War as I Knew It,* "Christmas dawned clear and cold; lovely weather for killing Germans, although the thought seemed somewhat at variance with the spirit of the day."

The 35th Division ate Christmas dinner in comfortable quarters in Metz, although Ray Huckaby remembered feeling like a "condemned human being" as he ate. Dad told me that lots of soldiers suffered diarrhea from that turkey dinner after so many months of K-Rations.

At 3 o'clock the morning after Christmas, Ray Huckaby ate a hot meal. By 4 a.m., he became part of a convoy being rushed north over 85 miles of bad roads, trails, and cow paths to the enemy breakthrough. The temperature was five degrees below zero. The troops travelled in trucks that were not covered with canvas. Therefore the soldiers were exposed to the elements as they travelled from Metz through Luxembourg City to the area of Arlon, Belgium, south of Bastogne. After 50 minutes of travel, there was a ten-minute bathroom break. Some men were so cold they needed help getting off the truck. Ray wrote that after several hours, "A few just urinated right in their clothing, which was at least four layers thick."

This was only the beginning.

ORVAL FAUBUS WROTE IN IN THIS FARAWAY LAND ... " *THE GERMANS USED THEIR RAILWAY GUNS ... " NEAR NANCY, FRANCE. NOTE THE RELATIVE SIZE OF THE THREE STANDING SOLDIERS COMPARED TO THE RAILWAY GUN.*

ALFRED, PROBABLY IN PETTENCOURT, FRANCE, FALL OF 1944.

Alfred

DEC. 26, 1944—JAN. 19, 1945
ARDENNES CAMPAIGN

BERLIN

DASH
TO
ELBE RIVER

BRIDGEHEAD
ACROSS
ELBE RIVER

BATTLE OF
'RUHR'
POCKET

Hannover
Magdeburg

LIBERATION
OF
VENLO

Hildesheim   Zerbst

ROER TO
RHINE
DRIVE

Wesel

LANDED ON
OMAHA BHEAD
6 JULY '44

Essen Dortmund

BASTOGNE
BULGE
BATTLE

Maastricht

SAAR DRIVE
INTO BLIES-
BRUCK, GERM?

REAK THRU
AT
ST. LO

CAPTURED
TORIGNY-SUR-
VIRE '31 JULY

BATTLE OF
FORET DE
CHATEAU-SALINS

STEMMING
VOSGES MT.
COUNTERATT'K.

FIRST LIBERAT-
ION CEREMONY
CHATEAUDUN

BLITZ
ACROSS
FRANCE

Metz

Hagenau

320th SAVES
LOST BATTALION
AT MORTAIN

Nancy

Chateau
Salins

PARIS

Joinville

ennes

Pithiviers

Troyes

Laval   Le Mans

Montargis

Orleans

FOR THE 320TH REGIMENT OF THE 35TH INFANTRY DIVISION

MAP FROM STORY OF 320TH INFANTRY:
**BATTLE OF THE BULGE / BASTOGNE AREA**

7. THE ARDENNES CAMPAIGN BATTLE OF THE BULGE / BASTOGNE

December 16, 1944 – January 25, 1945
For 320th Regiment: December 26, 1944 – January 18, 1945

*T*he Battle of the Bulge, as this campaign came to be called, was fought in the Ardennes Forest. Germany's initial goal was to control all the roads leading in and out of the city of Bastogne. Therefore the Battle of the Bulge, Bastogne, and the Ardennes refer generally to the same campaign.

Researching and organizing the Ardennes Campaign was very difficult. During much of this time period, Orval Faubus (320/35th) was hospitalized, leaving me without his day-to-day journal, In This Faraway Land. I followed Dad's battalion within James Huston's (134/35th) journal, Biography of a Battalion, and within the history of the 6th Armored. With so much written about this largest land battle in history, the number of potential sources is overwhelming.

I casually asked Dad, "What was the worst part of the war for you?"

He hesitated and quietly responded, "Bastogne."

Don May said, "Alfred, you are a hero. I have a lot of respect for anyone who was at the Battle of the Bulge. You have gone to hell and back."

* * *

The German goal of this campaign was to race to Antwerp, split the American and British forces in two, and capture that most important deep-water port in Northern Europe. Antwerp was crucial to our supply lines. Hitler himself orchestrated the timing and the path through the Ardennes Forest, which extended from northern France into Belgium and Luxembourg. He believed the large dense forest, the rough terrain of hills and gorges, poor weather, and the holidays would hinder the Allies.

Instead of racing to Antwerp as planned, the Germans were held up by the intentional placement of the 101st Airborne in Bastogne. Seven spoke-like highways radiated out from this city. Whoever controlled those roads would be able to move troops and supplies and gain the upper hand.

Frequently, this campaign is noted for its element of surprise by the Germans. In *Sitting Duck Division*, John Morse believed United States military intelligence should have detected the German build-up. It started in October and involved at least 200,000 enemy troops, almost 2,000 big guns, and 1,000 tanks. He asked, "Why would it be a surprise for Germany to use the exact same path they used in World War I and again in 1940 to invade France?" He also wrote that women behind the American lines rushed from house to house, probably warning each other of the impending attack and the need to move out of their homes.

John Morse was part of the unfortunate 106th Infantry Division with no combat experience when he became part of a thinly guarded defensive line in the Ardennes on December 10. This was expected to be his calm introduction into the war. The 106th Division was responsible for 27 of the 88 miles of the battlefront. This was more than five times the typical distribution for a division, which then created large gaps along the line.

Some soldiers reported they could hear enemy tank noise and vehicle movement, especially at night. Another soldier said, "Sometimes, when the wind was right, we could hear music and singing." American headquarters reassured these soldiers that the Germans had simply made recordings to "spook" the American troops.

During a trip to Luxembourg, I discovered *"The Bulge" Remembered*, a brochure that marked the 60th anniversary of the battle. One paragraph reported that several citizens from the small Luxembourg village of Bivels escaped from German custody. They reported a massive concentration of German troops and equipment in the Bitburg area, but their warnings to the Allies were ignored.

Before the attack, U.S. General Bradley commented, "If they will come out of it and fight us again in the open, it is all to our advantage." On the night after the initial attack, General Patton wrote, "This was the first official notice we had of ... the antici-pated German assault."

Whether the attacks against Allied lines were allowed intentionally or by complacency is not known. No matter what the upper echelon knew, the troops were completely caught off guard. They were vastly outnumbered by the Germans who

broke through the weakly defended Allied lines in the heavy fog of early morning December 16. Steady streams of civilians fled the area, and some American troops withdrew because so many company commanders were missing after the first day of the attack.

* * *

At a graduation party, I was introduced to John, a veteran of the Battle of the Bulge. I sat down next to him and asked what group he served with.

He softly answered, "The 106th."

I said, "I know what that means."

The average ratio of German infantry to American was more than three Germans to one American, and at some points, six to one.

I asked John, "Do you think the Battle was a true surprise?"

ORIGINAL PILLARS IN THE BACKGROUND, REPAIRED PILLARS IN THE FOREGROUND. ST. LAURENTIUS CATHOLIC CHURCH, SAARBURG, GERMANY, BOMBED DECEMBER 23, 1944.

He said, "I know my boss did not know," and then he added, "We did hear their horses." Their horses transported their artillery.

* * *

The weather for the Battle of the Bulge started with a heavy fog and mist, exactly what the Germans wanted to prevent Allies from flying. "The fog moved over our base like a blanket, and you could not even see a few feet in any direction," Charles Haskett of the 8th Air Force wrote in the *Bulge Bugle* (August 2014).

For a week after the initial German attack, the fog continued, but finally on December 23, cold, dry winds cleared the skies and allowed the Allies to carry out air attacks.

* * *

By chance, 60 years after the war, my family visited St. Laurentius Catholic Church in Saarburg, Germany. This church housed an original baptismal font from 1575, and it was bombed by Allies on December 23, that very first day of clear skies. Functional smooth pillars were built after the bombing to replace the more elaborate 100-year-old fluted pillars that had been destroyed. The congregation expected to replace the simple, basic pillars, but in the end they decided against it. A brochure in the church explained that the "old and new parts of the building give evidence of the destructive power of our century."

* * *

The original assignment for the 35th Division was to break out to the Lutrebois-Harlange Road, south of Bastogne. That road fed into the Arlon-Bastogne Highway and continued into Bastogne, if the 35th could gain control. Eventually the 35th Infantry and the 4th Armored Divisions were to secure the Longvilly-Bastogne Road, heading northeast out of Bastogne toward St. Vith. Allied troops fought to open corridors through the German lines, while the Germans continually attempted to close them. Basically, the Allies fought for a month to take back the land the Germans had captured in the first days of the attack.

Casual history tends to infer that the Battle of the Bulge was basically decided when the 4th Armored Division made contact with the 101st Airborne in Bastogne on December 26. However, even from the perspective of the 101st Airborne, their task was far more difficult once they went on the offensive, as compared to initially being surrounded. James Huston wrote in *Biography of a Battalion*, "Indeed, American losses sustained after December 26 exceeded those from the preceding ten days, including all the units that had been overrun in the German's initial breakthrough."

During the early morning hours of December 27, some soldiers of the 320th waded through the icy, waste-deep waters of the Sure River. After crossing the river, the 320th advanced four miles through knee-deep snow to liberate the Luxembourg towns of Baschleiden, Flebour, and Boulaide, about nine miles southeast of Bastogne. There is a memorial in Boulaide that says:

Á LA MEMOIRE DES
VAILLANTS SOLDATS
DE LA 35e DIVISION
D'INFANTERIE U.S.
1944-1945

...in the memory of the valiant soldiers of the 35th Division of the U.S. Infantry.

On that same day, even though contact had already been made in Bastogne with the 101st Airborne, the surrounding areas were not yet under Allied control. During the night of December 27, snow blew horizontally, and the temperature dropped on each successive day and night as Scandinavian arctic air brought a blizzard. The soldiers became exhausted just moving through the snowdrifts. Temperatures could plummet at night to minus 10 or 20° F. Patton described it as "hideously cold." Others called it "arctic hell." "White hell." "Frozen jungle."

Some of the infantry froze to death in their ice-walled foxholes because they were not supplied with proper clothing for sub-zero temperatures. "Finish the war in '44" was a popular slogan, but the war did not end as hoped. Priority had been given to shipments of ammunition and gasoline rather than to winter supplies. The winter boots and gear did not arrive on the front lines until after the Battle of the Bulge. At times, American combat soldiers took clothing for their own use off dead Germans.

Some soldiers tried to sleep while standing in groups of three. They placed their arms on the shoulders of the other two men, forming a tripod by leaning inward to avoid lying in the snow. Other soldiers used branches from evergreen trees for ground cover. Troops from both sides could freeze to death if they were not evacuated within a half hour after they became casualties.

Newspapers and draperies were scavenged from bombed-out houses and stuffed into regular boots to try to keep feet from freezing and occasionally even turning black. Building a fire to stay warm was problematic because it attracted the attention of the enemy, as did lighting cigarettes. Whenever Dad saw photos from the Ardennes, he looked for soldiers huddling behind tanks. He remembered how everyone tried to stay warm with tank exhaust or by using the tanks as windbreaks. He permanently lost feeling in the tips of his fingers because they had frozen so often during this time. After being home, it took two years for Robert Phillips to put on socks without pain.

Bill Mauldin, a popular American cartoonist, created World War II cartoons with his weary and scruffy infantry characters named Willie and Joe. These cartoons were widely distributed to the army, throughout the United States, and abroad. In one cartoon, Willie and Joe scraped back snow while digging a foxhole in the frozen ground. Tree bursts were sending shrapnel in every direction; the caption read, *Willie, this makes me miss that warm summer mud.*

Another problem for our troops was that it was not easy to detect the enemy because they used smokeless and flashless powder in their rifles and machine guns. Some Germans camouflaged themselves in the snow by wearing white capes. Some dressed in American uniforms, carried captured weapons, drove American vehicles, and spoke perfect English. This caused great confusion, so a password was established every day at noon. In *Biography of a Battalion*, James Huston gave the example of a guard saying the word "Revolution" to which Americans were to reply, "French."

Occasionally, when Americans did not know the password of the day, they were killed by their own troops out of impulse or fear. Other soldiers with slight speech impediments were killed because they stammered, stuttered, or could not clearly pronounce the password.

In addition to the extreme cold, many infantrymen did not have access to basic clean drinking water. Water was delivered to Ray Huckaby (134/35th) on December 27, but it froze and burst its container, according to his written memories in *A Soldier Remembers*, published in *The Bulge Bugle* (February 2008). For him, that was the last water he received for almost two weeks, until the morning of January 10. He could eat snow, but every time a shell hit and exploded, it left a black ring about fifty feet across. After repeated barrages, clean snow could only be found in one-to-two inch layers between thinner layers of dirt, burnt shell powder, pine needles, and bark splinters. A cup of snow produced about a sixth of a cup of water. By the time Ray actually received drinking water, he was warned to drink it slowly, or it would all be thrown back up. With the combination of almost two weeks of highly concentrated rations and the lack of water, constipation became another discomfort for the soldiers.

Ray and his foxhole buddy alternated hour-long guard duties while their muscles quivered constantly from hypothermia. They were afraid to sleep because the quickest way to freeze to death was to be still.

In the dark of night, Ray could barely see a blanket that he wanted for warmth. When he reached for what he expected to be the blanket, he almost grabbed the frozen arm of a dead soldier. Later, he expected to find his military pack that he had dropped earlier in the snow, but he discovered the snow-covered mounds were not packs but dead soldiers from his company. That was the precise moment Ray vowed he would never return to the battlefields where he fought.

Alfred

* * *

Almost 60 years after the war, my brother Bob casually asked Dad whether he wanted something to eat as they drove through the tiny village of Dane on a wintry day.

Dad answered, "It's hard to believe in da war, we went four or five days without eating anyt'ing except hard candy bars [D-Rations] dat made you t'irsty."

He also recalled how they fought four or five days with no sleep.

On another bitterly cold January evening, Bev pushed Dad in his wheelchair back into the nursing home where one of the staff members greeted him. Dad told the woman: "People t'ink dis is so cold. In da service, it was dis cold and I didn't know where to sleep. Wit' a pick and an ax, I could not always dig a hole because of da frozen ground. Da woods were better for blocking da wind, but we could not build fires because of being seen. A big coat might work, but it did not cover everyt'ing."

Then he added, "I don't know why I t'ought of dat."

* * *

Leonard Huskey (2nd Infantry Division) was in the Battle of the Bulge with one woolen army blanket. He told me in a phone conversation that he also had a long woolen coat, but he left it behind when they advanced because it got wet and then froze. He could not deal with the coat along with the mortars he was responsible for.

* * *

I asked Dad, "Did the military supply you with enough clothing?"

He asked me, "How could dey?"

* * *

* * *

The Allies expected the Germans to counterattack if the weather would again limit our ability to fly. That is exactly what happened when weather conditions deteriorated to clouds and overcast on December 28. Allies could not fly; therefore German tanks moved more freely around Bastogne. Various types of weather continued to restrict our flight through January 3. At times, snow drifted to more than five feet.

Patton wrote, "How human beings could endure this continuous fighting at sub-zero temperatures is still beyond my comprehension." In addition to the cold and the snow, there was lengthy darkness, which extended everyone's dangerous guard duty at night. In Bastogne on December 16, sunset was around 4:30 p.m. and sunrise was after 8 a.m.

All commanders, German and American alike, tried to keep battles away from little hamlets because this type of combat was time-consuming and indecisive. However, the weather and the geography were so difficult that both sides tended to gravitate toward any type of shelter.

On December 29, Germany's General Manteuffel created an overall plan against the continued influx of Allied troops. According to the website for the United States Army Center for Military History in Washington D.C., "The operation [German] would be in three phases: first close the ring once again around Bastogne; second, push the Americans back to the south; third, with reinforcements now on the way, take Bastogne in a final assault." The 35th Division would be greatly impacted by this plan. They would have to resist the Germans pushing back to the south.

Alfred

On December 30, the Germans attacked. Patton stated in his memoirs, "This was probably the biggest coordinated counter-attack that troops under my command ever experienced."

At that time, Dad's 320th was involved within a group of buildings in Harlange, called the Furhman Farm. Along with Villers-la-Bonne-Eau, these were the primary areas of enemy resistance, both about six miles southeast of Bastogne. German paratroopers had occupied Villers since December 19, and they saw themselves as favorites of Nazi Hermann Goering. By the end of the month, Joe Demler (137/35th) of Port Washington, Wisconsin, was captured and became a prisoner of war at Villers -la-Bonne-Eau.

* * *

I first learned of Joe Demler about 60 years after the war from Laurie Arendt's *Back from Duty: Ozaukee County's Veterans Share Their Stories*. Joe's biography included a photo of him weighing a skeletal 70 pounds and a quote, "We were sent to Metz, France, where we joined the 35th Division."

I sent a note to Joe about my interest in the 35th Division, along with my contact information. I acknowledged he may not be comfortable talking to me, which I understood and fully accepted. Joe called a week later and apologized for the delay. They had just installed new carpeting. Friday at 2 p.m. would be a good time for us to talk at his home in Port Washington, so I copied a few pages from *35th Division: Trail of the Santa Fe Division* that pertained to Joe's capture.

When I first met Joe, I asked, "So you were in the 137th Regiment?"

Joe answered, "Yes."

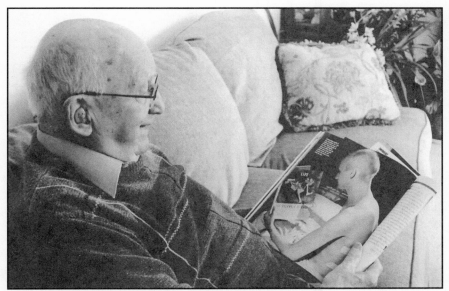

JOSEPH DEMLER, LOOKING AT A PHOTO OF HIMSELF LOOKING AT A PHOTO OF HIMSELF. PHOTO BY KATE MOORE, 2005.

"K or L Company?"

My interview questions were not typical, and Joe's wife called from the next room, "Are you writing a book?" At that time, I really did not know.

I said to Joe, "A picture speaks a thousand words, but that photograph of you weighing only 70 pounds speaks far more than that."

Joe's parents had been informed he was missing in action. A family friend saw the published photo and said to his parents, "I think that could be Joe." Joe said to me, "I was told the photo would never be published, but it was too good for selling war bonds."

Alfred

As we talked, he glanced out the window near the kitchen table with tears welling up in his eyes. He recalled the German prisoner-of- war camp, "Every night, they'd carry bodies out."

Since World War II, newspapers had called and asked for Joe's perspective on hostage situations. He told them, "It is too difficult to talk about it."

When I left that day, he called to me from the front door of his immaculately maintained white Cape Cod home, "You can come and talk to me anytime."

I sent Joe additional information from my research, and Joe replied in a letter, "I also want to thank you for getting the map from Keith Bullock of where I was captured. I did not know the name of the town. The last letter you sent was with the picture of *LIFE* magazine… I guess I was in *LIFE* more than any POW in World War II and after."

The after-action report said of Joe's capture, "Companies K and L were slowly being cut to pieces by tank fire and flame throwers." Reinforcements from Lt. Colonel Peiper's 1st SS Panzer Division, *"Leibstandarte Adolf Hitler,"* moved into Villers on the morning of December 30. This group acquired the nickname of "Torch Battalion" as it moved through Russia and burned villages. It was also responsible for the massacre of over 80 unarmed prisoners of war near Malmedy almost two weeks earlier. The 1st SS Panzer Division began as a unit serving as Hitler's elite personal body guards, but it eventually evolved into a full-sized division. It was diminished in the early fight for Bastogne but was functioning again and supported by the 14th Parachute Regiment.

Joe also wrote in his letter to me, "We were in one of the stone houses where the tanks shot their 88 shells through the front of the ground floor. I was on the second floor, and I flew halfway to the top. I sure will never forget that. That is the reason that I never got a word from anybody that was with me... as the rest were either killed or they died in POW camp." A postscript added, "You can see why I do not go to the reunions. I don't know a soul."

Joe was liberated about three months after his capture, weighing just those 70 pounds, too weak to rise from his bed. Given another three days of neglect, doctors estimated he would have died from starvation.

* * *

A plaque at nearby Lutremange, Belgium, commemorates the combat at Villers-la-Bonne-Eau and reads:

> **On December 30, 1944, the Germans launched a counter-attack designed to break supply lines. Elements of the 1st SS Panzer Division entered Villers-la-Bonne-Eau, where the K and L Companies of the 137th Regiment were trapped. More than 200 soldiers became missing in action. The German prisoners later said the SS had used flamethrowers on the houses held by the American soldiers, and most of them burned alive.**

On this single day, more than 6,000 rounds of artillery fell on the little village of Villers-la-Bonne-Eau. The village consisted of just seventeen houses.

* * *

Sixty years after the Battle of the Bulge, my family of four visited Villers-la-Bonne-Eau in Belgium. It had been completely rebuilt after the war. Graves were grouped within terraced plots, surrounded by variously colored small stones, in a neatly tended cemetery. As I stood alone between that cemetery and the steepled white church tucked into the side of a hill, I thought about Joe Demler's terror at this very spot where I viewed a peaceful, green valley with scattered buildings.

Several months later, I was stunned to discover one simple sentence in the after-action report for the 320th. On January 1, Dad's 1st Battalion attached to Joe Demler's 137th Regiment. In other words, Dad's unit filled the ranks for Joe and for all those killed or captured two days earlier. Their assignment was to gain control of Villers-la-Bonne-Eau and open the roads to the east. Dad's 1st Battalion remained attached to the 137th until control of the all-important road junction near Villers was assured.

GERMAN STEEL-BAR REINFORCED CONCRETE BUNKER NEAR VILLERS-LA-BONNE-EAU AT LUTREMANGE, BELGIUM.

On New Year's Eve, Orval Faubus wrote in his journal, "I know that in this frozen, flame-lit, thunderous vortex of hell, there are many who welcomed this New Year who will not see its first dawn, and many more who will not survive its first day."

At this point, Allied victory was still not certain. General Patton wrote in his diary on the afternoon of January 4, "We can still lose this war." He admitted this was the only time he ever said such a thing. The fight just to capture and gain control of the city of Bastogne lasted two more weeks after this journal entry by Patton.

Then a Siberian weather front brought more snow that week, and our troops could not dig in. On January 6, Dad's

OVERLOOKING VILLERS-LA-BONNE-EAU, BELGIUM, WHERE ALFRED'S UNIT REPLACED JOSEPH DEMLER'S UNIT, WHICH HAD BEEN CAPTURED.

battalion was attached to the 134th Regiment in the area of Lutrebois, according to Huston's *Biography of a Battalion*. Lutrebois was a couple of miles south of Bastogne, now part of the present-day city. There were attacks, counterattacks, and counter-counterattacks. If air support could bomb, strafe, and keep the enemy in their foxholes, our troops could overrun German positions. However, sufficient numbers of aircraft simply were not available. Rather than having the benefit of air support, the artillery of the 35th Division fired more than 41,000 shells on German positions from January 3 to 7, averaging five shots per minute for these five days of battle, according to a plaque located at nearby Lutremange.

* * *

During this campaign, Dad described how Jeeps carried wounded soldiers with broken backs, legs, arms, or shot-off limbs out of the woods. After hitting bumps in the terrain, the wounded would scream and swear, "You sons of bitches!"

Dad asked me, "What else could we do? We had to get dem out." Medical supplies were not always available for the wounded, and at times Cognac was used as an anesthetic.

* * *

By January 8, the weather was a bit more bearable with temperatures around –5°F and with less wind. A couple days later, there was a pause during which hot food and the first replacements of the campaign arrived.

It was not easy to be a lonely, individual replacement or to fight with replacements. James Huston wrote in *Biography of a Battalion* that when "...former rear-area clerks and cooks had been transferred to combat duty," casualties even among officers increased because the new replacements were unfamiliar with combat, commonly afraid or careless, and needed more guidance.

Leonard Huskey felt sorry for replacements because they were given little respect and undesirable duties. Both Dad and Robert recalled replacements getting out of transfer trucks and being killed, almost immediately, before they climbed a hill to get into position. Many replacements died before anyone knew their names.

Merle Koontz (HQ/2nd/320) said he was haunted all his life by a tearful replacement soldier, a nice-looking blonde, who held out his M1 rifle and said he did not even know how to load it (*35th Infantry: Trail of the Santa Fe Division*). This soldier had been transferred as a former airborne mechanic to a very likely death in the infantry.

* * *

Robert told me, "Some were found with their full field pack, a sign of a brand-new replacement." He explained, "The old guys just tied a blanket with a rope and hung it over their shoulders."

* * *

On January 11, Americans attempted to occupy the woods east of Lutrebois. Their path was littered with dead Germans, killed by 100,000 rounds of artillery shells. Dad spoke of pulling sleds out of the woods with bodies of dead Germans mixed with dead Americans. They were then piled together on trucks. Other frozen bodies were dragged by tying wire to their arms or ankles. James Huston wrote that crews worked for four days to remove the dead with trailers and two Jeeps, four to five men per vehicle. They still had not finished the task when they were ordered to move to their next assignment.

MEMBERS OF "320TH INF RGMT" IN BASTOGNE, JANUARY 1945, FOUND BY FAMILY FRIEND MATT ENGELS AT NATIONAL ARCHIVES, COLLEGE PARK, MARYLAND. THE SOLDIER ON THE BACK SIDE OF THE FIRE HAS SIMILAR FEATURES TO ALFRED.

Medic LeRoy Maleck (137/35th) was searching for a location to set up a medical aid station when he came upon the flattened village of Villers-la-Bonne-Eau. In his book *What Am I Doing Here?*, he described how he and a friend entered what remained of the small church tucked into the hill at Villers. Most of the roof was gone, but a chandelier and part of the balcony remained. Upon a closer look, the chandelier held the upper half of a German soldier. A lieutenant from graves registration found the lower part of a body on the balcony.

Then LeRoy approached a structure about a block away from the church, but instead of it being a building as he expected, "It was a huge, long, rectangular stack of frozen German bodies, possibly thousands of them." He added, "Thank God for the cold weather, or the stench would have been unbearable."

* * *

The actions of the 35th Division during this campaign are memorialized in a park-like setting near Lutremange, five miles southeast of Bastogne, where a German steel-bar-reinforced concrete pillbox still remains. A plaque was dedicated by an association called, "The Triangle of Destruction." It honors the 35th Infantry Division for its sacrifices in liberating their small Belgian towns. The last words of the memorial are:

> **The triangle formed by the villages of Lutremange, Villers-**
> **la-Bonne-Eau, and Lutrebois was literally plowed by the bombs. The Germans held onto the terrain like nowhere else in the Ardennes. In Lutrebois, only five houses remained standing. At Villers-la-Bonne-Eau, with 17 buildings, only three remained. Numerous civilians lost their lives during the combat. Hundreds of acres of woods were totally pulverized, and the fields were covered with bodies and craters. Everywhere there were burned-out tanks, charred vehicles, and complete destruction. From the testimonies of the soldiers themselves of the 35th Infantry Division, these battles were the most terrible they had to wage in Europe. The soldiers of the 35th Infantry Division fought in the freezing cold and snow, against determined German soldiers in order that today we can live in freedom.**
>
> **May their sacrifices never be forgotten.**

* * *

Remembering the battle, Dad twice lamented to me, "All dose bodies covered wit' snow."

alfred

After researching Dad's route, it is unlikely that he saw the fallen soldiers from the Malmedy Massacre mentioned earlier. Over 80 unarmed American soldiers were gunned down by Peiper's 1st SS troops on December 17. The action most likely would never have gained international attention except that an Associated Press photographer took a photo in early January before the bodies were removed on January 14.

Dad's minimal description was more probably the corpses of slain Nazis mentioned in *Story of the 320th Infantry*. They "froze in the snow in the grotesque positions in which they had fallen" in the area of Bastogne. Only four enemy soldiers escaped death by surrendering. The other 76 corpses "were not removed for several days because of the terrain," and they were never removed from Dad's memory.

* * *

Veteran Jack Foy emotionally stated during a commemoration of the Battle of the Bulge, "The war may have ended 64 years ago, but for us, it never ended. The snow-covered mounds, once men, frozen arms, legs, seemingly beg us not to forget." (*Bulge Bugle,* May 2010)

* * *

On January 12, the 320th was attached to the 6th Armored Division and relocated to Bastogne to join elements of the 101st Airborne, the 4th Armored, and other units. Then they moved east of Bastogne, where Germans had occupied excellent defensive positions for more than three weeks.

The 320th was ordered to do a straight line attack across snowy fields just before dawn on January 15 in order to capture Oubourcy about four miles northeast of Bastogne. There had been no artillery preparation, no initial tanks, no cover, just standing infantry so as to completely surprise the enemy. Robert Phillips recalled, "We were pinned down for hours in open fields." Eventually the troops broke through the German perimeter to capture the town.

Captain Norman Carey (320/35th) described the process of capturing Oubourcy in *35th Infantry: Trail of the Santa Fe Division*, "These Germans were ordered to hold the town at all cost, to the last man if necessary, and they fought with fanatical zeal." *The Stars and Stripes*, a newspaper that reports on matters affecting the United States Army, simply said, "The 320th Infantry captured the town of Oubourcy," but higher officers commented the town looked as bleak as Saint-Lô, and it was a miracle they had made it.

Captain Carey also wrote that two D Company machine gunners were killed that day. I gently asked Dad whether he remembered that situation. Either he did not remember it, or he did not want to talk about it. Sometimes it was difficult for me to tell the difference.

I spoke with Robert Phillips more than any other veteran, and every time I had a conversation with him, he told me about his best friend and foxhole buddy, Albert Gibeau. Also, without fail, Robert reminded himself that Albert's death on January 15 at Oubourcy was not his fault. He reassured himself, "It would have happened anyway."

Robert had encouraged Gibeau to accept a battlefield commission as a second lieutenant in Dad's 2nd Platoon. Robert said, "He was already doing the work, and he may as well get paid for it." Gibeau was reluctant because every 2nd Platoon

leader had not survived two weeks in that position, but with his wife's approval, he accepted the promotion. Albert Gibeau was killed in Oubourcy as he rested against a building after removing his helmet.

Orval Faubus believed a helmet made little difference in life or death. A helmet was mostly for morale purposes because Faubus said, "A hard-flying shell fragment or bullet can slice through one as if it were paper." Captain Carey and others believed Gibeau was hit by an American 81-mm mortar round that fell short.

Robert said, "I made a promise to him to take stuff off his body and send it to his family."

* * *

Dad rarely spoke of war, but our family had all heard of "Stud," whose real name was Herman Hinson. Because of his importance to Dad, I was obsessed with finding him, and my obsession only got worse when I thought Stud could be the other soldier in the foxhole within the National Archive video mentioned earlier.

I scoured the Internet for connections, and I made cold calls. I wrote letters to American Legions, who do not seem to receive mail. I found the same incorrect Herman Hinson from two directions, once through his wife and once through his daughter. A bank even delivered one of my letters to an employee that I hoped would be a relative. Each time something would disqualify my newly-discovered Herman Hinson. One did not have a middle name. One was not tall enough. Another did not have enough dental work done immediately after the war. One never served in World War II.

HERMAN HINSON, "STUD."

I finally found the only child of "Stud" after Dad had passed away. I used a mix of genealogy, libraries, and obituaries, churches, and funeral homes in North Carolina, and then I wrote to Stud's grandson, who kindly called me to give contact information for his mother in South Carolina.

Shirley Hinson Bragg always thought her father's nickname was "Spud." She wrote to me, "Mother said he had kitchen duty and peeled lots of potatoes, which is how he got his nickname." From his family's respect and love, "Spud" seems more appropriate, but his military buddies clearly called him otherwise. Shirley discovered one of my father's letters in a box of mementos. Dad had written to her father after the Battle of the Bulge:

Alfred

January 1945
Hello Stud,

*Received your letter today and was sure glad to hear
from you. Sorry to hear that your back is still giving
you trouble, but I think you'll live. I hope. We did not
know if you maybe went back to the States like so
many others. If you do, be sure and let us know
because we would demand a bottle of something
good to drink.*

*We are all fine, just like always, except that I'm in, or
rather back in, D Company, but so far I had a very
good go here, and hope it stays that way. Never had
to walk yet when we moved, and when the Co goes
to some town when they ain't fighting in the front, I
have to go with the Lt. to find room for them in town.*

*Are you still sleeping with boards under your
mattress? Well it can't be worse than some of the
foxholes we had. I hope this war will be over soon. I
don't like that word, foxholes.*

*Ack-Ack hasn't been around here lately, Griff said,
but when we see him, we'll say hello to him for you.
Everybody sure was wondering where you're at.*

*And about those pictures, I think Perone does not
want anything. I gave him a haircut, and he said that
was all he wanted for what I owed him. I will ask
him, and if he wants some money, I'll pay for you.*

*Yes, we had a good meal on Xmas, and glad to say we
had it in Metz. We came back from Germany just
before Xmas. We sure travelled a lot since you were
gone. After Xmas, we went to Luxembourg, and now
we are in Belgium. I suppose you maybe know that*

by reading the paper. We got replacements in Metz.

Oh yes, Stud, Griff said the gang is not like it used to be. Like last night, Griff said that Kramer was going to hit Eikerle with a bottle. Of course, he was drunk. They found some down in a basement some place, and they have a lot of trouble with the guy who took my place. Jack said they complain about a guard now, but they are still together. Lt. Duffy is in charge now as Capt Vignes and Capt Kolmer got hurt at the same time. The bed roll truck backed over a mine some place, and it was one of our own. They will not be back for a while.

How do you really feel about being back? I suppose it would get awful tiresome in a hospital. If this darn war was over once, like we always said, then being in one place with nobody shooting at us, it would not be so bad.

The Germans wanted to get smart and push us back, but it did not work so good. Of course, I suppose it didn't help us any, and then again, maybe it is going to make them much weaker in Germany. Well, Stud, I'll close for now. Was very glad to hear from you, and I will go to the boys to see if they want to send along a few lines, and I hope that this letter finds you in good shape again, and that you'll be back soon if you want to. Anyhow, I hope you are fine. I am and hope to stay that way.

Your pal,
Hot Papa

Alfred

Written on the bottom of the letter is a note from Benjamin Lane:

> *Hello you old chicken thief. It is still rough in the*
> *E.T.O.*
> *D Co. runner*
> *Lane*

* * *

Dad had written in his letter to Stud, "...they are having a lot of trouble with the guy who took my place." Sometime during January, Dad had become a translator rather than a gunner. The 35th Division was taking a lot of prisoners, and Robert said, "If I had the authority, I would use your dad as an interpreter. A division was lucky to have one man who could do that."

* *

On January 16, the 320th took the town of Michamps and cut the Bourcy-Longvilly Highway while our own planes accidentally bombed our own soldiers. An after-action report included the remark, "...friendly aircraft bombed Michamps with some disruptive effect on our troops."

From the history of the 6th Armored Division, Dad's 1st Battalion aided the 6th Armored and the 101st Airborne in six of the "nine long, bitter cold days...to push back the enemy four miles." This word "push" may elicit reactions as to whether the Germans should have been pushed back, as Eisenhower ordered, or pinched off as preferred by Patton. Don May agreed with Patton and used this difference of opinion not to vote for Eisenhower in the presidential election eight years later.

The 4th Armored Division broke through to the 101st Airborne in Bastogne on December 26, but it took weeks of combat to secure the area. In historical accounts, the campaign is frequently oversimplified and almost exclusively focused on Bastogne. Instead, the Battle of the Bulge was a very complex battle, still the largest in the history of the United States Army, involving over a million American, British, and enemy soldiers. It took 41 days to push the Germans back to the original break-through line, and according to the statistics in the *Wisconsin State Journal*, January 17, 1944, the battle covered 1,200 square miles. Some say Germany basically ran out of fuel and was unable to get reserves to their Panther and Tiger tanks.

As mentioned earlier, the Luxembourg government produced *"The Bulge" Remembered* in commemoration of the 60th anniversary of this battle. The statistics for the Ardennes Campaign vary among sources, but this particular publication lists the losses:

American losses:	German losses:
18,500 killed (about 450/day)	29,800 killed
46,200 wounded	34,450 wounded
10,900 captured and missing in action	22,500 captured and missing in action
75,600 total (about 1,800/day)	86,750 total
	Belgium and Luxembourg civilians:
	3,800 killed and wounded

Other sources report 81,000 American casualties and more than 100,000 for the Germans.

As far as the loss of soldiers from the 320th Infantry Regiment during this campaign, Orval Faubus wrote, "...we went into the Ardennes with over-strength companies, more than 186 men and officers. Some companies came out with only 31."

* * *

I said to Dad, "I know what you had to do in World War II was bad because I have been reading. The 101st is mentioned frequently, and their casualty rate is recorded as 150 percent. Do you know the casualty rate for the 35th?"

I answered my own question, "Over 180 percent."

I continued, "When I watched parts of the *Band of Brothers*, I heard a comment about 70 days of continuous combat for the 101st. Do you know how many days you had of continuous combat?"

I knew Dad would have no response, so I answered, "162."

I added, "I even found that Eisenhower said the 101st got enough attention for the Battle of the Bulge and that the 4th Armored and the 35th deserved more."

James Huston, in *Biography of a Battalion*, included a memorandum from General Eisenhower to generals Bradley and Devers, suggesting some divisions had not been recognized for their contributions. Eisenhower acknowledged the heroic actions of the 101st Airborne Division in Bastogne, and then he added:

> *... in many instances other units have performed in equally gallant fashion---and under almost equally spectacular conditions...Little has been said of the exploits of the 4th Armored, or of the*

> *35th and other units in battling their way forward*
> *under appalling conditions to join up with the*
> *Bastogne position.*

For the first time, I noted the tiniest hint of relief in Dad's face. I acknowledged what he had done, but more importantly, General Eisenhower had also.

The 6th Armored Division, which had the highest casualty rate of the armored divisions in the European Theatre and fought with the 35th Infantry Division, was even more neglected in recognition. As written on the website of the 6th Armored Division:

> *It was disillusioning and bitter for us, who had*
> *come in at the most crucial time and had borne*
> *the brunt of all the highly geared enemy pressure,*
> *had thrown back with heavy losses his every*
> *counterattack, had without sleep or relief fought*
> *him tooth and nail until this terrific drive was*
> *slowed down to a standstill, to have our coura-*
> *geous stand so conspicuously ignored by the*
> *world. We wondered with no little amazement if*
> *this war was fought by Public Relations Officers...*

Patton bragged about his Third Army because he had moved his troops faster than anyone, including generals Eisenhower and Bradley, thought possible. Patton wrote, "During this operation, the Third Army moved farther and faster and engaged more divisions in less time than any other army in the history of the United States—possibly in the history of the world."

* * *

* * *

Six decades after the Battle of the Bulge, Sara Rosenberry travelled from her assignment at the American Embassy in Luxembourg to visit her mother at the nursing home in Lodi, Wisconsin. She asked the staff whether any resident was a veteran of the Battle of the Bulge, and the staff directed her to Dad. Sara impacted him tremendously when she spoke to him about the appreciation of the people she had met in Luxembourg.

Dad asked, "Dey remember?"

"Darn right, they remember," Sara said.

Sara gave a speech during the summer prior to the 60th anniversary of the Battle of the Bulge. The speech was given to returning veterans of the 35th Infantry Division at Clervaux Castle in Luxembourg:

> *I am very honored to be here today representing the American Embassy in Luxembourg and in particular our Ambassador, Peter Terpeluk, who is a great patriot and supporter of the commemorations of the Battle of the Bulge. No state has more soldiers resting in the American Military Cemetery at Hamm than does his, Pennsylvania.*
>
> *While there may be something very official sounding about being a diplomat at an American Embassy, it is often a very personal experience.*
>
> *The Ambassador tells every audience he is the luckiest ambassador in the entire world. Serving in Luxembourg is always a pleasure, of course, but being here at this time is a true honor as it allows us to witness something very special.*

Most of us in the public service, and particularly those of us who chose to serve our country overseas, are motivated by something we cannot really explain even to ourselves. We know we are trying to live up to something that we recognize as being important and larger than us but something we do not entirely understand. Those of us serving in Luxembourg at this time -- who have the opportunity to meet you, to talk to you, to hear your story, to look you in the eye – I think we finally do understand. We realize that we are spending our lives trying to match what you did here. Thank you for being our heroes and our inspiration.

Many of us serving today—whether in Africa, Sarajevo, Afghanistan, China, Washington or Luxembourg—were born of the greatest generation. Your sacrifices and contribution made possible our legacy. Thank you for what you have given to my generation, my daughter's generation, my future grandchildren's generation – whether American, Luxembourger, French, or even German. Of course, we cannot match what you did, but we can dedicate ourselves to protecting that legacy and passing it on.

Today is particularly special and personal for me.

I am here not just as the representative of the United States Embassy, but also on behalf of a veteran of the 320th Regiment of the 35th Infantry Division. His name is Alfred Endres, and he lives at Good Samaritan Retirement Home in Lodi,

Alfred

Wisconsin. He was with you all the way from Normandy to the very end.

Like many veterans, he never talked about his experiences, and it is only recently that his family really began to understand all that he had been through and all that he had done. His medals are now framed on the wall of his room, and he is now telling his story. It is one of serving as a gunner in the hedgerows in France, of walking endless miles in the snow behind tanks, trying to stay close to absorb the warmth of their exhaust. He pulled bodies – American and German mixed together as the result of successive attacks – from foxholes in order to be able to retake a position. As he put it, no one should ever have to do that again.

I have had the honor of hearing his story when I visit with him during my trips to my home state of Wisconsin. When I told Alfred about all the things the people of Luxembourg do to ensure that what he and others did and sacrificed will not be forgotten, he looked at me and asked, almost in astonishment, "They remember?"

Darn right they remember, Alfred.

When I heard the 35th was returning, I sent word back that I planned to be with you today. I will be sending Alfred pictures of this day and, with your permission, your best wishes. I want him to know that, even if he was not able to attend, we were thinking of him and all the others of the 35th who could not be here.

The United States and Luxembourg shared a deep bond forged by circumstances and sacrifices of those days. I want to especially thank CEBA and the United States Veterans' Friends and also the Government of Luxembourg for ensuring that the bond remains strong and that there is always someone here to greet and honor them. It is a testament to their dedication that, to quote our Ambassador, "No U.S. veteran or soldier's family need walk alone on these hallowed grounds."

Thank you to all.

From Sara's conversations with Dad, she relayed to me, "Your dad also served as a scout at times, which meant crawling ahead with a radio on a long wire. Sometimes he crossed wires that connected German scouts to their bases." He could speak German, and therefore he was able to translate the transmitted messages.

Sara invited my family and me to visit her in Europe. There, she drove us to various memorials in the area. General Patton is buried at the Luxembourg-American Cemetery in Hamm. At that cemetery and at the national Liberation Memorial at the crossroads of Schuman's Eck, maps with colored arrows depict the movements of military units during the Ardennes Campaign. I noticed the length and the number of arrows associated with each unit. At first glance, the greater amount of color seemed to indicate a greater contribution to the Battle, but then I realized the relatively few and short arrows of the 35th Division indicated the intensity of their fight. The soldiers of the 35th could not move very far or fast because their battles were so difficult.

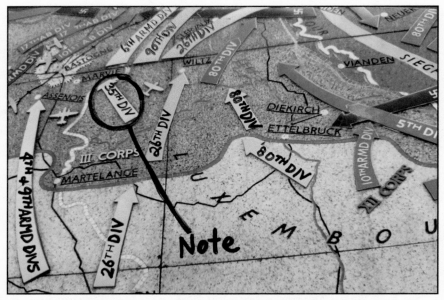

Alfred

THE RELATIVELY SHORT ARROW FOR THE 35TH DIVISION INDICATES THE INTENSITY OF COMBAT. LUXEMBOURG AMERICAN CEMETERY, HAMM, LUXEMBOURG.

For Dad, the Battle of the Bulge was the worst of his war experiences. I read letters by a 35th veteran that did not show any of Dad's emotions. Dad was on the front lines, and the other veteran, as he said, had a "pretty good job" in headquarters. On December 31, Dad was about to enter Villers-la-Bonne-Eau to replace Joe Demler's unit, which had been captured after an attack with tanks and flame throwers. This other 35th veteran was far enough away in headquarters to comment on an "occasional burst of machine-gun fire" which marred the beauty of the snow and the pines. He felt sorry for the infantry "in the foxholes on days and nights like we are having," so he understood the cold, but he had no concept of the reality of their combat.

* * *

The wife of a World War II soldier told me, "I know war must be bad because my husband never wanted to visit where he had served."

I asked, "Did he serve in Europe or the Pacific or …?"

She replied, "He was a cook in Texas."

This woman believed that cooking in Texas had the same impact and trauma as front-line combat. I was so stunned on the phone that it took me a few seconds to start breathing again.

* * *

A young man approached Dad as Bev pushed him in his wheel-chair on a sidewalk one day. The man put his hand on Dad's shoulder and said, "I know what you went through because I was in the army, too."

The words were kind, but the young man had never been in combat. Dad remained silent, accepted the good intentions, and was most likely fully aware of this man's ignorance about the realities of war.

* * *

I commented to Dad, "I read about a soldier who said the Battle of the Bulge was a good experience."

For a man who was slow to react and soft-spoken to a fault, Dad responded immediately and harshly, "Who said dat?"

"Just someone I read about," I said.

Dad replied, "Den he doesn't know much!"

Alfred

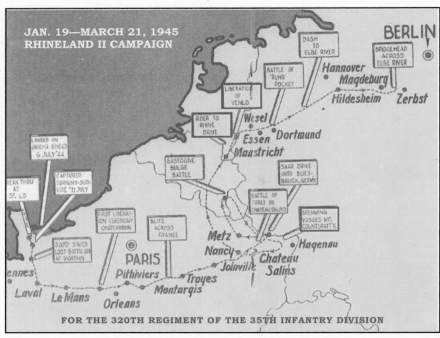

MAP FROM STORY OF 320TH INFANTRY:
VOSGES MOUNTAINS, ROER TO RHINE DRIVE AND VENLO

8. RHINELAND CAMPAIGN PART II

January 19, 1945 – March 21, 1945

O n January 19, most of the 35th Division was trucked in strict secrecy back to Metz. Orval Faubus wrote, "Shoulder insignia must be covered and vehicle markings obliterated." That did not sound like the ten-day to two-week rest everyone was hoping for after the Battle of the Bulge. The men were quartered in some dirty stone buildings on the southern outskirts of Metz, and for the next three days, they cleaned up, ate hot meals, and picked up replacements.

Dad and Ben Lane reconnected with Roland Dewald, the manager of the bathhouse, and he gave gifts to the two soldiers in return for their fruit and chocolate on Christmas Eve. Ben received a medallion honoring the first cross-Atlantic flight in 1936 of the *Hindenburg*, an 804-foot hydrogen-filled, rigid passenger-carrying airship. Dad was gifted a pinkish-gold ring with the French words for *"More than yesterday...Less than tomorrow*," which our family treasures, and each of his five daughters eventually wore.

Within days, Eisenhower's headquarters ordered most of the 35th Division to move 90 miles to join the Seventh Army. Generals Bradley and Patton strongly protested, and Patton wrote, "The 35th had been in actual combat with the enemy every day except five since the sixth of July, and I had only just succeeded in getting it out of the line."

However, there was a threat of yet another German offensive, sometimes called a "Little Bulge," in the area of the Vosges Mountains about 25 miles southeast of Saarguemines. On January 23, the troops moved in extremely cold and windy weather to await the German offensive.

Howard S. White (320/35th) wrote in his war memoirs, *The Eyes Have It!,* that in the Vosges Mountains, they used previously built German foxholes, wide enough for two men to lie down and roofed with logs. The snow was eight to ten inches deep and artillery flew overhead, but the new assignment near Wingen, France, was a welcome relief compared to what they had just been through near Bastogne.

ALFRED, FRONT ROW RIGHT, PROBABLY IN THE VOSGES MOUNTAINS, JANUARY 1945. OTHER POSSIBLE SOLDIERS ARE MITCHELL, HORN, NELSON, AND LYNCH.

When possible, Jeeps delivered food in insulated containers so it was reasonably warm when it was served. At other times, the troops ate K-rations. A three-man rotation allowed for one hour on guard duty and two hours of rest in the foxhole. Orval Faubus wrote in his journal, "The personal feelings of most of us are that we'd like to spend the rest of the war here if the Russians can end it before too long."

Shoepacs, which could have prevented frostbite in the Ardennes, finally arrived. Now their usefulness in the snowdrifts of the Vosges Mountains would be short-lived because the German attack never developed. In a week, the 35th Division prepared for a 292-mile troop movement to join the Ninth Army.

Patton had assumed the 35th Division was only on temporary loan to another command. He wrote, "We also got information that the 35th was going to the 9th Army instead of coming back to us. From a sentimental and morale standpoint it is unquestionably a mistake to move divisions from one army corps to the next." He added, "This division was one of the oldest in the Third Army and had always done well."

At the nursing home, Dad said of his division, "Dey never made much of us den, but dey seem to now."

While 800 men of the 35th Division travelled by trucks and Jeeps, the vast majority of the division relocated by means of old World War I "40 and 8" boxcars, built with wooden slats like cattle cars in the United States and intended for 40 men or 8 horses. At almost 300 miles, this was one of the longest infantry moves during the war, moving from the Vosges Mountains in France through the Ardennes in Luxembourg and Belgium to the area of Maastricht and Sittard, Holland, near the German border. Traveling in this fashion is probably how Dad spent his 27th birthday on January 31. Most of the trucks and Jeeps arrived February 1st after driving over roads caked with ice, with shoulders that were still mined. The train arrived on February 2.

Robert Phillips remembered travelling at night and attempting to be secretive, "We covered up all the markings and identification on our vehicles that indicated who we were, but when we got there, we found leaflets dropped by the Germans that said 'WELCOME 35th DIVISION'."

Howard White (320/35th) recalled a brochure from the Germans in Sittard saying, "We fought against your fathers in World War I," and "The 4Fs are taking care of your wives and girlfriends." (4Fs are considered unfit for military service.)

The 35th was now inside the German border for the second time. Their ultimate goal was to complete the Rhineland Campaign by removing Germans from the west bank of the Rhine River. However, the 35th first needed to cross the Roer River, as it was named in Dutch and French, or the Rur River, as the Germans called it, but not to be confused with the Ruhr River, which is a tributary of the Rhine.

In the flat lowlands of the Roer River Valley, the roads and fields were muddy with melted snow, yet iced on some mornings. The British warned the Americans of land mines and booby traps scattered by the German troops. Civilians had evacuated, and enemy snipers and machine gun nests were hidden in houses and within bushes. Now on German soil, there would be no friendly French civilians to rout out hidden Germans, and French resistance fighters could not serve as guides.

In addition, there was a constant threat the Germans would open the river dams and flood the flat landscape. This eventually occurred and raised the level of the Roer River by four feet and increased its width from 30 to 300 yards, and in some places, as much as 1.5 miles wide. The flooding delayed the Allied attack for a couple weeks until February 23.

* * *

Almost five decades after the war, back in Martinsville, Wisconsin, the children of Dad's sister, Catherine Endres Kalscheur, discovered a letter Dad had written to their family. In the letter, "Vmails" were mentioned. Vmail was short for Victory Mail, and it was a system used to correspond with soldiers abroad. Letters were censored and copied onto thumbnail-sized microfilm. Upon arrival at their destinations, the images were then blown up to

Alfred

about four-by-five inches, 60 percent of their original size, and printed back onto paper. This process reduced the weight and bulk of shipping by more than 90 percent, giving priority of space to the transport of war supplies.

Feb 5, 1945

Dear Catherine, Jim, Mark, Phil, and everybody,

I received your letter today and was glad to get it. I also got one from the Simons, one they wrote Jan 17 and two Vmails from Celia. They were from Jan 8 and 15, so tell them that I am glad to hear from them. I would like to write to everybody, but I haven't got that much time tonight, and they don't want us to carry letters with addresses on them.

A little while ago I wrote to the Simons when we were in France. Then the other day I wrote home that we were in Holland, and I'm writing to you that we are in Germany. Sure got around these last few days. In less than a week, we have been in five different countries…France, Luxembourg, Belgium, Holland and Germany…and seven different countries now since I've been over here. Sure will be glad to get back to the one and only U.S.A. The war news sounds good again, and I hope it keeps on, and then maybe the war will soon be over.

How are Celia and Barbara? Still fine, I hope. By now Rita and Edward should have their baby. When this family gets together, there are a lot of babies around. Soon Eileen will be five months old. Time goes fast. I hope that soon I can be with my family. It is nine months today that I last saw Louise and soon nine months overseas, and on the 6th of next month, three years in the army.

Well, anyhow, I'm still fine and hope to stay that way, and let's pray now already that our kids don't have to go to any war, as we all know it's bad, not only for soldiers or rather servicemen, but also for those at home and for sure people over here.

I'm sending some old German money along in this letter. I don't know if you care for it or not. I don't know how many different kinds of money I sent to Louise already. I sent two different boxes of souvinirs, spelled wrong, but I guess you know what I mean. Anyhow, I hope she gets them. Most of them I got in Metz from a good swimmer who runs a bath house where we took showers.

Well I'll close for tonight. Say "Hello" to all the rest for me, and tell them that I got their letters. I hope that everybody is fine. I am, so til next time...

Love,
Alfred

I noticed the timing of the letter and asked Dad, "This letter was written shortly after the Battle of the Bulge, and you said you were fine. Were you really fine?"

He said, "What else could I say? When guys would say dey were fine, I t'ought dey were nuts, but den I did da same ting."

Alfred

Around this time, Dad probably had a chance to bathe again. Orval Faubus was delighted to take a bath on February 9 and again on February 13 in a wonderful stone building with hundreds of baths and plenty of hot water. A sign at the mine entrance in the town read "All Allied servicemen are welcome to have a bath on the coal miners of (a Dutch town Faubus could not remember)."

On February 13, author Faubus also wrote, "Picture that stuck in my mind: The rear-echelon soldier walking down the street of a Dutch town with a gorgeous woman on each arm, as our battle-stained doughboys moved up to the front."

And within the same journal entry:

> There is no way for me to express to you the
> depth and sincerity of my desire to make others
> see the horror and the cost of war. I have never
> really tried to do that in my letters for censorship
> rules would not permit it … I think if everyone
> fully understood what war is like, there would be
> no more conflicts of this kind.

Dad similarly said to me, "Tell da main guys who start da wars to go to da front, and see how many wars we'd have."

Dad wrote another letter to his friend, Herman "Stud" Hinson, which his daughter discovered within a box of keepsakes more than 65 years later:

Feb 23, 1945 Germany
Hi Stud,

I received your letter the other day, so I'll answer it today as I have some writing time.

Everything is fine, and so am I. Boy, Stud, we really did some travelling since you left us. There in one week, we were in five different countries. But the one I want to see soon is the United States. Say, Stud, I was very glad to hear that you are going to the States, even if I wanted to see you again, but if anybody can get out of this mess, more power to him.

Oh, yes, the same day I got your letter, Ack-Ack stopped here, and I asked about your gas mask, and he said he turned it in, so I suppose the stuff is gone, but I still got the straight razor, so if you want it, I'll send it to you.

Well, there is no grave digger now the gang is broke up. Nelson, I think, went to C Co. Griff was at the kitchen B Co, but said he was getting a transfer, and so is Jack Cramer, and I believe so is Eckly. Gregier is now a squad leader in D Co, the machine guns. I only seen him one or two times since he is in D Co. So the whole gang is broke up, and I think A and P guys do the guard. I liked it very well when we were together, and I like it very well here in D Co. Lane and Hager often talk about what we did together. Hager always says there isn't anybody who can make him laugh more than Stud did. Remember when you was talking to Murphy, and he had a few drinks. Well

Alfred

Hager said he had to leave. He was getting a side ache from laughing. We did stuff we will never forget. Sure would be nice to get together some time after this mess is over with. Maybe we will.

Well, Stud, I'll close for this time and hope that you are fine and get to the States. I'm fine and so is my wife and baby, and hope I can be with her soon. I know how much you will enjoy being with your wife and Shirley.

Til next time, Alfred

The following letter to Stud from Ben Lane was also enclosed:

Feb 23, 1945
Germany (Damn it)

Hi Herman,

What is all this turkey shit I hear about you going to the States? What are you doing? Running out on us? All kidding aside, it would be swell if you could get back there. All the more power to you. I sure am not enjoying my stay here. Sure hope Adolf quits soon.

Hot Papa is doing a good barber business. He will soon have me talking German. Some of the boys call him the Boche. Sgt Gregier is in our company now.

The worst part about this place is there is no chickens. So we have to eat army chow. I haven't killed a chicken in over two months.

I didn't have much luck with the poker game. I owe Poppa $21.50. We play a little after each pay day.

The doughnut wagon was here today. Good thing because we had K-rations.

Well, I must bring this to a screeching halt for this time.

Best of luck,
A pal,
Ben

* * *

There was a major bombing raid in February on the German city of Duisburg, a raid Faubus described to be "about the most terrifying thing in the world," The next morning Dad's 1st battalion attacked at 3:30 a.m. to cross the Roer River and eventually reach the Rhine. By March 1, the 320th was about 23 miles behind the defenses of the Siegfried Line, the western approaches to the Rhine River, also called the Westwall by the Germans. Germany was no longer protected by its reinforced concrete "dragon's teeth," minefields, barbed wire, bunkers, and diagonally placed steel beams, which acted as a barricade against Allied tanks and troops. The 320th seized 16 towns, turned back into Holland, and liberated Venlo.

On March 2, thousands of delighted Dutch residents, led by priests wearing orange robes, some weeping for joy, poured out in the streets of Venlo to greet their liberators after more than four years of Nazi occupation. Some said they had been hungry all that time.

Alfred

Marge Bullock, wife of Keith Bullock (137/35th), posted the following newspaper clipping on the 35th Division website:

VENLO FALLS TO 320th ATTACK
By Wes Gallagher, Omaha World Herald Correspondent

VENLO, HOLLAND (AP) – This forgotten Dutch city Sunday was the most news-hungry and deliriously happy community in Europe.

Venlo was freed three days ago by the Thirty-fifth Infantry Division, but still is suffering from a celebration hangover.

The welcome given the doughboys of the Thirty-fifth was the most tumultuous ever given an American force by a liberated city, according to the officers and men of this division – and they have fought across France from St. Lo to Nancy and have known how liberated cities react. Everyone in the town was wearing orange caps or carrying orange flags and they just sort of went crazy when we entered," one officer said. "They yelled and held up five fingers, indicating the Germans had been on their backs for five years."

Seventy percent of the once tidy city has been destroyed. Only 15 thousand of its customary 60 thousand population remain.

For two years, Venlo has been without newspapers. Under siege, its electricity was knocked out and radios were useless. Although in the very front of the fighting, it has had little idea of what has been going on.

The Americans brought in nine truckloads of food with them, so there was enough to eat even though nearly everything else was lacking for comfortable living.

Sixty-one years after the liberation of Venlo, the *Santa Fe Express* published a request from Venlo resident Hugo Levels. He had been born fifteen years after the war and asked for information from February 28 to March 1, 1945. He wanted to preserve and keep alive the history of the Liberation, especially for the younger people. On that anniversary, another Hollander, Jan Saris, wrote on the 35th Division website, "The 320th is very close to my heart. Lots of warm regards from your city here, Venlo."

* * *

Then, for the third time, the 320th invaded fifteen miles into Germany, capturing Straelen, Nieukirk, Sevelen, Kamp, and Kamperbruck. In Sevelen, stacks of German propaganda leaflets were found. The 35th Division patch was beautifully reproduced, and the ink was still wet on the bold red print, welcoming the 35th to Holland. The leaflets were intended for the American troops and warned that it would be impossible to cross the Roer River defenses. That is precisely what the troops had just done.

The 320th captured the towns of Oemten and Rheinberg on March 3 and on March 4, Kamperbruck. On some days, there was heavy enemy resistance from prepared entrenchments and buildings, according to after-action reports. Even so, the list of liberations grew with Hogenhof, Alspray, Saalhof, Schmitshof, and Bauern. On March 8, fierce house-to-house fighting ensued before taking Huck and Millingen. Drupt, the final objective, was only four kilometers from the Rhine, and at this location, the Allies suffered heavy artillery and mortar fire.

Some German troops were dressed in American uniforms, and every house and building was fortified. Resistance was described as fanatical, and eight units of Hitler's best troops were identified, including elements of three paratroop divisions. Historically, the Rhine River was the great barrier guarding

Alfred

Welcome, Men of the 35th Division

Considering the fact that you are newcomers, we would like to do everything to make you feel at home. We extend to you a cordial greeting and a hearty welcome to the Rur Valley.

We regret that you must come to this unpleasant district, but, as usual, you have to take over this section where the air is heavy with lead.....

You have tried to veil your arrival here by doing such things as removing your divisional insignias. Nevertheless, a little bird told us all about it.

Before you arrived, there were other divisions here who didn't fare so well....They all got knocked about a bit. You can see that you won't have an easy time of it against the Rur defense lines.

As we said before, we shall try to make you feel at home. We hope to make every day here seem like the "the glorious Fourth" - there'll be plenty of fireworks.

WE KNOW WHAT YOU ARE MEANT TO DO.
WE KNOW, ALSO, WHAT YOU WANT TO DO.
YOU WANT TO RETURN HOME AS SOON AS POSSIBLE!!!
(BETTER ACROSS THAN A CROSS)

GERMAN PROPAGANDA LEAFLET.

Germany from invasion from the west, even going back to the days of Caesar. Because the Germans were unable to withdraw their heavy guns and ammunition back across the Rhine, they used everything at their disposal to fight the 35th.

By March 11, the 35th was on the west bank of the Rhine River while a major German industrial area, which fed supplies to the war effort, was on the other side. This area was known as the Ruhr Valley, 8,000 square miles of huge factories and coal and iron mines, with thousands of skilled workers, many of them underground.

The 35th breathed a sigh of relief to learn they would not be in the first wave to assault across the Rhine. On March 12, James Huston wrote, "For the first time since landing in France, the entire 35th Division was to have a period of rest."

In *Biography of a Battalion*, James Huston further described there was no relaxing of discipline. There would still be drills, marches, range firing, bridge guarding, and inspections of housing, kitchens, clothing, and equipment. There were strict measures to prevent looting. Reports of rape were to be investigated at once. There was a $65 fine for fraternizing with the residents and a $2 fine for not saluting, wearing a knit cap without a helmet, or other uniform violations. AWOL soldiers (absent without leave) were to be immediately checked. Steps were to be taken to prevent the spread of venereal disease. No riding of bicycles, motorcycles, or unauthorized vehicles. This was still the army, and the war was not yet over.

Alfred

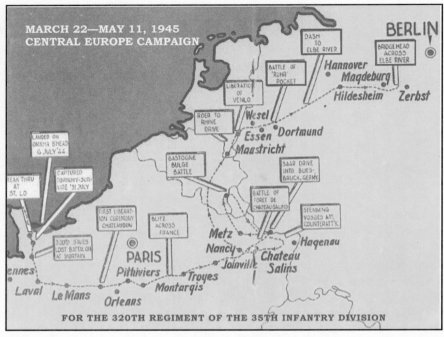

Map from Story of 320th Infantry:
***Ruhr Pocket, Dash to Elbe River,
and Bridgehead across the Elbe***

9. CENTRAL EUROPE CAMPAIGN

March 22, 1945 – May 11, 1945

At this time, Orval Faubus was again hospitalized for three weeks. He had an abscessed tooth, an infection, hives, and an appendicitis attack. He said of his hospitalization, "Life here is different, vastly different from the front. There is much suffering of course, but the strain of battle is missing. There are soft voices and the occasional lilting laughter of a feminine tone, something we have not heard in many weary months." Faubus also noted that hospital staff members who had been under fire were more sympathetic to the wounded than personnel who had never experienced combat.

Back on the front lines, the 35th Division had to cross Germany's greatest waterway, the Rhine River, before reaching the industrial area of the Ruhr Valley. Parts of the 35th provided artillery fire on March 24 to aid other divisions in crossing a northern portion of the Rhine. The river had been already been crossed in the south, first at Remagen, a few weeks earlier. This combination of these two crossings would eventually seal off the Germans in the "largest pocket of envelopment in the history of warfare," according to James Huston in *Biography of a Battalion*.

General Patton crossed the Rhine River on March 22. Considering Patton's personality and the river's psychological importance to Germany, Patton could make a statement by urinating into it. Orval Faubus wrote in the closing days of the war, "I saw picture postcards of General Patton...standing on the bank of the Rhine River, 'taking a leak'...Below the picture were the words, 'If they had turned me loose, I would have done this six months ago.'"

By March 27, the 35th Division was more than three miles beyond the Rhine River with the goal of ultimately taking control of Germany's main highway, the *Autobahn*. This area of the Ruhr Valley was in ruins from multiple attacks by hundreds of Allied heavy bombers. Yet, many of the coal and steel industrial plants were still intact, some with smoke rising from their stacks. Robert Phillips said, "Fighting in the Ruhr Valley was bad. There was intense fire coming from all the buildings and all the factories."

Eventually, Allied troops overtook industries such as the Rheinbaden Factory and the Moeller Coal Mine at Gladbeck. More than 6,500 displaced people from France, Belgium, Holland, and Italy had huddled in fear for five days during Allied bombing at these two sites. Before the end of March, the 320th Regiment fought for two days near the Emscher Canal to take the Prosper Coal Mine. At this location, 8,000 to 10,000 German and foreign workers had been held hostage in tunnels by armed guards.

Suddenly, the Ruhr pocket was swarming with people. Many of them were women who had been kept in barbed-wire stockades, beaten, and raped. Faubus estimated up to half of them were pregnant. Newly released forced laborers, weak and sick, clogged the roads as they started walking toward their homelands, possibly hundreds of miles away. The prisoners of war (POWs) were generally in worse condition than the forced laborers because laborers needed to have enough strength to work. At rare times, laborers had been treated well.

Orval Faubus was overwhelmed with a liberated camp of about 1,100 British and American prisoners of war. They were dirty, covered with lice, some unable to stand. These prisoners of war had been marched back and forth across Germany, alternating their direction to avoid either the Russian or the American forces approaching from opposite sides. One prisoner of war had kept a daily record that showed the survivors had walked 1,400 miles. Many died or were killed along the way.

Faubus wrote the average person would expect these newly liberated prisoners to have "an attitude of great joy... such was not the case. These POWs, like combat veterans, had been drained... Their pale, flaccid faces showed little, if any, emotion."

* * *

Once, during a television documentary on concentration camps, my brother Bob asked Dad, "Did you ever see anything like that?"

Dad said, "Lots of it. I don't know how one person can do dat to anot'er person."

When I made plans to speak about World War II to a Cedarburg High School history class, I asked Dad what I should tell the students. He replied, "Tell dem about da chicken." Everyone in our family knew the story.

Newly released prisoners trudged through a little village where a small amount of shelling had killed a chicken. A woman from a nearby house ran outside and grabbed the dead chicken so the meat would not go to waste. She disappeared into her house and returned outside a short time later to throw the chicken guts on a pile of garbage and manure in the yard. A starving man, who was passing by, snatched the raw intestines and voraciously ate them. Dad said, "...as if it was good meat." Another time, Dad witnessed prisoners eating grass upon their release from a camp.

* * *

On April 6, General Eisenhower wrote to the Chief of Staff, "... we must pause to digest the big mouthful that we have swallowed in the Ruhr area...There may be 150,000 German soldiers left in the area, but a number of these will change into civilian clothes...we will capture at least 100,000..." In the end, James Huston noted in his book that over three times that number of enemy soldiers were captured there.

The 320th Regiment was attached to another division for an attack on Dortmund on the western side of the Ruhr Valley, but suddenly the 320th was ordered back to the 35th Division to rush to the Elbe River, nearly 200 miles away.

Then, in the very early hours of April 13, the troops awoke to hear that President Franklin Roosevelt had passed away the day before.

Don May said, "Some soldiers cried." President Roosevelt had been in office for twelve years, and many soldiers wished he could have seen victory.

At the same time in Berlin, Hitler learned from one of his most devoted followers about the death of President Roosevelt. In *Rising Sun: Volume 2,* John Toland wrote that Joseph Goebbels told Hitler, "Fate has laid low your greatest enemy. God has not abandoned us ... A miracle has happened."

The presidency transferred to Harry S Truman, who had served with the 35th Division during the First World War. He understood the front-line soldier, and he said, "I know the strain, the misery, the utter weariness of the soldier in the field. And I know, too, his courage, his stamina, and his faith in comrades, his country, and himself."

* * *

During the war, some prisoners had been forced to work in the German war industry, such as in the production of German airplane parts and weapons. Then, toward the end of the war, the Germans feared that if these slave laborers were suddenly liberated, they could turn against their guards or pass along detrimental information about Germany to the Allies.

During the first week of April 1945, Allies had been advancing toward the general area of Mittelbau-Dora, a labor camp near Nordhaussen, Germany. A couple thousand prisoners of war were loaded onto freight cars to be transferred to other concentration camps, farther ahead of the approaching Allies. Some of the sick and lame had to be carried, and some were shot where they fell. Bread was the only food thrown into the freight cars to sustain the prisoners for seven days.

On April 13, the prisoners were ordered off the freight cars because railroad tracks near the medieval town of Gardelegen had been bombed. More than 1,000 prisoners were marched several miles by SS troops and forced into a large grain barn made of stone. Some prisoners escaped and hid in the woods,

but they were then hunted by townspeople, who were worried about retribution and their own safety as German citizens.

The prisoners initially were told they would spend the night in the barn before being handed over to the Americans the next day. The sick were carried in first, and the rest followed. The prisoners were ordered to sit in straw that was knee-deep and had been soaked with gasoline. Then the straw was torched while the doors were barricaded. Those who tried to escape were shot, and according to reports, the shooting continued for half the night.

The SS hoped to kill any survivors the next day and then cremate or bury the remains to get rid of the evidence. In the morning, the SS returned and offered medical help. Any survivor who responded was shot. In the end, one of the few silent survivors lay buried under dead bodies. He had stumbled the previous night and was covered by others who had been killed by machine guns.

The 102nd Infantry Division was first to arrive in Gardelegen and to discover several emaciated prisoners lying in the road, holding up their hands to draw attention to themselves. According to the history of the 102nd Division, soldiers attempted to save a prisoner by cradling his head and letting water drip into his mouth from a canteen. They opened a ration and placed shavings from a chocolate bar into his mouth, along with a crushed cracker. Within five minutes, the prisoner was dead. It happened again, and a medic told the soldiers not to feed anyone, "You will kill them." The soldiers had difficulty ignoring the raised hands of fallen prisoners, but there was nothing they could do to help them.

SIX HUNDRED CORPSES FOUND IN SMOLDERING BARN NEAR GARDELEGEN, GERMANY, APRIL 1945. CHARLES OVERSTREET COLLECTION, FLORA PUBLIC LIBRARY, FLORA, ILLINOIS.

The troops of the 102nd Division assumed the smoldering barn had been ignited by artillery fire. Then the awful stench hit them. Almost 600 charred corpses were found in the barn and 400 more in nearby trenches. Heads and hands stuck out from the dirt under the doors where prisoners had tried to dig and claw themselves out of the barn. Most of them had burned alive.

From April 13 to 15, Robert Phillips and Dad's 1st Battalion had been moving toward the Elbe River when it passed through Gardelegen and witnessed the aftermath of the killing. Robert took photos of the barn and sent copies to me from his album with his words, "Bodies were stacked four deep where they tried to escape." He further described to me in a phone conversation what he had witnessed:

> *You could tell the war was close to being over*
> *because the Germans were trying to cover up their*
> *mistakes. Gardelegen was different than Dachau.*
> *It involved mostly slave labor, Czechs and Polish*
> *wearing black and white pajamas. Many dead*
> *bodies were in the ditch when we got there.*

Major General Frank Keating, Commander of the 102nd Infantry Division, ordered several hundred men from Gardelegen to stand and wait in line. Robert said of the townspeople, "They were forced to stand where the awful odor made the most impact." Then each one of them was given a dead body to wrap in a white sheet and bury in a separate grave.

Stories appeared in New York Times and The Washington Post on April 19 and in Life magazine on May 7. Stories of German war crimes were welcomed because General Eisenhower wanted to distract the press from reporting stories about atrocities by our Russian ally and the killing of innocent civilians by Allied bombing.

A sign posted at the burned barn, written in both German and English, reads:

GARDELEGEN MILITARY CEMETERY
Here lie 1016 Allied Prisoners of War who were murdered by their captors. They were buried by the Citizens of Gardelegen, who are charged with the responsibility that these graves are forever kept as green as the memories of these unfortunate souls will be kept in the hearts of freedom-loving men everywhere.

On the 55th anniversary of the massacre, a memorial ceremony was held where the citizens have maintained the cemetery and added a museum. They preserved the last remaining wall of the barn, which contains plaques from many of the fourteen countries that lost victims, along with a plaque from the 102nd Infantry Division that reads:

> May the memorial be a
> "cry for freedom and peace"
> by the victims of this massacre, their
> homelands and our two countries.

* * *

After passing through the horrific scene at Gardelegen, the 320th Regiment continued toward the Elbe River, about fifteen miles south of Magdeburg. Arriving on April 15, they had moved 275 miles in 48 hours by means of 2.5-ton trucks, a definite advantage for the mobility of our soldiers.

At the Elbe River, the 83rd Infantry Division had been ordered to stop the German advance. The river was the line of demarcation between Americans coming from the west and Russians coming from the east. Roosevelt from the United States, Stalin from Russia, and Churchill from England had agreed upon this dividing line.

A regimental combat team from the 320th was attached to the 83rd Division. Then they were ordered to cross the Saale River to reinforce the only bridgehead at the Elbe River. Another bridgehead in the north had just been lost to the enemy. The 83rd Division, with the 320th attachment, was closest of all units to the

German capital. They were close enough to see the bombing of Berlin but still not able to hear it.

A pontoon bridge was eventually built over the Elbe River and became the first army project dedicated to the newly named President Harry S Truman. It was made of hollow, boat-like structures filled with air, and lashed together from bank to bank with a road laid on top. The bridge was vulnerable to bombs, artillery, and floating mines that could break the ties or puncture the pontoons. Soldiers with rifles and carbines stood a few feet apart on the bridge to explode potentially destructive mines in the water.

If the bridge was destroyed, Americans would be caught on the enemy's side of the Elbe River with no means for escape. Our soldiers were bombed several nights in succession, but then on April 20, it seemed a major Russian drive would save our troops from more combat.

However, Hitler was intent on destroying that pontoon bridge. He gave personal instructions in Berlin to a team of seven naval swimmers. They were to equip themselves with underwater suits and gear, carry large charges of explosives, float downstream to the bridge, and destroy it. Orval Faubus described the swimmers, "The Nazis wore tight-fitting rubber suits and helmets with wool camouflage hoods...Their faces were blackened...and they were equipped with pistols, knives, and waterproof watches." The water was rushing and cold, and the swimmers could not hang onto their explosives. The frogmen climbed out of the water, flitted from tree to tree, and eventually surrendered to a couple of soldiers from the 320th Regiment. The swimmers were then questioned at headquarters.

* * *

A few years before Dad passed away, he told my sister Eileen in a phone conversation, "Da swimmers probably did not know da war was over or did not want to believe it." He gave very little context, so I am still surprised such a comment made enough sense to Eileen that she relayed it to me. Much later, I discovered the story of Hitler's frogmen in the journal of Orval Faubus. It occurred in the final days of the war, shortly before April 22.

I wondered why the strange swimmers were still important to Dad. Had he heard about them? Had he witnessed them? I believe it is likely Dad translated for them during questioning at 320th Headquarters.

* * *

With the war almost over, there was speculation as to where Americans would meet the Russian forces. "News correspondents moved along the front while trying to guess the place where contact would be made," James Huston wrote in *Biography of a Battalion*. A signal was arranged to avoid any mishap. The Russians would send up two red flares to be answered by three green flares from the American troops, with both armies being aware of possible fakes by the enemy.

Orval Faubus wrote in his journal that the 83rd Infantry Division, with an attachment of the 320th, was the first American unit to meet the Russians at the Elbe River. However, the official publicized meeting of the two countries occurred later at Torgau on April 24 at 4:44 p.m.

* * *

At the nursing home, Dad knew exactly where he had been at the end of the war. "On da river," he said. The end of the war for him just meant the day he learned the war was over. The official signing of the treaty was a bit later.

I asked, "How did you find out the war was over?"

And he answered, "Someone on da ot'er side told us."

"What did you do?" I asked.

"Not'ing different," Dad answered.

"No excitement?"

"No."

"Calm?"

"Ya."

"Just relieved it was over?"

"Ya."

With a bit more prompting, Dad said one of the few Americans walking on the Russian side of the Elbe River informed him the war was over. Robert agreed, "We knew the war was over before anything was signed."

* * *

Around this time, Ernie Pyle, a treasured correspondent, was killed in the Pacific Theatre of Operations. He was known as the "Foxhole Reporter" because he always sought the company of the foot soldier, and he described the conditions from the front lines more accurately than any other writer. In his book, *Brave Men*, Pyle wrote:

> *The front-line soldier I knew had lived for months*
> *like an animal and was a veteran in the fierce*
> *world of death. Everything was abnormal and*
> *unstable in his life. He was filthy dirty, ate if and*
> *when, slept on hard ground without cover. His*
> *clothes were greasy, and he lived in a constant*

*haze of dust, pestered by flies and heat, moving
constantly, deprived of all the things that once
meant stability – things such as walls, chairs,
floors, windows, faucets, shelves, Coca-Colas, and
the little matter of knowing that he would go to
bed at night in the same place he had left in the
morning.*

A similar type of quote from Pyle is included within the front pages of Dad's *Story of the 320th Infantry*. Don May had spoken fondly of this writer before I understood Ernie Pyle's importance to World War II veterans.

* * *

Because Dad could speak German and some Russians understood the German language, he was told to inform a group that their liquor could have been poisoned. Dad cautioned the Russians, "You should be careful because a soldier died from poisoned vodka last night."

The group of Russians responded in raucous laughter, "What's one?"

About 9,000,000 Russian military were killed in World War II, compared to about 415,000 American soldiers. That is a ratio of more than twenty to one.

* * *

On April 24, troops from the 35th Division captured SS Major General Heinz Jost, the head of the Gestapo in foreign countries. They also captured Clauswitz Task Force Commander Lt. General Unrein riding a bicycle in civilian clothes.

More than 1,500 Allied prisoners of war were liberated near the Elbe River and taken to Graesleben Airfield, where they ate

their first meal, intentionally simple, because of their emaciated condition: soup, coffee, pudding, and bread.

The 35th Division was then relocated to the Hanover area around April 27 to clear out remaining enemy, assist with hospitals, help with thousands of displaced people, and "occupy and govern."

Hitler's death just days later on April 30 was ambiguous at the time. I remember hearing decades ago that Hitler married Eva Braun, and suicide was their honeymoon. The *Wisconsin State Journal* reported on May 2:

> **General Dwight D. Eisenhower revealed today that there was some evidence that Hitler really was dead – but that it indicated the Fuehrer died of a brain hemorrhage, not fighting to defend Berlin, as Radio Hamburg reported... It was possible that the Nazis had covered up his death for several days in order to build up the legend of a hero's death.**

Then, on May 5, with only three days remaining in the war, Patton entered a brand-new armored division into service, one which had not yet served in any capacity. The division wanted to be part of World War II history, and Patton wrote that he "was glad to get them (in)." These late additions became veterans of World War II but barely part of the war. A person once told me, "Everyone does the same thing."

* * *

On the evening of May 6, Dad acted as a translator when he accompanied a captain and a Jeep driver to scout out lodging for a future move by the 320th. The search was near the location of Frank Poelluci, the buddy with whom Mom and Dad had shared an apartment in Arkansas thirteen months earlier. Because of turmoil at that site, Dad was not able to connect with Frank, and therefore the search for housing just continued.

Robert Phillips also helped with lodging for American troops. He told me, "German women always pointed down the street when they were approached. 'They were the Nazis! Take their house!'"

* * *

The war in the European Theatre was finally over. The *Wisconsin State Journal* (May 8, 1945), reported the general atmosphere in Madison, Wisconsin:

> **Tavern and liquor stores in city and county were closed all day in keeping with the request that celebration be avoided and production of needed war supplies continued without letup. Lights on theater marquees and in store windows will be permitted for the first time in four years. The capitol dome was spotlighted Monday night. Although riotous celebration was reported in some neighboring counties Monday night, police and sheriff's officials said all was quiet in Madison. The city's reaction was a contrast to Nov. 11, 1918, but at that time the Allies did not have Japan to lick.**

After the first week in May, the 35th Division's total count of prisoners of war was over 31,000. The 35th had endured ten months of war and travelled over 1,600 miles in combat, serving within all four of the American armies and on the soil of five countries. In terms of battle casualties alone, the 35th ranked seventh highest out of 60 infantry and armored divisions in Europe.

Two months earlier, Faubus had written, "I never thought any infantryman would last that long, but a few have."

Dad and Robert Phillips were two of them.

This clover was found 57 silent years after WWII in the army trunk of
ALFRED N. ENDRES

Frontlines/Machine Gun
35th Infantry Division
All 5 ETO Campaigns
264 Days in Combat
180.9% Casualty Rate

10. WAITING TO GO HOME

May 9, 1945 – October 12, 1945

A fter the European war officially ended on May 8, 1945, combat veterans were initially relieved and happy just to be alive, but gradually life evolved from the selfless aspects of combat to irritating military hierarchies and inspections. Pettiness replaced comradeship. It was discipline for discipline's sake rather than for survival. The motto all along had been, "Get it over with and go home." Now everyone just wanted to go home.

Orval Faubus wrote in his memoirs, "… no one was happy. Everyone, it seemed, wanted to go home at once, or else to run around Europe, or engage in black market activity." A few soldiers jumped ship, returned to camp, and hid out in order to steal and sell army supplies until they were caught.

On an airplane flight from Kansas City to Milwaukee, I met the daughter of this type of veteran. It was such a stark contrast to Dad's military involvement, and yet this daughter was comfortable and proud enough to tell me of her father's experiences. He developed his salesmanship for his eventual occupation by selling United States government property in the Philippines during and after the war. He possibly returned home a wealthy man.

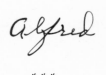

Alfred

* * *

There were many soldiers devastated by their injuries, but some were almost too difficult to comprehend. On May 18, Orval Faubus wrote his final journal entry as he recovered from an appendectomy. As he transferred between hospitals, he sadly recalled a soldier who had lost both arms and legs in combat. My neighbor Gordon Sorensen cared for this type of casualty at Wood Veterans Hospital in Milwaukee, Wisconsin, during one of his college summers following World War II. Friends of this veteran picked him up from "Woods" Hospital, took him home, and partied with him each weekend. Gordon told me, "Every Monday he was a mess, and I cleaned him up. Then his friends would pick him up the following weekend to drink again. When I told him I would be leaving my job, he cried."

* * *

One of Dad's assignments during Occupation was to collect German firearms and smash them on stumps. Reluctantly, he confiscated a meticulously maintained pistol from a sobbing German woman. It had been powdered to prevent rusting. Maybe her husband had died in the war. Maybe the gun was an heirloom. Dad would have softened and allowed her to keep it, but his partner would not.

With Dad's ability to speak German, he was able to ask German civilians how Hitler had risen to such power. Decades later, he explained to me, "Dey said dere would be small meet-ings at night. Anyone who went against dose ideas would be dead in da street in da morning."

Further, one of my friends relayed to me that her German cousin had told her, "The people had almost no option but to join the Nazi Party. If they did not, they would likely lose their jobs." She added, "Hitler also instilled a hugely needed sense of pride to a country that had lost the First World War and was economically and emotionally devastated."

* * *

At the nursing home, Dad and I casually looked at photos. He was disgusted when he recognized a particular officer. When I spoke with Robert about the same officer, Robert recalled, "No one liked him. No one. He gave our cigarettes and candy rations to the German girls he shacked up with." Robert continued, "After the war, someone took a shot at him while we were in formation. I was supposed to inspect and smell every rifle to figure out who had done it. I would not have turned the guy in anyway."

Several years later, Robert discovered an interesting photo while looking at his World War II album. A triangular black tab held each corner of the photo onto its page, and one of the tabs partially covered the name written on the top corner: "Andres – German Interpreter & Gogal, Munster 1945." Endres had been misspelled with an "A," as in "Andres." It was Dad and Louis Gogal, the same soldiers who were in the foxhole from the National Archive video. Unfortunately, Robert did not find that photo until three years after Dad's death. It may have elicited a comfortable, if not pleasant, memory for Dad.

For this photo, the two veterans stood in front of a beat-up Jeep with a vertical steel bar welded to the front bumper. The top

Alfred

Andres—German Interpreter + Gogal
Munster
1945

ALFRED ANDRES [SIC] AND LOUIS GOGAL IN A PHOTO FROM ROBERT PHILLIPS'S SCRAPBOOK, MUNSTER, GERMANY, 1945. ALFRED IS SMOKING. ERNIE PYLE WROTE THAT MANY SOLDIERS STARTED SMOKING TO CALM THEIR NERVES AFTER LANDING ON D-DAY.

of the bar was bent at a 45-degree angle. During the war, the enemy strung wire across roads. If a Jeep's windshield was down, the steel wire could decapitate the passengers. If the windshield was up, the wire might damage the Jeep or knock it off the road. Therefore the vertical bar was added to cut those wires and prevent casualties.

The photo in Robert's album had been taken in Münster, Germany. The 320th Regiment occupied that area until May 29, as Robert recalled. On that day, Dad was granted a furlough to London. His "Combined Leave Pass and Railway Ticket" was later stamped on both June 13 and June 14 when he returned.

Within a couple days of Dad's return from London, he received a letter at his 35th Division address from his first cousin Leo Lochner:

> *June 17*
>
> *Alfred,*
>
> *Just a few lines. We are not doing very much these days. Do not know what is to become of us here. Some of the fellows heard we are going home in about two months for a furlough and then, well I suppose, to Japan. Don't care too much for that. Have had enough of this shit.*
>
> *I just got back from Rome last night. Sure am worn out. Fifteen hundred miles. It is not much fun driving that far in a truck and only five days to make it in.*
>
> *We got beer today and kind of feel like hanging one on. Do not do near as much drinking as I used to. Can't do anything when you do start feeling good. Have a dance now and then but can't talk this Italian no how. Every now and then, I run into someone that can talk German. That is more my line, but I have forgotten a lot of it. Well, will sign off hoping to hear from you some time. Hope to see you soon.*
>
> *Leo*

* * *

Dad was most likely transferred out of the 35th Division before July 1 because he did not participate that day in the ceremony honoring his battalion with a Presidential Unit Citation. It was

Alfred

awarded for the rescue of Bob Esser's battalion at Mortain, and the ceremony was held at the repaired Santa Fe Stadium in Koblenz, dedicated also that day to the 35th Division.

The stadium had been originally built in 1920 by American engineers and then utilized during Occupation after the First World War. The French later used the stadium for soccer until Germany took control in 1929 and held track meets, football games, and horse races there. James Huston explained further about the stadium in his memoirs, "In 1932, an afternoon crowd of 15,000 people had gathered to hear Adolf Hitler plead for election to the German presidency."

The stadium was badly damaged by bombing during World War II, and James Huston wrote, "...engineers of the 35th Division had worked with several hundred German prisoners— and used 150 truckloads of rubble to fill craters in the field—to repair the stadium for its dedication July 1." Following those dedication ceremonies, a baseball game between the 35th and 106th Divisions was played that day. It was one of the big sporting events after the war. Had Dad been there, I expect he would have played in the game because he had been a pitcher on a local baseball team before the war.

A point system had been developed to prioritize soldiers for discharge. Soldiers could not be in combat forever without eventually breaking down, so one point was given for each month of total service (42) and another point for each month abroad (16). Eileen's birth awarded Dad points (12), in addition to five points for each of Dad's five campaigns (25). A total of 85 was considered "high-point."

According to the Advanced Service Rating (ASR) on Dad's discharge papers, he had 95 points. This qualified him to be transferred out of the 35th Division with the intention of speeding his return to the United States. On the other hand, soldiers with low points could be transferred to the Pacific Theatre, where the war continued. It was advantageous for Dad to go home, yet he was separated from his friends, those who silently understood what they all had survived.

Unfortunately, the system did not work as planned. The lower-point soldiers from the 1st Battalion returned to the United States several weeks before Dad's departure. He said, "I could not get upset about it, but da low-point guys were writing us letters from home." There were hundreds of thousands of GIs who qualified for discharge, but they remained somewhat stranded in Europe because there were not enough planes, ships, and trains to transport them back to their families.

* * *

On Mom and Dad's second anniversary, August 14, 1945, Japan announced its surrender. The *Wisconsin State Journal* reported the next day:

> **...for the first time since rationing started on May 15, 1942, gasoline would no longer be rationed. Nor will canned fruit and vegetables, fuel oil and oil stoves ... But rationing of meats, fats and oils, butter, sugar, shoes, tires and other commodities will continue indefinitely.**

* * *

It seems Dad was transferred a couple times. Eventually he received a ration card from the 254th Infantry Regiment of the 63rd Division. According to that unit's history, the 254th was re-

staffed with the high-point men from other divisions. I found
Dad's name among a list of thousands from the 63rd Division.
Only a handful of soldiers had two question marks after their
name, and Dad was one of them. When he shipped home, the
right sleeve of his woolen Eisenhower jacket bore the patch of the
35th Division, and on the left sleeve was the patch of the 63rd.

Dad's duffel bag was tagged "from LeHavre" (France) on
shipment number RE 7342-G. Eventually he boarded the *RMS
Queen Mary* at Southampton, England. For use during the war,
the ship's elegant furniture and fixtures had been removed. Bunk
beds had been installed. It was painted camouflage gray and
called the "Gray Ghost," the largest and fastest troop ship. The
Queen Mary was able to deliver troops between the United
States and England in five days. During the war, Adolf Hitler

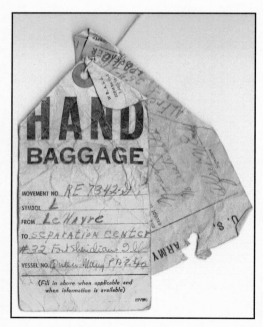

***ALFRED'S LUGGAGE TAG FOR HIS
RETURN VOYAGE ON THE* QUEEN
MARY, *SEPTEMBER 1945.***

had supposedly offered a quarter of a million dollars to the captain of any German submarine who could sink it.

After the war, the *Queen Mary* carried almost 15,000 (14,938) troops plus its crew on each voyage, almost five times as many passengers as when it was used during peace time. Now it is a museum, docked in Long Beach, California.

The veterans were each furnished with a blanket, and with so many men, they slept in rotations. During Robert's trip home, also on the *Queen Mary*, Robert said of the soldiers, "Half of them slept on the decks." Likewise, everyone ate in shifts, twice a day rather than three times, and no one complained because everyone just wanted to get home.

Wisconsin veterans were listed within a fragile, torn newspaper clipping found in Dad's army trunk. The article was titled, "*Queen Mary* Brings Badgers Home." I was able to contact several veterans who returned to the United States with Dad on that voyage.

The wife of an Air Corps radio operator from Brookfield, Wisconsin, shared information with me from the back sides of photos hung on the walls in her home. A woman from Beloit, Wisconsin, told me her husband served as a rifleman, and she added, "He has memory problems, but the war still haunts him."

Alvin Schaal was also on that list of returning veterans. He served with an anti-tank unit attached to the 36th Division and was later transferred to the 63rd, as was Dad. Alvin spoke with me at length from his garage in snowy Gillett, Wisconsin, while he took a break from snow-blowing his driveway at the age of 88. His group had been routed through Austria before being quarantined in England. The soldiers were not able to go

Alfred

CERTIFICATE OF RETENTION AND CUSTOMS DECLARATION
(Strike out portions inapplicable)

1. I certify and declare that the following items of Government property were purchased by me and are my personal property:

1- belt WAIST web
1- CAP. DArresion
2- DArWers Cotton
1- Necktie
2- pAit Socks
1 Cotton UNdershirt

Name *Alfred N. Endres*

Rank and arm *Pfc Infantry*

2. As his commanding officer, I certify that the above named E.M.
_____ has, by the authority of the theater Commander, been authorized to retain the following items of captured enemy material, and has evidenced to me his right to possess the items of British, Russian, Canadian

Captured Enemy Material

1 Vesta 7.65 pistol #138711

Allied Government Material

Date 9, 9, 45

John D. Con
1st Lt. C.E.

3. The following Customs Declaration will be accomplished in all cases. In addition the Customs Declaration tag will be accomplished and affixed to the container.

CUSTOMS DECLARATION

I declare that all items listed herein consist of personal and household effects either taken abroad by me or acquired abroad, for my personal use, except the following:

(Here list items
or write
"No exceptions"
as appropriate)

No exceptions

Date 9, 9, 45
Signature *Alfred N. Endres*
Rank and ASN *Pfc. 36737118*
Type of container *Duffel Bag*
No of tag _____

ALFRED'S CUSTOMS DECLARATION, SEPTEMBER 9, 1945.

anywhere and did not have money that was accepted, even by the Red Cross. Before boarding the *Queen Mary* to sail September 23 to 28, Alvin and his group bivouacked near a rabbit farm where their only entertainment was watching rabbits dig holes. While on the ship, he remembered candy bars being constantly available.

I asked Alvin whether he had received a Purple Heart, and he responded, "What good are they? My mother's brother died in World War I, killed by an artillery shell. I saw and heard too much about that Purple Heart. I did not want one, would not take one if they gave it to me." He never reported injuries because if a soldier left for treatment, he may never get back to his old group.

Alvin said of the enemy, "The Germans could put a mortar shell in your back pocket."

He also summarized a foot soldier's general knowledge of the war:

> *Headquarters never told us where we were going or what the objective was. We would be holding or fighting during the day, and then we would have to move at night, always digging a foxhole. In a couple of hours, we would move again, and dig another foxhole. We always had to be in a hole, with our heads below the dirt, so tanks would not run over us.*

I asked, "Do you ever have dreams about the war?"

"Lots of 'em," the 88-year-old replied.

* * *

Alfred

ROSTER OF WISCONSIN RESIDENTS ON THE QUEEN MARY PRINTED IN THE MILWAUKEE SENTINEL, SEPTEMBER 28, 1945, INCLUDING ALFRED N. ENDRAS [SIC].

During the war, German and American troops tried to kill each other. Yet, a couple of months after its end, Orval Faubus and his driver offered a ride to an exhausted German soldier walking along the road. The Americans then drove in darkness to deliver their former enemy to his family, and they heard a most joyous reunion when he arrived home. Before the Jeep left, the German soldier ran out with a bottle of wine in appreciation for the ride.

En route to Europe, it seemed most soldiers trash-talked Germans, which probably bothered Dad. Sixteen months later, he was relieved to hear any comment that affirmed his heritage. He told me, "On da way home, some guys said, 'Dose were da best people over dere.'"

Alfred

IN MEMORIUM

In this long and agonizing trek from St. Lo through Bastogne to beyond the Elbe River hundreds of 320th soldiers have fallen, their blood soaking into the dust, or the mud, or the snow.

This brief and inadequate story of the regiment is dedicated to those of the fallen who never rose again, and to those who have been maimed in body or spirit for life.

There is a lasting monument to these glorious comrades in the hearts of those of us who remain. Let us fight in the time to come for a greater monument to them—an enduring peace, a peace which will make their supreme sacrifice for their country even more sacred.

— 54 —

FROM THE FINAL PAGES OF STORY OF THE 320TH INFANTRY.

11. BACK IN THE UNITED STATES

After September 28, 1945

First at Camp Kilmer, New Brunswick, New Jersey

Dad's ration certificate, dated September 23—29, 1945, was for "embarking or debarking personnel only" at any Camp Kilmer Exchange. He was entitled to one carton of cigarettes, 32 cigars, or eight ounces of smoking tobacco. The first meal for the returning veterans included half a head of lettuce and a steak. Ben Lane (320/35th) said the food was so foreign to his body, it made him sick.

Each soldier received a 29-page pamphlet to help with the transition back to civilian life. It included everything from celebrating one's return to accessing chaplains. One of the rules specified, "Do not carry knives and pistols on your person— leave them in your luggage."

In addition, the booklet offered suggestions for behavior:

- You will get a swell feeling inside when you toss a snappy 'highball' (salute) at an officer and he tosses one right back at you. It makes you feel part of the same swell team.

- Don't ruin it right off the bat by going out and getting "stinko" or seeing if you can run the tap dry the first night.

Alfred

BE AVAILABLE AT ALL TIMES

There's an awful lot of work necessary to get you out of here and on your way to the Reception Station nearest your home where your leave or furlough will be issued. We don't mind working around the clock to accomplish this. But you've got to help us. Stay on the ball. If you go "goofing off" so that you miss your processing or miss a meeting that is essential, you not only jeopardize your chances of leaving but the chances of all the men in your group. So play it smart—stay together and be available at all times as a group, until your entire processing is finished and your Unit or Group Commander dismisses you. Then check frequently as we may not be able to give you much advance notice on your departure.

[2]

APPEARANCE AND CONDUCT

You're the "returning hero" to your family, friends and community. They'll be looking at you as the Army's representative. You will be on display, so to speak. So don't be a "Sad Sack." You've been through a lot—why spoil it by looking and acting like anything but what you are—a good soldier. It'll mean a lot to everyone—you, your family, the Army, and the community—and hike up your morale and pride plenty to know you are making a good impression. A complete uniform—including the cap and insignia — is required on the Post at all times. If you are in cottons you do not have to wear a necktie on the Post. Off Post and on departure you are required to wear one. So get in the swing of things right away.

[3]

DRESS CODE FROM CAMP KILMER PAMPHLET NO. 1, PAGE 3, "INFORMATION FOR ALL PERSONNEL RETURNING FROM OVERSEAS."

MILITARY COURTESY

That's not just something they write manuals and Army Regulations about. It ties in greatly with your appearance. There are certain traditions in civilian life which mean a lot to the folks and to society. In the Army we also have very fine, deep-rooted traditions. You know them—but naturally have had other things to think about while overseas. But now that you're back, just as you'll have to think a bit about your manners, stop and think about your military courtesy. You get a swell feeling inside when you toss a snappy "highball" at an officer and he tosses one right back at you. It makes you feel part of the same swell team. We insist on military courtesy on this Post to help you "get in the groove" right away.

[4]

INTOXICATING LIQUOR

We know you've been away for a long time and have had to do without a lot of things. But you're home now and will be able to do all the things you have probably dreamed about. Don't ruin it right off the bat by going out and getting "stinko" or seeing if you can run the tap dry the first night. Enjoy yourself—but take it easy. There'll be plenty more nights and plenty more occasions to have a swell time. If you get all "slopped up" here you may get into trouble or may even miss your train home. That would certainly not be such a hot way to start off that long awaited stay at home. Honestly, it won't pay!

[5]

ALCOHOL USE FROM CAMP KILMER PAMPHLET NO. 1, PAGE 5, "INFORMATION FOR ALL PERSONNEL RETURNING FROM OVERSEAS."

- You're the "returning hero" to your family, friends, and community.

- You will be on display, so to speak, so don't be a "sad sack."

- You've been through a lot—why spoil it by looking and acting like anything but what you are—a good soldier.

* * *

Dad was discharged as a Private First Class. I asked him at the nursing home, "Were you ever offered a promotion?"

He answered, "Lots of times, but it was always more risky. I always wanted to stay out of dat business. How could I tell somebody else to do what I didn't want to do?"

* * *

Endres, Cross Plains, Discharged from Army

CROSS PLAINS — Pfc. Alfred Endres, a veteran of action in the European theater, has received an honorable discharge after serving since Mar. 6, 1942. He was overseas with the 35th infantry division for 17 months.

The Cross Plains veteran, the son of Mr. and Mrs. Nick Endres, wears five battle stars on his ETO ribbon, the Distinguished Unit citation, the Expert Infantryman badge, and the Good Conduct medal.

His wife and their daughter, Eileen, lived at Lodi during Pfc. Endres' service.

ENDRES

Mom and Dad happily reunited at the train station in Madison, Wisconsin, and beamed in a photo taken at the Endres homestead with their 13-month-old, firstborn child. Mom wrote on the back of the photo, "October 13, 1945. Alfred arrived in Madison at 5 a.m. this morning. Eileen and I were there to meet him, and we stopped at Sally's on the way home." Mom added later, "Eileen went to him right away. Of course, I had told her all about him."

"ALFRED ARRIVED IN MADISON 5AM THIS MORNING. EILEEN AND I WERE THERE TO MEET HIM." (EILEEN WAS EXACTLY 13 MONTHS OLD.)

Dad's sister-in-law Rita recalled that a military letter had been sent to the wives and parents of returning veterans. Mom had explained the contents to Rita, "Do not ask questions. Do not make them relive it. Leave it behind." Mom would have been first to honor the letter's directives, but Dad's sister Sally unknowingly asked him, "What was it like?" More than six decades later, one of her children remembered his answer, "When you have to jump over dead bodies, you do not want to talk about it."

Don May recalled, "We were told just to forget. We were told lots of things went on that should not have. You are going home. You are discharged. Forget the war."

Dad said to me, "I tried not to remember." That is different than trying to forget. He knew his memories could not be wiped out.

Robert admitted, "My nerves were shot. It took three years for me even to start to recover." He buried the war for almost forty years until he attended the reunions of the 35th Division and began to talk of his experiences. As a farmer with eight children, Dad did not have the freedom, or possibly the desire, to seek out reunions, so his box of war memories remained locked. Luckily for us, the lock basically worked.

As I researched, I found a veteran's daughter who said of her father, "He went from pole to fence post" as he drank his way through life after the war. Another shared that her father paced at night with a knife and was eventually institutionalized.

About seventy years after the war, Michael Phillips wrote an article in the *Wall Street Journal* called "The Lobotomy Files." The article described the effects of brain surgery performed in the late 1940s and early '50s to control the behavior of at least several thousand veterans who were psychologically damaged by World War II. Michael Phillips wrote, "The surgery left them little more than overgrown children, unable to care for themselves. Many suffered seizures, amnesia, and loss of motor skills." This was before the antipsychotic drug of Thorazine was readily available.

* * *

Presidents sometimes say that military training will prepare people for jobs in civilian life. James Graff (134/35th) laughed at such a comment, "I was a rifleman in the infantry. The only

training I received was how to kill the enemy. You couldn't do that when you got home."

"…Veterans were at a disadvantage. Many were worn and weary, others shell-shocked and wounded…Many veterans had lost, or failed to develop a civilian skill," Orval Faubus wrote *In This Faraway Land.*

When Dad returned home after the war, his brother Edward offered him a job with his excavating business, but Dad probably needed to be his own boss and deal with things his own way, although life may have been financially easier as an employee of his brother.

* * *

Shortly after the war, Dad observed a veteran entering a Lodi area dance hall. Someone shouted, "How many Japs did you kill?"

PALLBEARERS FOR CLASSMATE JOE KRUCHTEN. L TO R: VICTOR BRAM, OSCAR STATZ, WILBERT GROSSE, ART KUEHN, ALFRED ENDRES, AND NICK MAIER.

The veteran paused and answered, "Twenty-two!"

Dad said, "He did not kill 22, and how would he know?" Dad added, "Dat is too many," and then under his breath and almost to himself, "And not dat many."

From a more recent war, a veteran chooses to answer that same question quickly and without explanation. He says, "Eighteen," just to eliminate conversation.

Dad also recalled a World War II veteran who publicly boasted of his war experiences. Dad asked, "How can anybody be happy about killing people when dey have parents and sisters and brot'ers?" The room fell uncomfortably quiet. Some veterans thought only of killing enemies; Dad could not shake the fact that the enemies were human.

Then three years after Dad came home, the body of one of his childhood friends was returned for burial. All of Joe Kruchten's six classmates from St. Martin's Grade School in Martinsville, Wisconsin, served in World War II. They also served as pall bearers for Joe. Dad remembered Joe as being very bright. The group posed for a photo at the Endres homestead down the road from the church.

* * *

Shortly after I began my research, I shared with others what I was learning about war and my father, and I cringed at some of the responses because they felt like tiny slaps in the face. Comments came from people from all walks of life who spoke with me in stores, on sidewalks, in the back of churches, on the phone, at celebrations, and at tables where I was graciously invited to eat with them. I was disillusioned as I choked down aspects of their kindness and began to understand my father's silence. For

those who do not understand and refuse to listen, words are inadequate. For those who experienced the trauma, words are not necessary.

Steven Melnikoff (175/29th) spoke with me on the phone. He said, "Talking about the war just brought back bad memories. Nothing good had happened, so we coped by not talking. It took many, many years for me. I could not make it to Europe for the 50th anniversary of D-Day because I was not mentally ready, but I went for the 60th."

Rafael Alvarez, a museum technician at Fort Bragg, explained it to me in an email, "We learn to put certain memories in the dark areas of our minds and hearts, hoping they stay there and don't come out. But there are times when something will trigger those feelings to return…"

For some veterans, flashbacks can be triggered by firecrackers or even the smell of coffee or freshly moved dirt. Buried memories have impact.

One of my students enlisted at the age of 15 into the military of El Salvador, during a war when it was common to mount heads on fence posts. Eventually, he fled his country and realized the impact that war had on him. When he drank alcohol, he cried, and when he held a gun, his hand became physically warm.

The brother of another one of my students had nightmares, which disrupted her family's life. She did not understand her brother's frightful behaviors. Yet she was aware that he had picked up a helmet to find parts of his friend's skull and brains still inside.

Murray Leff (137/35th) wrote of World War II, "Once I saw a G.I. glove lying next to a tank destroyer. Elated, I reached down to pick it up, only to discover a wrist protruding from it. For many years thereafter, I felt it was necessary to fold gloves in half."

* * *

While teaching math at Milwaukee Area Technical College, I noticed an aging tattoo on the forearm of my student Dan. The most distinct words were "Never Again." After several months of teaching him, I asked him whether the MC stood for Marine Corps.

Dan said, "I served in Vietnam in Da Nang."

I commented, "Da Nang is very familiar. If I have heard of the place, it must have been bad."

"It was all bad," he answered.

I explained to Dan how my father had just begun to talk about World War II after 57 years. Then, as Dan tried to explain why a veteran may have difficulty talking about war, tears welled up in his eyes. As quickly as I could bumble my way through the difference between basic memories and those with emotions still attached, we returned to something easier, yet despised—math word problems.

I shared that story of Dan and his tattoo to a small group of people at a holiday gathering. When I finished, a man said, "My sister is immature, too. She cried in the grocery checkout because she could not be home for Thanksgiving."

I was stunned. According to this man, the Vietnam veteran, who dragged bodies out of danger while being fired upon, was immature.

alfred

A couple of months later, I met Dan in the hallway at school and asked, "Do you ever get angry with what people say about war?"

Dan replied, "Lots of times."

I added, "I have never served in combat, and I am constantly appalled."

* * *

The editor of a local newspaper captioned a reenactment photo, "Romance in War."

"What do you think about a title of 'Romance in War'?" I asked 94-year-old Robert as he made plans to attend the 35th Division reunion.

He said, "Those two words do not belong together. There is nothing endearing about war, but not many people know it."

Consider the following description by Donald Schoo, a veteran in the 633rd Anti-Aircraft Artillery Battalion, who wrote in *The Bulge Bugle* (August 2014):

> **You are always cold or hot, it is raining or snowing, you are thirsty, tired, have diarrhea, your feet are sore, you are dirty, itchy and you stink. You hurt all over and chafe, afraid because a few miles away, an enemy artilleryman is about to kill you, or just over the next hill an enemy infantry is going to try to kill you before you kill him.**

In addition to the concept of romance within war, I struggled with books that included too many words like adventure, heroics, and exploits, and I kept tallies on the inside cover just to irritate myself. Even Patton used the term "valor of ignorance" to describe the confidence and bravery of those with little or no combat experience.

* * *

As I drove to the nursing home, I listened to Andy Rooney's *My War*. He had been a correspondent for the military publication, *Stars and Stripes*, and he created images that helped me understand the war. There were descriptions of dead soldiers hanging on fences and other visuals that made me tear up when I realized what my father had witnessed without our previous knowledge. Eventually, however, I found fault with Andy Rooney describing the war as fascinating. I wrote to him, "My father found no pride or glory in what he was asked to do. He would never use the word 'fascinating' to describe his war experience. In fact, he used virtually no words at all."

Andy Rooney wrote thousands of letters in response to those sent to him, but I never received one. I want to believe he understood what I had written.

* * *

"Overall it was a great adventure," a veteran said in an interview for a locally published book. Another veteran was quoted, "Through all the combat I was in, only one person was hit," while a third said, "There were a couple scary moments."

Compare those comments with the words of rifleman Lloyd Barnett (137/35th) in *Santa Fe Express* (January/February 2011), "I hate to admit it, but I got so hard-hearted over there I could have seen my mother dead, and I would not have stopped….There is just no way you can tell somebody how really bad it was. Every morning when you woke up, you did not expect to live."

* * *

Alfred

Decades after Dad's return, Mom said of him, "He came back a changed man." By the time Mom had passed away and Dad lived at the nursing home, my siblings and I retrospectively recalled only a few examples of the war's impact on our father.

He rarely used a gun after the war even though officers had used his expert-level marksmanship scores (minimum of 36 hits out of 40 targets) for their own promotions. Dad was only being kind when he agreed to go deer hunting with my brother's newly widowed father-in-law. Dad noted, "It is different being in da woods wit' a gun when no one is shooting at you." He fell asleep in a tree that day with no intention of shooting anything.

My brother Jerry remembered how a neighbor, Leonard Theis, bought a gun and was unable to hit anything with it. Dad shot three times at a target and found the gun to be a little off, but all three shots were within the area of a quarter. Dad told Leonard, "You just have to aim and allow for da way you shoot."

Leonard said, "Okay, you allow, and shoot that sparrow on the roof."

Dad did not want to damage the new roof on the barn, but Leonard insisted. Dad shot, hit the bird, and Leonard's brother responded in the Theis accent that elongated every vowel, "No wonder we won the war."

Dad attended fireworks because he rarely refused any invitation, but my sister Yvonne said, "He tried to like fireworks for us, but he thought they sounded like war."

And when my sister Del offered to take our parents to Germany about five decades after the war, Mom was willing to go, while Dad remained quiet. Our distant cousin in Germany had said, "Your father can speak low German with the best of them." It seemed Dad would enjoy Germany, but since he never wasted time discussing what might not materialize, he did not say much about the trip. When it became more of a possibility, he finally said, "I have already seen it. I do not want to go." He later added, "I was dere once. Dat is enough."

* * *

Sixty-three years after the war, Ray Huckaby (134/35th) choked up on the phone as he told me of his conversations with his father at the family store in Alabama. His father was a veteran of the First World War, and he understood war, listened to Ray, and did not judge him. Ray felt those conversations helped him heal and re-enter civilian life, but he added, "There were lots of suicides."

When Ray returned, he was also asked, "How was it?" He said, "Those people had no more clue about war than a possum. They did not want to hear about it anyway." Therefore, Ray quit talking.

I loaned out Gerald Linderman's *World Within War* to a man after the book had helped me understand my father's experiences. As the man prepared to return the book to me, I was ushered to a small built-in bookcase where a copy of Tom Brokaw's *Greatest Generation* was accidentally pulled from the shelves. *World Within War* had already been placed on a table, so it was a not-so-subtle way of showing me which book this man preferred. I understand.

Brokaw's book is a feel-good book in which our veterans emerge from the war with self-confidence and determination, with "passions and discipline that had served them so well in war," and with prior "qualities intact and reinforced." Brokaw focuses on a very small group of successful people with five decades of accomplishments after the war. As for the man who returned the book *World Within War* to me, Ray Huckaby had already explained it, "He did not want to hear about it anyway."

In his final years at the nursing home, Dad asked Eileen whether she had access to the *History Channel.* "I can take it better now," he said. However, that was not the case at the nursing home when some cable networks had broadcast continuous coverage of a military invasion. The nursing home staff noticed behavior changes in Dad, and our neighbor once switched the television channel out of concern that Dad was being negatively impacted.

World War II Memorial, unknown location. Jerry Simon points to his Uncle Alfred's name.

12. MILITARY MEDALS

S ara Rosenberry wrote to me that her years within the United States Embassy in Luxembourg had taught her, "American soldiers went home to a relatively undisturbed world where no one had any idea what they had been through in war. This made it more difficult for the American soldiers to heal. In Europe, on the other hand, civilians understood what had really happened and what their soldiers had done."

* * *

About 60 years after the war, I received John Walsh's bright green three-page newsletter for the members of the 320th Regiment. That is when I learned about the French Legion of Honor Medal. Dad had not felt any sense of pride when the United States awarded him a Bronze Star, but he was impacted by Sara Rosenberry's comments about foreign appreciation. Therefore I decided to nominate Dad for the French award. I submitted his discharge papers, a letter of recommendation, and a copy from the newspaper about Ben Lane and Dad's Christmas in Metz, France, 1944. Once I had done my part, I did not give it any more thought.

It had been almost four years between Dad's receipt of the Bronze Star and my nominating him for the French Legion of Honor. I had learned a lot about medals and our reactions to them. In life, we most often accept what reinforces our existing

beliefs, whether it is about prejudice or politics or war. It is easy for us to notice the examples that confirm our beliefs and discard those that do not.

If a person is only exposed to the honor of military medals, one only sees the honor in them. I emailed a short paragraph to a woman about Dad's reaction to the Bronze Star and his comment, "I do not know why you should get medals for killing." This woman's husband had served in the military for years, and she quickly responded, "But what did he think of his Bronze Star?" I tried to make sense of her question because I thought Dad's comment had already answered it. Bewildered, I sighed and deleted her email.

Months later, I stopped to visit my childhood dentist, Dr. Bohlman, on my way home from the nursing home. It was a beautiful autumn day, and he was raking leaves on his front lawn. He had served as a dentist for the Marines at Camp Pendleton, where he observed the fragile state of veterans and the look in their eyes as they returned from the Pacific. He offered to work on their teeth, trying to delay their return to civilian life because they did not appear ready for it. Typically, the veterans declined because they were so desperate to get "home," a place that would probably not feel the same as before combat.

I told Dr. Bohlman about Dad associating a medal with killing and the woman's question, "But what did he think about his Bronze Star?" In defense of this woman's seeming lack of understanding, I casually added, "She is an intelligent woman."

Dr. Bohlman minced no words, "She is not!"

As I drove home to Cedarburg that afternoon, I thought of Dr. Bohlman's statement about the woman's intelligence. Sometimes our beliefs and emotions run so deeply that we lose our ability to be objective. Objectivity is the essence of intelligence, according to Marilyn vos Savant. She was once listed in the *Guinness Book of World Records* under "Highest IQ," a category that has since been retired. The military woman could not fathom that my father would not honored by the Bronze Star. She had lost her ability to be objective.

For a soldier to receive a medal, someone has to witness the action, survive it, and have the ability and time to write it up. Composer Frank Loesser wrote the words for the song, "*Oh, they've got no time for glory in the infantry.*" Orval Faubus wrote in his journal about Mortain, "Many heroic deeds today will be unknown and unsung for both the doers and the observers may well perish in the struggle."

At other times, staff members could be awarded medals without ever hearing the whistle of a bullet, simply due to the honoring process.

The Combat Infantry Badge (CIB) was the most valued recognition for the infantry. It is awarded for being in actual combat and experiencing deadly encounters with the enemy. It is based on company rosters, not an officer's recommendation. It is for what a soldier did, not for what someone said a soldier did.

A friend told me her brother threw all his medals overboard as he was returning from his duty in India during World War II. Likewise, Dad's Bronze Star brought no obvious satisfaction for him because he felt he had done what was necessary to survive. Yet Ben Lane, in trying to recall his and Dad's history within the

war, asked me on the phone, "Does your father have a Purple Heart?" Medals are still a tangible indication of one's experiences when there are so few words to describe them.

* * *

About five months after I submitted Dad's nomination for the French Legion of Honor, he received a letter from the Ambassade de France aux Etats-Unis, the Embassy of France in the United States. "I am pleased to inform you that by a decree signed by the President of the French Republic, you have been named '*Chevalier*' of the Legion of Honor."

The letter expressed kindness and gratitude, but since there was no mention of a medal or a presentation, I thought Dad had received an honorary title of *Chevalier*. Dad was touched by the letter and the certificate, which we framed for his wall. He asked me to send a thank-you note, so I chose to write to Bernadette Day at the French Consulate because hers was the only contact information I had:

> *Dear Bernadette,*
>
> *My father, Alfred N. Endres, veteran of World War II, received his certificate from the Embassy of the French Government. He asked me to thank someone, so I chose you.*
>
> *I thought you may find it interesting that he did not speak about World War II until after my mother died a little more than five years ago. When he received the retroactive award of a Bronze Star for his Combat Infantry Badge, he said, "I do not know why you should get medals for killing." However, when he received the*

certificate from you, he showed it to me and asked me to write a thank-you note.

The gratitude from people in Europe seems more important to my father than from Americans. He is fully aware that most Americans do not understand the reality of war whereas many Europeans saw it, experienced the bombing, grieved the death of civilians, lost their homes, their cattle, and their livelihoods. When Europeans offer their gratitude, it is with honor, respect, and humility, whereas American gratitude can be based on naïveté and national pride.

My father was touched by your gratefulness. Thank you.

* * *

I typically left home at 10:30 on Saturday mornings, stopped to eat at Culver's Restaurant in Columbus, Wisconsin, and arrived at the nursing home after lunch had been already served at "the boys' table" near the big window at the back of the dining room. The food actually was quite good, but I preferred just to visit with the men and not to eat with them. Only once Dad joked of the meal, "You do not have to ask for dat recipe."

One Saturday, at Dad's table, the conversation progressed from brownish oak leaves that may not drop in the fall to dances at Springfield Corners, where Italians occasionally came out from Madison to pick a fight. For the sake of conversation, I simply mentioned, "Dad got a letter from the French Government thanking him for what he did in World War II."

A tablemate joked to Dad, "I suppose you walked behind the tanks."

Dad said matter-of-factly, "No one did dat. Everyone was shooting at da tanks."

"Behind the trees?" the tablemate asked with a smile.

I knew that answer and said, "No, if artillery hits a tree, it sent pieces of wood and shrapnel into everything below."

The man continued, "I always wanted to be in the war....a *fraulein* on each arm."

I watched Dad's face for his reaction, but even with my life-long knowledge of the man, I detected nothing. The conversation changed, and eventually everyone left the table except Dad and me.

I commented, "He does not seem to understand what you went through."

Dad looked out the big window with a slight nod of his head toward the driveway. "What good does it do to have two guys out dere shooting at each ot'er?"

We left the dining room, and I slowly pushed Dad in his wheelchair down the hallway. Just as we turned to enter his room, he said something. I stopped, leaned around the back of his wheelchair, and asked him to repeat his words.

"Maybe it is good I touched da war. At least I know what it is."

Several months later, we were informed by the Wisconsin Department of Veteran Affairs that being named a Chevalier of the French Legion of Honor involved a medal and a presentation ceremony. Suddenly I realized I did not know much about it.

The National Order of the Legion of Honor had been founded by Napoleon Bonaparte in 1802. Our application moved from the French Consulate in Chicago to the French Embassy in

Washington D.C. to the final decision being made by the Legion of Honor Committee in Paris, France. Approximately one hundred medals are awarded to World War II veterans each year in the United States at a public ceremony on a patriotic holiday, starting 60 years after the war.

Dad's most significant medals were the Combat Infantry Badge, a Bronze Star Medal, and the Presidential Unit Citation for the rescue of the "Lost Battalion" at Mortain. He served in three of the four campaigns recognized for the liberation of France: Normandy, Northern France, and Ardennes. (He did not participate in Southern France/Provence.) The Chevalier award was to "acknowledge services rendered to France by persons of great merit."

I told Dad there would be a ceremony for the French Legion of Honor. He had a brief moment of pride, not acknowledging himself as a hero, but possibly as an honorable man doing what he believed was important in life. Dad said, "Not dat many would go for somebody else."

I considered Dad's comment in terms of how the United States created a massive mobilization during World War II to liberate the people of other countries. Sixteen million American soldiers had been involved in some capacity, along with efforts on the home front to ration gasoline, rubber, silk, and sugar and to recycle paper, tires, and scrap metals. There was a general focus by the entire country, something that has never been replicated.

Three days later, Dad's comment floated into my consciousness when I awoke. It had been so soft-spoken and without context that I did not fully understand its meaning. "Not dat

many would go for somebody else." He was not talking about the United States as a whole; he was talking about himself and his brother Edward.

It was not until the final years of Dad's life that I learned how he ended up in the military. I knew Dad did not enlist with thoughts of heroism, but I never knew how the events unfolded until my sister Bev received a copy of a history assignment written by the granddaughter of Dad's brother Edward. Stephanie, a Waunakee High School student and a generation behind us, knew the history that we did not know. She had written:

> *More than fifty years ago, after the attack on Pearl Harbor, government workers in charge of the draft for World War II came to my great-grandfather and asked him to make a choice. He was to choose which of his unmarried sons he wanted to send to the war and which of his sons he wanted to keep home to work on the farm. My great-grandfather told the workers that he could not make that choice, but they told him that he had to. Luckily for my great-grandfather, one of his sons volunteered to go to the war, taking the horrible decision out of his hands. My grandpa [Edward] was very lucky that day that his brother [Alfred] volunteered to go…I am grateful to my great-uncle for choosing to go to war. If he had not done that, it would have been my grandpa who went to war. If that had happened, my grandparents might have never gotten married, and I might not be here right now.*

Farming was an essential service, a deferment. Don May knew of farmers who were wealthy enough to buy farms for their sons, so they would not have to go to war, but that was never considered for Dad.

On that day in the nursing home when Dad had said, "Not dat many would go for somebody else," I had asked "Do you wish you had gotten out of the war?"

Dad answered, "Not really," but he was thinking of his brother Edward while I was thinking of one soldier out of sixteen million. The realization three days later brought tears to my eyes, a poignant example of "Greater love hath no man, that he lay down his life for his brother."

At another point in time, Dad said to me, "If I did not go, Eddie would have to go. I did not want dat." I guess that is why Dad never had any resentment about his lot in life. He had made the choice.

* * *

The French Legion of Honor ceremony was to be held on a patriotic sort of day, such as a special date in history or in our case, an election day. Our family was thinking the sooner, the better, so we had three weeks to organize our gathering. My brother Jerry shared that Dad no longer stayed awake for an entire Packer game, and he had only asked to leave the nursing home twice during the previous two months of Sundays.

Because of our choice for the date of the ceremony, the Consul General was not able to attend; however, the medal would be presented by someone from the Wisconsin Department of Veterans Affairs. The more I thought about an American presenting the French medal, the more uncomfortable I became.

Alfred

My entire premise was for Dad to hear appreciation from a country other than the United States. I felt Dad needed the authenticity of a French accent. He had never been impressed by rank or position, but an accent would be important, so I tried to think of anyone of French heritage who could present the award.

Pierre Briere, the chef at Elliot's Bistro in Milwaukee, Wisconsin, made a special dinner for Normandy veterans on the Monday evening closest to the anniversary of D-Day. He had been five years old when he crawled from ditch to ditch to find safety in Vignats while his hometown of Falaise was being bombed six miles away. During my research, I once emailed Pierre to ask a question about the Battle of the Falaise Pocket, which lasted ten days in August 1944. He responded, "With the concentration of all Allied forces (Americans, British, Canadians, Irish, Australian, New Zealanders, Czechs, Polish, and French), 14,000 soldiers in total were killed in four of those days."

Because of his helpfulness and kindness, I decided to send a letter to Pierre:

> _Dear Mr. Briere,_
>
> _My father served in the 35th Infantry Division during World War II, and his name has been on your D-Day dinner list although we have never been able to get him to Milwaukee from about a half hour north of Madison. You were even gracious enough to call me last year._
>
> _I have a question to ask, and in no way do I expect you to do this, but I need to be certain that I do not miss an opportunity._

On Tuesday November 7 at 11 a.m. in the activity room of the Good Samaritan Center (nursing home) in Lodi, Wisconsin, my father will receive the French Legion of Honor Medal for his partici- pation in the liberation of France. At this time, it does not seem anyone from the French Consulate is able to attend, so your kindness came to mind. Would you be able to present my father with the medal?

Thank you. I just do not want to later think, "I should have asked Pierre."

Sincerely,

Louise Endres Moore

Pierre called me, and he was irritated. His French accent had so many genteel consonants that I put a finger in one ear, closed my eyes, and concentrated on what he was saying. I missed some of his words, but I clearly understood Pierre to say, "This is unacceptable!"

Pierre called the consulate, and he threatened to call some- one in France, where he told me he used to be in politics and had connections. He said something to the effect that it could get ugly.

Less than two hours later, a woman named Matilde called. She understood why it was important for a French person to be at the ceremony. The consul could not be present, but the vice- consul would be there.

Shortly thereafter, I noticed in the local newspaper that Pierre was teaching a Thanksgiving cooking class at Webster Middle School in Cedarburg. I decided to thank him in person.

Alfred

After teaching my evening math class, I approached Pierre at his cooking class and jokingly introduced myself with a smile, "I am your girlfriend you have never met." His students were just sitting down to eat their class project of turkey and trimmings. I was able to thank Pierre and was treated to an unexpected Thanksgiving dinner. He understood Dad because he said he also "served in the military for two bad years and did not want to talk about it either." He added, "The Americans who liberated France are still my idols."

Then, as preparations continued for the French Legion of Honor ceremony, Dad fell when he did not ask for help out of his recliner. I sent an email to my siblings, "Remember how Dad never made it to Vonnie's Pearl Harbor commemoration because he broke his hip the day before? Dad fell last night and is confused today. He will probably be fine, but…in the back of my brain…November 7 is still a long way off."

Bob emailed back, "Jerry said the same thing to me today."

I awoke at 2 o'clock in the morning with a partial speech floating in my head, probably not as good as the one spoken in French on YouTube, but with enough thoughts that by 3 a.m., I decided to write them down, so I could sleep. And on a different night, I awoke in a mild panic. "Is this just too much for him?"

I emailed Matilde, "Attached is a three-minute 'speech' that I will give for my father. He is 88 years old, in a wheelchair, and would never want to give a speech, even if he were younger and healthier. He will sit beside me."

There is always a myriad of details for an event, but especially when the guest of honor is a health risk. The ceremony would be at the nursing home, so there would be no steps, minimal physical transfers, efficient timing, and the weather would not be an issue. My sisters Eileen and Del were coming from out of state with instructions for a very calm and relaxed Monday with Dad. Maintain his typical schedule and activities. On Tuesday, only Bev and Jerry should be in his room before the ceremony to dress Dad and keep everything low-key. We had about a three-hour window of time before he would tire.

A cousin happened to be travelling in France and emailed me to ask whether we needed anything. I asked for a little Calvados and ten small French flags, only if they were easy to find and to pack.

Dad's siblings, Edward and Celia, received hand-written invitations, while emails were sent to his nieces and nephews. Former neighbors. The Dane and Lodi Legions. The Mass group. We invited "The Breakfast Group," the monthly volunteers with whom Dad discretely tried to get as many strips of bacon as possible from everyone who passed near him. Dad asked to invite the wife of Bonard Leatherberry, his partner on the bus ride 64 years earlier when the young men were inducted into the army.

BG Andrew Schuster of the Wisconsin Department of Veterans Affairs planned the logistics for the day. He had been the Public Affairs Director for nearly five years and had never coordinated a French Legion of Honor ceremony, so Dad was

one of the first recipients in the state. He showed interest when I relayed Andrew's comment, and Dad was pleased that his siblings and a couple of nephews had sent early replies. Then we all held our breath that he would use the call light and remain healthy for the following weeks leading up to the ceremony.

13. FRENCH LEGION OF HONOR CEREMONY

O n the day of the ceremony, I did not go to Dad's room because I knew he was in good hands with my siblings Jerry and Bev. Television cameras arrived from two Madison stations, and the journalists were hoping for an interview with the guest of honor. They asked me, "Could we interview him?" "I just want to ask him a couple of questions." "Where is he?"

I had decided in advance that Dad should not be interviewed before the ceremony because he would not like the questions, and he did not speak well on camera. It would stress him and tire him, so we kept him hidden in his room prior to the ceremony.

The journalists were persistent, and after repeated requests, I escaped to Dad's silent room to hide out with him for the remaining twenty minutes. Dad was reclined in his chair, wearing his good navy-blue trousers, his dusted-off wingtip shoes, and a t-shirt. His eyes were closed. He always ran warm, so we waited until the final minutes to finish dressing him in his white shirt, red tie, and blue jacket.

Jerry said quietly to me, "You look like Mom when she was mad." It was the overwhelming interview requests. I looked out the window to distract myself.

After a few minutes, I asked Dad one of the questions suggested by a journalist, "What would you say if someone asked how you felt about this day?"

Dad was quiet. Then he softly said, "Dose dat like war should go fight it."

That definitely was not the answer a newscaster wants for the nightly news. If Dad was pressured for an interview, I knew it would not last long, and I relaxed.

The *Lodi Enterprise* described the beginning of the ceremony, "The sounds of the United States national anthem rang through the community room at the Lodi Good Samaritan Center—preceded by the melodic sounds of the French national anthem."

Dad faced the podium, along with one hundred guests, while local and state dignitaries spoke. Col John Scocos, Secretary of the Wisconsin Department of Veterans Affairs, commended Dad and soldiers in general who had returned from war with their humanity. It was true for Dad.

Granddaughter Tina said, "It truly amazes me that Grandpa remained so gentle and loving after what he endured."

Then Christophe Alamalema, the Vice Consul of the French-Consulate General of Chicago, took the podium. The *Lodi Enterprise* noted, "In a distinctive French accent, Alamalema spoke to the room crowded with Endres's friends and family, cameras flashing."

The vice consul said, "You gave your youth to this effort....The French citizens will never never forget." He spoke with kindness and appreciation, and then he concluded, "On behalf of France, I want to award you the highest award in France for your commendable deeds to protect my country."

"The French people do not take this award lightly," a French friend of John Walsh (320/35th) had said. Filmmaker Steven Spielberg received the award for his commitment to humanistic issues and in fighting hatred and intolerance. General Eisenhower had also received it.

I pushed Dad in his wheelchair to the front of the room for him to receive his medal, and after the presentation, I joined him next to the podium, holding his hand while I summarized his tour of duty:

> *France has been our country's ally for almost two and a half centuries, historically our first ally, and the country which gifted to us our precious Statue of Liberty as a gesture of friendship in 1885. Both of our countries have a proud heritage.*
>
> *It is with humility that Dad accepts this honor for he knows that many others served in the same cause during World War II and suffered similar hardships, some veterans serving in a different theatre of operation, others who are deceased, and those who have been without nomination. This medal is most important to him because his painful memories are best validated by those who fully understand war, those who have known the horror of war on battlefields within their own country. The fact that France is grateful and*

remembers after 62 years is far more important to Dad than other recognitions.

When I visited your beautiful country in the summer of 2005, I telephoned Dad, and he asked, "How did the beachhead look?" He was not involved in D-Day, but arrived, at the age of twenty-six, on Omaha Beach in July of '44 and fought his first days of combat in the Battle of Saint-Lô. Immediately thereafter, he served in Patton's Third Army, during which his 1st Battalion of the 320th received a Presidential Unit Citation for the rescue of the Lost Battalion at Mortain.

On September 13, while he fought in the area of the Moselle River near Nancy, his oldest daughter was born, Eileen, a child he doubted he would ever see. He spent the fall of '44 in the excessive rains of the Gremecey Forest, and after 162 consecutive days of combat, the 35th Division was relieved to Metz for only several days to receive replacements and celebrate Christmas. Before being rushed to the frigid, snowy Ardennes to fight in the horrors of the Battle of the Bulge, he and his friend gave their army rations of fruit and chocolate to the manager of the bathhouse in Metz to be used as Christmas gifts for his children. In January, the troops of the 35th Division returned to the Vosges Mountains, later leaving France to enter Germany where they met the Russians on the Elbe River.

It has been only in the past five years that we have come to understand Dad's experiences in World

War II. Prior to that time, we were not aware that he had been a machine gunner. We only knew he had been a chauffeur, a translator, and a barber.

Dad participated in three of the four major campaigns involved in the liberation of France, in addition to the Rhineland and the Central Europe campaigns. The 35th Division served 264 days in combat and suffered a casualty rate of 180.9%. He served the entire duration of his division's tour of duty.

Dad deeply appreciates the honor and gratitude from the French Government and its people. On the day I told him about this ceremony, he said of the people of France, "They know what war is," whereas "Here, people do not really know how bad it was."

At the very end of my speech, I added, "Alfred and his family say…" Then I directed the microphone toward Dad while we said in unison, "Thank you."

A luncheon followed with fun and appreciative guests. I served Calvados in plastic medicine cups to anyone who wanted to sample the apple brandy that soldiers discovered in barrels in the basements of Normandy farmhouses.

Don May and Dad had said this brandy was so strong it could be used in cigarette lighters, lanterns, and even to run Jeeps. Don remembered it as being 180 proof and capable of temporarily blinding soldiers who drank too much. Leo Treinen and Dad's brother Edward wanted a second shot of Calvados, but their wives stood behind them, gently shaking their heads

*ALFRED AND VICE CONSUL CHRISTOPHE ALAMALEMA TOASTING WITH
CALVADOS AFTER THE FRENCH LEGION OF HONOR CEREMONY, NOVEMBER 7,*

from side to side, so I pretended to become distracted and
moved on.

All in all, it was a very good day, and we knew it would
probably be the last gathering in Dad's life with this number of
friends and family. He enjoyed their presence.

Later as I watched the video of the ceremony, I saw that Dad
remained blank-faced and emotionless, and then I understood
the question from Matilde of the French Consulate, "Does he
understand?" The vice consul was so kind in his gratefulness,
but I suspect Dad looked at him, considered his young age, and
knew, as with most people, he did not know the reality of war.
Possibly Dad needed Pierre Briere to present the medal because
the chef had actually experienced the war.

FAMILY PHOTO AT FRENCH LEGION OF HONOR CEREMONY, NOVEMBER 7, 2006. TOP: DEL ENDRES, BOB ENDRES, BEV GORDON. MIDDLE: JERRY ENDRES, EILEEN WALDOW, LOUISE MOORE. FRONT: ALFRED ENDRES AND YVONNE ZIEGLER.

In truth, there was probably nothing that could impact Dad's feelings about war. If he ever felt pride that day, I never saw it. About ten days after the ceremony, I asked him, "It was a nice party, but you do not think too much of the medal, do you?"

He laughed, "It seems everybody else does."

Another time he said of the medal, "Dere were lots of ot'er people."

When family friend Matt Engels congratulated Dad on the phone about six weeks later, Dad replied, "I have medals I had to do a lot more work for than dis one." And Dad simply summarized to me the reason for his award, "I got old."

Alfred

Even though the French medal did not foster pride or ease his memories, Dad and the one hundred guests had a very pleasant gathering. The award acknowledged a part of Dad that few people knew even though he was 88 years old. Actually the ceremony seemed more important to the guests than to Dad because there were tears in some eyes, recognizing what this very ordinary man had gone through. Our family received compliments about the day for quite some time.

* * *

About two years later, I decided to nominate Robert Phillips for the French Legion of Honor Medal. He knew Dad had received it, but Robert said to me, "After 60 years, I am not interested. Maybe if I were a younger man..." I did not know what that meant, and I also knew he was not going to get any younger, so I wrote a letter and sent the necessary forms to the appropriate French consulate. Both men had a Presidential Citation on their discharge papers for the rescue at Mortain. I was quite confident Robert was eligible for the French award.

Eventually, Robert received the French Legion of Honor Medal and sent me the newspaper article about his ceremony, printed in *The Telegraph* of Macon, Georgia. He only hinted to me about his initial reaction to his award letter because it would seem unappreciative of my efforts. He actually tore the letter in half! He admitted to his friend's wife that he had ripped it up. She scolded him, and months later he told me that Ruth had said, "You should be ashamed of yourself." I smile as I imagine Robert taping the letter back together.

In the newspaper article, Robert said, "I did not do any more or less than any other man...."

I spoke with Robert many, many times during the final nine years of his life, and one of our phone conversations lasted two hours. Robert knew he had done more than some soldiers because he told me, "Even some men in the 35th Division did not know what war was." Another time he said of all soldiers, "A small percentage fought World War II."

Tom Brokaw's *Greatest Generation* includes the biography of a soldier who was "involved in combat several times." That soldier served for a time under Patton in a division with 34 days of combat and a casualty rate under 9 percent. Robert served almost 260 days in combat, much of the time under Patton, and within a division that suffered a casualty rate of over 180 percent. There is a huge difference even though both veterans received the Combat Infantry Badge. I believe Robert did not want to make comparisons to diminish anyone.

Robert, along with five other veterans, received the French Legion of Honor Medal in the presence of family members and friends at the home of the Consul General in Atlanta. In the end, I believe Robert was proud of the honor, and possibly more so, proud of it within his legacy to his family.

Alfred

*"I hate war as only a soldier who has lived it can,
only as one who has seen its brutality, its futility,
its stupidity."*

—Dwight D. Eisenhower
Address in Ottawa, Canada, January 10, 1946
Supreme Commander,
Allied Expeditionary Forces 1943-1945

14. AFTER THE CEREMONY

I had pretty well wrapped up Dad's story in my speech at the ceremony. At home a couple of days later, I responded to several emails, and I chuckled to myself, sitting at the computer, celebrating the success of the ceremony, and downing the final few drops of Calvados, straight from the bottle. I redirected my attention to our dining room table that had been the designated work area for World War II for the past five years. I wanted to do something more interesting than just organizing or writing. I preferred to research or to find people.

Mom had saved a letter in the farm's safe ever since she received it more than 60 years earlier. I reread the letter and decided to find Sophia Grecsek, one of the military wives from training, or possibly the baby, whose birth was announced on the tiny three-by-three inch enclosure.

> *Here I Am....*
> *Mom and Dad are mighty proud!*
> *The reason? I've arrived!*
> *And I'm about as cute a trick*
> *As has ever been contrived!*
>
> *Name Anna Mae Grecsek*
> *Date of birth Sept. 25*
> *Weight 7 lbs. 8 ozs.*
> *Sgt and Mrs. Edward R. Grecsek*

Dear Louise, Alfred, and Eileen,

Received your card and letter today and was very glad to hear from you and that Eileen is a good baby. Anna Mae is most of the time. She is a little nervous or something, and I do not dare let her cry too hard or she gets gas in her tummy, but she does not have spells often, so she really is pretty good. After she has her bottle, she wants to go to bed and does not want to be rocked hardly at all, so that helps as babies surely take the time.

Yes, Louise, we both had plans for our next baby, and I believe it would be the most wonderful experience in the world to go through together, watching each new development and then to be together in body instead of spirit as the last. But fate plays on different people at times, I guess. Things seem so unreal and at the moment so very cruel, but behind it all, God must surely have a reason, even though it is hard to bare. And it is with a heavy heart I write you this. We all had such grand plans for when this war is over and how happy we would be. But for some of us, and I guess I am not alone in it for it is happening all over the world, and I know Eddie would have been so proud and happy had he but had the chance to know of his baby girl. But maybe it was not meant to be that way.

I received a telegram from the war department the morning before I left the hospital that my darling had been killed in action September 17. If only he could have known. I am sure he is watching over us now, and he was with us when our baby was born, I feel sure. It seems so impossible that it could happen to Eddie. I do not know just where Anna Mae and I will end up for good yet. Eddie's sister is coming out next month, and we are going back to New York for a while and maybe will settle there. His folks are pretty bad now, and if they can get a little comfort by having our baby there, I'm sure it will do us all good.

That is about all for now. There is not much I can say when the bottom seems to have dropped out of everything. I do have two years of happy memories and can truly say they were happy ones, so with them and Eddie watching over always, we must go on.

Anna Mae and I send our love, and with you and yours, the best of luck. Give Eileen a kiss from Anna and myself, and regards to Alfred and all.

Love,
Anna Mae and Sophia

I remembered the name of Sophia Grecsek from old Christmas photos, but I had no previous knowledge of Eddie's death in war. According to the online ATT Directory, there were no Grecseks in the state of Oregon, which was the return address on the envelope of the birth announcement. In New York, there were five, so I made five copies of Sophia's letter and mailed them along with a note explaining my connection.

Several weeks later Anna Mae's cousin Jerry Grecsek called. He kindly promised to find "the baby," who was married and living in another state. Sophia had died about twenty-five years

after the war. He asked whether Dad might have stories of his Uncle Eddie, whom he remembered fondly from very early memories and from the stories of older relatives.

I did not expect Dad to tell me a story about Eddie Grecsek because I had tried to learn more about him previously to no avail. However, Eddie's nephew was so pleasant that I asked Dad again and was surprised when he started an unexpected ramble of stories. While he did not share any stories about Eddie, he started talking about another buddy, Frank Poelluci.

Dad explained, "Because I could speak German, I went ahead to find housing wit' an officer in a Jeep driven by Mitchell. We went near where Frank was. He was a good guy. We were wit' him and Margaret for Easter."

Dad had tried to arrange housing near Bochum, Germany, on the evening of May 6, two days before Germany's formal surrender. "Dere was a lot of commotion because a sergeant had been shot," Dad said. With all the confusion, he was not able to find Frank.

As Dad spoke that day in the nursing home, I recalled how Frank's wife Margaret had called Mom twice a year for 50-some years, around Christmas and then again for my parents' anniversary in August. Margaret called as usual about a month after Mom's death. Dad gave the news of Mom's passing too quickly, and Margaret hung up. Mom had been healthy for Margaret's December phone call; by August, Mom had passed away. When I heard Margaret had hung up on Dad, I called her, and she explained, "I do not hear well, and I knew I would not hear anything after that news."

During my conversation with Margaret, the 85-year-old offered to write her wartime memories. Her letter explained why Dad never found Frank while searching for housing in Germany at the end of the war:

I received the record of the trial concerning Frank's death. They were guarding prisoners in an old school house in Germany. A young soldier's date did not show up, and because he was partly drunk, he beat up the young girl who brought the message to him. My husband, a staff sergeant to the private, tried to stop the fight. The private said to my husband, "I'm not going to punch you. I'm going to shoot you!" and he did.

They said Frank was hit in the lower part of the stomach, but I say, right between the legs. This happened May 6, 1945, at 6 p.m. on a Saturday, two days before the war ended. Frank "came to" on Thursday, but when he realized his condition, he slipped into a coma and never came out. He died May 12, the day before my first Mother's Day.

I got the telegram the next Sunday, delivered by a soldier, who handed it to me and quickly left. I was living with my in-laws at the time and casually commented about the telegram, "He's coming home in October." That's what we were being told. It was ten minutes before noon, and I was about to cook macaroni.

Sitting at the kitchen table, I opened the telegram and read, "We regret..." I did not move. I could

not believe it, but my brother-in-law Joe, looking over my shoulder, told his mother, who started screaming and pulling her hair. About a month later, they had a Mass for him, and I got a big flag. Being he died in a hospital, I know I have the right body.

Initially he was buried in Holland, but a colonel came to me in October 1947 to ask whether I wanted to have Frank's body brought home. I had the wake at my apartment after his body arrived at 2 p.m. on a Friday afternoon, October 17, 1947, in a light green coffin with a big flag over it.

The soldier who was to guard the coffin had family living nearby, so we allowed him to spend the night with them. Frank's two brothers, my sister, some friends, and I stayed up all night. The guard returned at 7 a.m., and a burial Mass was held at 9 a.m. at St. Mary's, with a cemetery in the back, a block from my house. Everyday Fran and I could visit the cemetery, which we did for twelve years until we moved.

I have a black marble stone on his grave with his regiment on it. My name is not on it as I feel he never really belonged to me. I still try to get there a couple times a year.

Dad did not hear about Frank's death until he returned home. Margaret had written to Mom, but I suspect Mom did not want to relay such upsetting news.

That day in the nursing home, Dad said, "He was one of da best guys I knew. When I found out he died, I felt like a rock."

Uncharacteristically, words continued to flow from Dad's mouth. I stood up from the bed and listened to his every word. It was as if a floodgate had opened. I grabbed a couple of Christmas letters from the card basket to scratch notes on their blank sides while I stood at the back of his recliner.

Dad recalled how he helped to arrange sleeping quarters, basically by forcing German woman and children out of their apartments in order to house our soldiers. "Kicking dem out," Dad called it.

He explained that he was supposed to tell the women in German, "Get da hell out of here…and t'ings dat were even worse. I did not do it as I was told. I would not say dat to a cow." Some soldiers said, "We cannot do that to the German people," while others responded, "I would like to kick every one of them in the head. They were to blame for Hitler for sure."

Most guys were the rougher variety when taking over German housing. If a woman wanted to speak in German, Dad was sent to translate. The women had no say in their evictions. They were upset and cried. Dad said, "Sometimes dey called me an asshole…or worse."

To my surprise, Dad's recollections continued. During the war, he paid attention to the direction of moving deer to stay away from the enemy's approach, and he added, "Everyt'ing was sort of lucky for me, being on da burial squad and da gunner squad." I kept scribbling notes as Dad's thoughts flowed. He spoke of "dead bodies floating in water," and how the movie *Saving Private Ryan* was "just a touch of it because it went on for so long." He did not believe the opening scene was acting. He

was convinced it was actual footage of D-Day. He said to me, "It was not make-believe. I *know* it wasn't."

Suddenly he jolted me into the present by asking, "Did you put on da light for da bat'room?" If he had previously asked me to press the call light, I did not hear him, but I doubt he did so. His recollections stopped so suddenly, so abruptly, I was stunned. I wanted a video of what had just happened during those five to ten minutes.

As I drove home that night, Dad's comments ran through my head. I thought of his words, "dead bodies floating in water," but I knew the 35th had not been involved in D-Day. From my research, I knew the entire tour of duty for the 35th Division so well. It seemed Dad needed to tell me something. I had asked Dad a question about Grecsek, but instead, other memories flowed from the floodgates. At 10:20 p.m. I emailed my siblings:

> *I have little notes written in all directions on the backsides of 3 papers, one being our own Christmas letter from last year. Actually I am too tired to organize it all. There are some confusing things for me. I really think Dad was with a different group for a short amount of time, but…? Also Dad told me a long time ago that he did not land on Omaha Beach a month after D-Day.*
>
> *Dad said there were floating bodies when he landed on the beach, but the 35th got there a month after D-Day. I have to organize these little notes, but to heck with it tonight. I'm tired.*

Bev responded the next day, solely to me, "He may be thinking he does not have much time left."

15. A DISCOVERY

D ad's comment about "dead bodies floating in water" haunted me through Sunday. On Monday morning, I studied a May 1944 letter sent to Dad from his mother-in-law, my Grandma Miller, to which I had never given much attention previously. It had been rerouted so many times to find Dad, with so many stamped and written addresses, that I could not imagine anyone knowing where it had been versus where it was going. I wondered how the envelope survived the war. Possibly Dad had sent it home because he mentioned he was not supposed to carry letters. His small, empty spiral notebook in his army trunk, which he probably had carried throughout the war, was water-marked, whereas this envelope was not stained.

The envelope began its journey to Dad on May 4, 1944, postmarked in Lodi, Wisconsin, and addressed to his training unit, Company H of the 174th Infantry.

The forwarding address that appeared first on the envelope was "325th GLDR." I assumed it was a minor error for Dad's 320th Regiment. With millions of servicemen around the globe, a discrepancy of one number seemed minor, but I did a quick search on the Internet. My eyes widened as I stared at the screen. GLDR was an abbreviation for glider. A unit of the 325th had landed amphibiously on the beaches on D-Day to reinforce the 82nd Airborne. I was stunned. How could I have missed this piece of information when the 325th appeared twice on the envelope, once on the front and once on the back?

There was no way I could drive to Lodi or wait until Saturday to visually watch Dad's reaction and body language as I usually did. I had to call him.

I chatted through a bit of small talk before I asked, "You didn't do D-Day, did you?"

His answer was simple. "No." That was it. I wonder whether he would have said anything if I had not asked the next question.

"When did you go?"

He answered, "Da next day."

I continued, "You went in a boat?"

"Ya."

"Were Germans still there when you landed?

"Ya."

"Were they shooting?"

"Dey shot at da water. Guys went down like flies getting killed. I t'ought nobody could live t'rough dat shit."

We talked a bit more, and then I transitioned to birdseed and squirrels so our conversation would leave him with something other than the war on his mind. I paced around the house. I was overwhelmed for hours. I had been so confident in my acceptance speech for the French Legion of Honor Medal—confident, yet wrong. In front of two television cameras and a hundred guests, I had said, "Dad was not involved in D-Day but arrived, at the age of 26, on Omaha Beach in July of '44 and fought his first days of combat in the Battle of Saint- Lô."

Everything made sense now. I had tried so hard not to exaggerate any of Dad's involvement that I actually had diminished it. I emailed my siblings:

> I am still sort of shocked that Dad had to do D-Day+1 along with everything else. I assumed he was with the 35th and only with the 35th the entire time. It is bad to get injured, but it is also bad to never have a break from combat. We are very lucky to have had a loving, sometimes quirky, father. It could have left him angry, bitter, and hateful.

One of Eileen's friends described her father-in-law, a veteran of the 29th Division: "He became a bitter alcoholic, and I never saw him even smile."

One of my co-workers was proud of her father, yet admitted to me, "At least your father came home a nice man. Mine did not."

Dad never liked the television show *M.A.S.H.*, and a woman told Eileen that her father did not allow it to be watched in their house. He had lied about his age to go to war and then never talked about it. He said, "There was nothing funny about Korea."

I had been researching four years when I observed a man watching the movie *Saving Private Ryan* on television in his home. He shouted, "Get those Germans! Kill 'em!" Then he noticed I was in the room. I could not remain silent. I was calm and simply said, "My father was a front-liner, and he said the enemy was forced to do the same things he had to do. He told me, 'They had families too.'"

Later, I described that scene to Dad, and he was visibly disgusted, "Who said dat?" His reaction was gruff and far

stronger than I would have expected, so while I could have explained my connection, I said, "Just a man I know."

Dad said, "Dey t'ink it is like deer hunting."

* * *

When I was first learning of my father's war experiences, a woman offered a quick explanation for my dad's pained memories. I would hear it again from others. It was so simple.

"Some can take it, and some can't."

The woman continued, "My father laughed and laughed at the hilarious things the monkeys did on the beaches." She did not consider that even monkeys know not to hang around during an invasion, and beaches are only part of combat during an actual assault and shortly thereafter. Soldiers either make it ashore, or they are pushed back into the sea.

* * *

In the nursing home, Dad and I once spoke with an older man wearing a veteran's cap. I asked the man whether he had served in World War II. He answered, "I served in Korea…and also in World War II." When I asked what group he was in, his story began:

> *I served in a unit that was connected with the Air Force. There were planes that were being blown up by spies when our pilots were in them. Once they called me to help with that. I said I would if Garcia could go with me. We were really close friends. I had a 30, and Garcia had a 45 revolver. Boy, mine was some gun. It shot so straight. We were down there, and a guy came out of the plane. I told him to halt, but he wouldn't, so I*

pointed my gun and shot. He fell straight to the ground. We found out later that the spy worked in the mess hall, and he was one of them planting bombs in the planes.

As this man described the event in detail, I wondered whether some veterans could talk more casually about war because of a shorter amount of time on front-line duty. I glanced at Dad, and our eyes met.

The man continued, "Patton even sent my mother a letter, which made her very proud. She carried it around and showed it to everyone."

I assumed it must have been a form letter because Patton led an army of several hundred thousand soldiers, and it would have been unlikely that Patton knew of this singular incident. I became more skeptical and asked, "How old are you?"

He replied, "77."

I confirmed his age when his birthday was posted at the nursing home. This storyteller had been just sixteen years old on May 8, 1945, the final day of the European Theatre of Operations. Though I knew some veterans lied about their age to serve their country, this man graduated from high school in 1947. Patton had died almost a year and a half earlier.

Shortly after I heard this tale, I spoke with Robert Phillips on the phone. As I relayed the story, Robert softly gave his perspective, "He did not do anything."

"What did you say?" I asked.

"He did not do anything."

Alfred

I asked Dad whether he could tell in a relatively short time what a veteran had done in the war. Dad just asked, "Oh, you mean da braggers?"

Joseph Demler answered the same question, "Ya, the fakers and the players."

I read an article that each year in Wisconsin, several families are shocked after they request military honors for their deceased loved ones and discover their "veteran" was either dishonorably discharged or never served in the military at all.

One veteran, who had slept in a bed each night during his military service and never feared for his life or took the life of another human, called out casually to me, "Just tell your father to talk!" A different World War II veteran suggested Dad's lack of conversation was from age-related memory loss.

Over time I came to understand the voice inflections and the combat descriptions of the most involved soldiers. I learned by talking with and observing Dad, Joe Demler, Robert Phillips, Ray Huckaby, Leonard Huskey, Ben Lane, and others.

Robert told me, "I can tell right away whether a person did much in war." He said of a relative, "He did his part, but it was different."

* * *

Suddenly it made sense that Dad could have been part of the beach assault because bits of information and his comments all fit together. When I had called Dad during our trip to France two years earlier, he had asked, "How did da beachhead look?" I was surprised the beaches were so important, but I rationalized they probably were still quite dramatic when the 35th landed a month after the invasion. When I first read my summary of the

Normandy Campaign to Dad, I had stated there was a month between his arrival in Europe and landing on Omaha Beach.

He quietly said, "Not dat long." I assumed his timing was off.

My brother Bob relayed to me a comment from Don May. Don had said, "It had to be later on D-Day or maybe the following day because bullets flew into the boat when the door opened." I dismissed Don's theory because I knew the history of the 35th Division so well. I considered myself a good listener, but I was faced with the humble realization that I had quit listening when I felt I knew everything about the subject.

* * *

While in high school, Bev wrote an unimpressive report about D-Day, bad enough that the teacher required a parent's signature on the graded paper. Mom was cooking while Dad was opening mail at the kitchen table. Neither was happy about the grade, but Dad found it incredulous, "Ach! I was in it."

Bev shared that story when I first started researching Dad's war experiences. I took his comment to mean, "I was there," as in England, in the general area. Later Bev laughed about Dad's reaction to her paper, "He said he was there, but he still never told me anything for my assignment."

Dad's reaction to the beginning of *Saving Private Ryan* was more difficult to discount, but I assumed the first scene was familiar to him from another setting, possibly a river crossing of which the 35th Division had many.

* * *

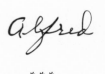

Alfred

* * *

Prior to the French Legion of Honor ceremony, I read my speech to Dad for his approval and asked, "Is that okay?" He approved it, but Bev, who had witnessed the reading, thought Dad had said something more similar to, "Good enough." He probably did not want any more questions and did not want to think about the war anymore. However, when I so publicly stated that he had not been involved in D-Day, he may have realized he needed to tell us the rest of his story that he assumed we already knew.

Ken Burns directed and produced *The War*, an American documentary and television mini-series. It premiered shortly after Dad's death. Ken Burns said of World War II veterans, "In the sunset of their lives, a few of them have realized that their memories are our inheritance."

It seems Dad realized his story was ours.

16. ALBERT SIMON'S BRONZE ARROWHEAD

A researcher from a national military museum spoke willingly and freely with me about D-Day+1. Then he asked, "When did your father arrive in Europe?"

I held my breath because Dad's arrival from the States was very late relative to D-Day+1. It seemed unlikely that in just five days, along with thousands of other soldiers in western England or Wales, he could be transported to replacement depots, to ports of embarkation on England's southern coast, and then finally embark onto boats, transfer to Higgins boats, and assault the beaches of Normandy.

"June 2," I said.

"It is not possible. It is too late to get the troops into position."

"But you do not know my father," I insisted. "He would not make it up."

Dad's cousin Jean Wipperfurth Lenling, who had lost her only sibling in the Battle of Saint-Lô, told me during my research, "Your father would be the last person to exaggerate."

I had more questions to ask of the curator, but the conversation from that point was brief. My subsequent phone messages

and emails went unanswered. I had lost a powerful resource for information.

I decided to ask the discussion group of the 35th Division Association whether anyone had been involved in an assault landing. When I emailed about my father speaking of "dead bodies floating in water" on D-Day+1, the first response was, "Reports that we were in action on D-Day are in error."

Even though two other members of the group mentioned their fathers' possible involvement in D-Day, others latched onto that first response. One wrote, "Now is the time to set the record straight."

Another added, "You hit it on the head. That should put a stop to all the email that has been sent." Half-inch type screamed at me from the computer screen. I felt attacked. Eventually, I decided it was probably a vision problem rather than hostility for such oversized font. Yet, the swarm of negative responses had cut me off from yet another source of information. I was on my own.

So discouraged, I was ready to give up my research, but after three days, I emailed my siblings, "I am back in the saddle again." I had to ignore those comments, and I was determined to find the truth for my father.

The historian was correct to protect the story of the 35th Division. He said privately to me, "Once an error gets into print, it takes on a life of its own." While I incessantly searched for individual connections between the 35th Division and D-Day, I became more aware of erroneous information in print. A western university website claimed an alumnus had landed on D-Day, was in combat for a week, and then was killed in action on July 13. As a mathematician, I knew the numbers did not add up.

Only two of those three conditions could be true, and it is most probable this veteran landed with the 35th Division on July 6 rather than on D-Day, June 6. I pointed out the dilemma, but the alumni website chose to delete the phrase of a "week-long combat." I highly suspect that change is a distortion of history and will falsely live on as fact.

Of my possible D-Day connections within the 35th Division, I found only one veteran, Donald A. Miller, who had received a Bronze Arrowhead on his army discharge papers for an assault landing. Donald A. Miller was shipped to Europe May 12, arrived May 27, participated in D-Day, and was eventually

ALBERT SIMON DURING TRAINING AS A RIFLEMAN. AT THE AGE OF 38, HE ARRIVED IN EUROPE ON JUNE 2, 1944, WITH ALFRED. HE RECEIVED A BRONZE ARROWHEAD FOR AN ASSAULT LANDING. JUNE 6, 1944, D-DAY, 6:30 A.M.

assigned to I Company of the 320th Regiment, the same regiment as my father.

After my failed attempts to get information from the military museum or the 35th Division website, I developed a new plan. I would try to obtain Albert Simon's discharge papers because I knew he had shipped out to Europe with Dad. Albert never married nor had children, which is the usual route to obtain records. Eventually I discovered a helpful woman at the Wisconsin Veterans Museum in Madison. She seemed open to a request from Albert Simon's niece, who was also my first cousin Marjorie Simon. Marjorie immediately sent a letter requesting her uncle's discharge papers. The national museum probably could have found those records for me in thirty seconds. Instead it took three months for Marjorie's efforts to confirm what I had surmised all along.

Thirty-eight-year-old Albert Simon had arrived with Dad in the European Theatre of Operations (ETO) on June 2, 1944, and was later awarded a Bronze Arrowhead for an assault landing. Albert, a replacement without personal connections to anyone in the 29th Division, was thrown ashore at Omaha Beach four days after he arrived in Wales. He was involved in the worst of D-Day at 6:30 a.m. on June 6, following almost two weeks of no exercise and lousy food on a ship.

According to the 29th Infantry Division Historical Society, Albert was most likely a member of F Company of 116th Regiment. He may have landed in front of strongly fortified Les Moulins on Dog Green Beach, or he may have drifted a bit to the east where half of the troops became casualties within 45 minutes.

I found no military expert who believed soldiers could be assigned within four days to assault the beaches. I understood the timing problem because of the logistics of moving so many troops. Albert had to be transported from his ship to a replacement depot to a port of embarkation. He then boarded a vessel and ultimately transferred to a Higgins boat. Bad weather delayed the amphibious assault 24 hours to June 6. It seems impossible, but the Bronze Arrowhead on Albert Simon's discharge papers proved otherwise. His documentation also proved it was possible for Dad, with one extra day, to do exactly what he said he had done. It was a bit of a victory for me, a civilian female.

The majority of the 29th Division had trained and built comradery along the Southern coast of England during the spring months of '44. In that area, thousands of residents had been ordered to evacuate, so the 29th could have large-scale practice landings. They used live naval and artillery ammunition on this coast that was similar to Normandy. It is unlikely Albert had such training, although it probably made little difference on Omaha Beach on D-Day. All was chaos, and nothing went as planned.

The Germans had built thick concrete bunkers on the 100-foot cliffs overlooking the beaches. Advance naval bombardment never touched these bunkers or the obstacles intended to disrupt a beach invasion. This lack of aerial preparation partially stemmed from the military goal of surprising the enemy. In addition, night skies and clouds obscured targets, and the Allies feared hitting their own troops. Therefore, much of the shelling went long, sometimes several miles inland. In addition, Allied intelligence underestimated the number of weaker enemy troops, which were replaced before D-Day with the veteran German 352nd Infantry Division. Ultimately, the Allied infantry had to face fully intact enemy defenses on Omaha Beach.

Germany reasoned that if the Allies would assault, they would do so at high tide when boats could move in farther on the beach. This would minimize the distance soldiers would have to run through mines and barbed wire to get to the relative safety at the base of the cliffs, out of the target range of the bunkers 100 feet above them. German Field Marshall Rommel had been so confident there would be no attack during such poor weather that he had gone home near Ulm, Germany, for his wife's 50th birthday on June 6.

Both Don May and Dad believed we were lucky to have won the war, one that Germany had already been fighting for nearly five years before D-Day. Don May further explained, "Hitler did not allow his generals to make any decisions, and no one ever wanted to wake up the madman." When German General Rommel was informed of the invasion, he said, "My God! If the 21st Panzer can make it, we might be able to drive them back in three days." Don May added, "If Hitler had sent Rommel's tanks to the area sooner, we would have been creamed...food for the fish."

Hitler thought Normandy was just a minor attack, and the major assault would still occur at Calais, France. An attack at Calais would involve crossing just 22 miles of water whereas there was at least 100 miles to cross from the English ports where most Americans embarked for Normandy. Hitler could have called up 50 divisions from the European continent to rush to

Normandy to fight off the attack, but he did not do so. Even as D-Day proceeded, German commanders pleaded with Hitler to change his strategy, but he kept tanks and troops in Calais.

Of course, the Allies intentionally misled Hitler by positioning Patton in England across from Calais, France. Patton was placed in charge of a ghost army, which included the 35th Division on paper, along with other American and Canadian divisions, a few that did not exist and none that were actually there. It was a pretty elaborate hoax with rubber inflatables, vehicles made out of fabric or wood, tent cities with mess halls and hospitals, and fake tire tracks that would look real to the German Air Force from an altitude of 33,000 feet.

Patton was the perfect commander to fill this role because Germany perceived him as very important. Actually, he was in a bit of trouble with Eisenhower. Patton had become a political embarrassment in April when he publicly declared that the United States and England would rule the world after the war. Obviously this offended our other allies. A year earlier, Patton created problems for himself when he impulsively hit a soldier in the head who was suffering from battle fatigue. This is now called post-traumatic stress disorder or PTSD. General Patton said, "...I'll stand you up against a wall and have a firing squad kill you on purpose. In fact, I ought to shoot you myself, you goddamned whimpering coward." He waved his pistol in front of the soldier's face. A hospital commander intervened. Therefore Patton was being disciplined a bit when he was ordered to passively remain in Calais.

To prevent assault landings on the beaches, Germany had created obstacles. Wooden stakes pointed out to sea, and ramps sloped toward the shore. Additionally, the ramps were topped with jagged steel edges that could rip open the bottom of a boat, flip it, or detonate a mine that may be attached to the ramp. Belgian gates were positioned at the line of low-tide. These Belgian gates were 9×6-foot heavy steel fences with mines secured to their uprights. Hedgehogs were scattered about. They looked like oversized jacks from the "ball and jacks" game, each angled prong being about 4½ feet long.

In preparation for the assaults, sea vessels circled miles offshore in very rough water. Troops vomited into paper bags, into their helmets, or on themselves. They transferred into smaller landing crafts, landing at low tide, tired, wet, cold, and seasick. Some said they were too sick to be afraid. At times, the boats bottomed out on sandbars, but when the soldiers disembarked, the water was over their heads. Some immediately drowned with their heavy packs. Dad said of the movie *Saving Private Ryan*, "Dat is how it was. Some sank and some came up right away."

The enemy opened fire on the soldiers as they unloaded. One veteran described the scene as similar to a shooting gallery at a carnival. Soldiers were shot in the back by some of their own troops because they fired wildly at the enemy. The troops had trouble advancing without tank and artillery support. Eventually smoke obscured the beach, making it impossible to identify one's target. The beach reeked of death and gunpowder amid deafening noise from fifteen concrete and steel strongholds that contained German snipers, *Widerstandsnests*," (resistance nests). On Omaha Beach, the *Widerstandsnest* strongholds numbered from 60 to 74 and spanned the five-mile-long crescent-shaped beach.

In Stephen Ambrose's *Citizen Soldiers*, Lt. Charles Stockell recalled the image of two soldiers lying on the beach with their arms wrapped around each other in death. Both feet were blown off one of the soldiers. Another veteran described a man crawling inch by inch up the beach with one of his eyes hanging out its socket and onto his face. It did not take long for the tide to begin to rise. Then, wounded soldiers drowned among the body parts and dead bodies in the bloody, red waves.

Movie-goers speak of the intensity of the first 20 to 30 minutes of the movie *Saving Private Ryan*. However, some veterans say that is the only realistic part. To Dad, it was so realistic that my sister Yvonne relayed to me, "He wondered how cameras could have been there."

Albert Simon's nephew Gene told me, "In the landing, Albert lost his belt with his shovel, so he had to dig through rocks and rough dirt with his hands to create a hole to protect himself. His fingernails wore down, and the skin was scraped raw on his hands as he dug between dead bodies. It was noisy all night." The beach was littered with bodies that, from a distance, appeared to be driftwood. Later, the organized and stacked corpses looked like cordwood to Ben Lane (320/35th).

Historical movies and books frequently claim the Allies controlled the beaches by the end of D-Day, but it was more that we had won two small isolated footholds. During my research, I was verbally corrected by a high school history teacher, "It was more of a toehold rather than a foothold."

US General Bradley considered abandoning Omaha Beach, and even at 13:35 on the afternoon of D-Day, the German 352nd Division reported the assault had been hurled back into the sea.

If the invasion failed, Eisenhower had prepared a note which said:

> *Our landings in the Cherbourg-Havre area have failed to gain a satisfactory foothold, and I have withdrawn the troops. My decision to attack at the time and place was based upon the best information available. The troops, the air, and Navy did all that bravery and devotion to duty could do. If there is any blame or fault attached to the attempt, it is mine alone.*

Shortly after the beach assaults were regarded as successful, German General Rommel said, "…if I was commander of the Allied forces right now, I could finish off the war in fourteen days." Rommel's ability to do so may or may not have been valid.

Many Americans thought the same thing about winning a war against the tiny country of Japan. Don May recalled, "Some people said Japan was so small we could take care of them in two weeks. It took four years." Bob Esser (120/30th) said in an interview with the Wisconsin Veterans Museum, "Americans believed we would promptly stomp the Japanese, and it would be a minor inconvenience."

American journalist and war correspondent Ernie Pyle said, "Now that it is over, it seems to me a pure miracle that we ever took the beach at all." The National D-Day Memorial Foundation continues its painstaking research to determine a more accurate count of the soldiers killed that day.

Dad's friend Albert Simon continued fighting beyond Omaha Beach and was wounded twice in July and again in September for a total of 93 days of hospitalization. His niece Maggie told me, "Once Albert pretended to be dead when he was injured because he feared the Germans would bayonet anyone who was moving."

Albert's nephew Gene said, "Albert loved Bradley, respected Patton, and hated Montgomery." Albert was a boxer and won all his matches within his battalion during military training, but he was different when he returned home.

ALBERT SIMON WITH HIS BROTHER'S CHILDREN (L TO R): MARGE, JERRY, JANET, LOUISE, AND LUANA SIMON.

His niece Lorraine said, "They are always different when they come back from war." Albert was particularly kind to her family, whose father died suddenly at the age of 41, leaving behind eleven children.

Gene remembered, "Albert's hand shook so much that he could not get peas to his mouth when he was eating with a fork. Then he tried a tablespoon, but when he noticed everyone was watching, he quit eating the peas."

Gene said Albert spoke highly of Dad while asking, "What are the odds? How many guys survived that many days?"

Dad liked and respected Albert. "Albert was ahead of me," but then Albert was with the 116th Regiment of the 29th Division. He was ahead of almost everyone.

All of Albert's nieces and nephews with whom I spoke—Jim, Lorraine, Gene, Maggie, Luana and Marjorie—fondly described their uncle as quiet, handsome, strong, jovial, and kind. Albert was a "good guy" and had a lot of girlfriends. I never knew Albert, but it is difficult to accept his being thrown on the beaches four days after arriving in Europe.

An online historian wrote, "Arriving June 2 and then landing in Normandy June 6 or 7…there is a word for that, one that I do NOT like to type: Cannon Fodder."

One person told me, "No one was cannon fodder."

Another said, "Everyone was cannon fodder."

All D-Day units were reinforced by overages of 20 percent to cover the expected casualties.

Dad was strong. He was educated only through the eighth grade. He was considered an unskilled worker, and he could speak German. Albert, probably the same. Possibly Dad and

Albert did not score well on their Army General Classification Test, but it is painful to think of them as so callously expendable.

* * *

Glen Wiedenhoeft (320/35th) from Wisconsin trained replacements for the army. I spoke with his grandson, and I learned how one morning Glen awoke to find everyone had shipped out except him. He was told they "lost" his papers, whereas it seems to me he was being protected from becoming cannon fodder. Suddenly Glen was alone, separated from his unit, and without the mutual trust and loyalty that develops during training. He always felt badly that he was never able to say good-bye to his men, who may have died on the French beaches or in the Pacific theatre. At the age of 90, while Glen could not remember their names, he could still see their faces.

* * *

Walter "Hank" Harrington (320/35th) was not involved in Omaha Beach, but he fought in other traumatizing combat. He hoped a visit to the location of his worst battles would, as he said, "exorcize my troublesome spirits." In an article in *Santa Fe Express* (May/June 2008), he explained the impact of his anniversary date. "Your night's sleep is interrupted, and you break out in a cold sweat. Sleep comes in periods of short duration. You become very irritable and upset until the eight- or nine-day period has passed."

* * *

In the years following Omaha Beach and Albert Simon's tour of duty, he sometimes stared and possibly heard noises from the past. Nephew Jerry Simon remembered Albert's jarring reaction when a tool crashed to the floor in the carpentry workshop. On June 8, 1967, on the 23rd anniversary of D-Day+2, Albert asked for a gun to shoot a rat. Instead he took his own life. His war was finally over.

ALBERT SIMON'S GRAVESTONE IN ST. MARTIN CEMETERY, MARTINSVILLE, WI. (PHOTO BY ALISSA LORENZ)

17. A REPLACEMENT ON D-DAY+1

My research finally allowed me to understand Dad's spring of 1944. He was separated from his training buddies and transferred to American Ground Forces (AGF) Replacement Depot #1. Eventually, the system tried to train and assign soldiers in groups of four to improve morale, but that was not yet the case for Dad, who was an individual replacement and alone.

He was ordered to arrive at Fort Meade, Maryland, by rail before noon on April 29. Sometime during the month of May, General McNair visited Fort Meade and was pleased with the handling at the base of approximately 40,000 replacements.

Also in May, "8469 Repl" was written on the upper right-hand corner of one of Dad's medical forms, along with the words, "Shoes do not fit properly. Note to CO to have shoes changed." The designation of "8469 Repl" may be insignificant, or it may have been Dad's replacement designation, which could be historically interesting if records were ever discovered.

* * *

After a community presentation on D-Day, I introduced myself to the speaker. I said, "It seems my father was a replacement in June 1944." The speaker corrected me, "They were called reinforcements." I was quite certain the term in the book on my kitchen table was "replacements," though I did not push the

issue. I had bought the 492-page book, which was called a "pamphlet," on eBay when it was "Not available through GPO (Government Printing Office) sales." The title of the book was *The Personnel Replacement System in the United States Army*.

Prior to the term "replacement," there was an even more dehumanizing word used by the military. It was "package." A package was a group of 250 soldiers. According to a restricted document, the term of package was changed "in an effort to avoid any connotation which would indicate that personnel were considered as cannon fodder."

Package. Replacements. Reinforcements. The end result was all the same.

According to the personnel replacement book, each assault division was given about ten "packages" or 2,500 men to replace the expected casualties during the first ten days. However, this number of men was not adequate for the loss of troops once the Normandy Campaign was underway.

* * *

On May 21, Dad boarded a ship with Albert Simon, a kind, strong man with a crushing handshake whom Dad knew from home. Their ship was part of a convoy of 39. Thirty-five of those ships transported war materials, four carried troops, and three of those ships were bound for England. The fourth troop ship, the *SS Robin Sherwood*, docked in Wales, where Dad always said he had landed and then continued on to Belfast, Ireland. Unfortunately for researchers, passenger lists were intentionally destroyed in 1951 by the Department of the Army. I am curious about the casualty rate for the soldiers on that particular voyage and how many of the ship's passengers were replacements for the assault landings.

These voyages were neither pleasant nor comfortable. One soldier from the 475th Military Police described some of their meals as "green liver, usually leftover from breakfast, salthorse, and gray potatoes boiled in their jackets." Salthorse is a sailor's term for heavily salted, low-quality beef, tough to chew and even harder to digest.

The ships were forced to zigzag to avoid possible German U-boats (submarines) that were out to sink them. In the event of major injuries during storms or following an undiagnosed ruptured appendix, caskets had been stored on each ship.

Troops generally slept on their backs on two-foot-wide bunk beds, sometimes with equipment tucked under their knees. The

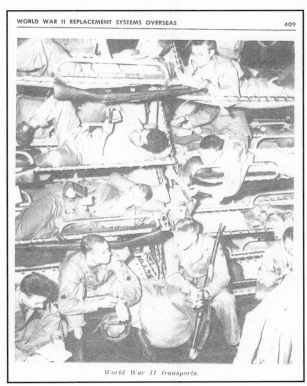

WORLD WAR II REPLACEMENT SYSTEMS OVERSEAS　　　　409

World War II transports.

Bunks on ships en route to war. Department of the Army Pamphlet No. 20-211, 1954, The Personnel Replacement System in the United States Army, Page 409.

bunks were positioned in rows with two-foot aisles on only one side and then stacked tier upon tier with only two feet vertically between the bunks, sometimes five to eight deep. Soldiers climbed a ladder and then moved into a horizontal position before sliding into their beds, kind of like closing a drawer. Some ships were so crowded that soldiers slept on or under tables or hung in hammocks. Dad said, "Da sickest ones seemed to be on da top."

There was no racial integration during World War II, so African-American GIs were housed in worse conditions, hot and foul.

* * *

Many times, the over-crowded ships reeked of vomit. Dad did not get seasick, but many others suffered. Albert Simon gestured toward a sick soldier and said, "Let's go cheer him up." Weak from vomiting, the soldier maintained his sense of humor and joked, "Christopher Columbus was a brave ol' boy."

From Dad's perspective, all the soldiers on the ship were trash-talking anything German, which was his full heritage. He never let on that he could speak the language because he was 26 years old with a pregnant wife at home. He was afraid he could be forced into dangerous assignments if it was known he could speak German.

Dad described how some celebrated the end of the week-and-a-half voyage as the ship pulled into Cardiff, Wales, on May 31. They grabbed life preservers and tossed them high into the air. Then everyone watched as their survival equipment disappeared into the cold waters and sank. At least the life preservers had given them the feeling of security during the voyage.

It took time to process the thousands of arriving soldiers, so Dad and Albert Simon did not set foot upon the dock until June 2, two days after their arrival, which is the same amount of time Robert Phillips recalled for his voyage. Albert was probably sent to Fowey, England, where the 116th Regiment of the 29th Division embarked for Omaha Beach.

In our final conversation ever about World War II, Dad said, "Albert was ahead of me," and "Da first bunch got clipped," meaning mowed down. Don May thought Dad could have been assigned to a later group of the 29th Division, but there is no way of knowing because there are few records for replacement troops.

Dad recalled how he had been rushed by train after he arrived in Europe. The train actually used its lights, which was not common at that time for reasons of safety and security. He said, "Dey wanted to get us dere as fast as dey could." It seems he was transported from Cardiff, Wales, in a train, probably crowded and seatless, the only restroom being a hole in the floor. Dad told me, "Dere was a hole in da middle of da car, and lots of guys were sick." Possibly they had been given too much food upon their arrival after almost two weeks of questionable food on their troop ship.

On D-Day, Dad sat on a hillside with a group of soldiers and listened to an officer, "It did not go as we hoped, but we are there. We are on the beach." Many of the gathered soldiers cheered the invasion. The group was further advised, "Don't cheer too loud. You will get your chance. You will be there tomorrow."

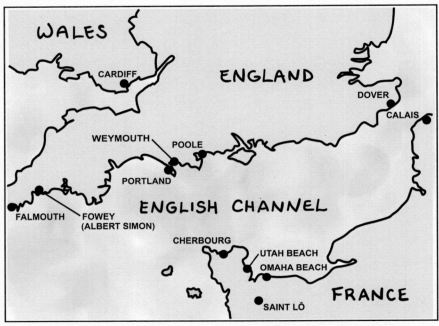

LOCATIONS OF INTEREST FOR THE ASSAULTS OF FRENCH BEACHES, ALONG WITH ALFRED'S AND ALBERT'S ARRIVAL IN THE EUROPEAN THEATRE OF OPERATIONS. ILLUSTRATION BY MEG MOORE, 2017.

It is difficult to know where Dad boarded a ship. If he boarded somewhere along the southern coast of England, it would have been west of Southampton because that was the main assembly area for the British. Some of the troops destined for Omaha Beach embarked from ports like Weymouth, Portland, Poole, and farther west from Falmouth and Fowey. When a shipment of soldiers was about twelve miles from the beaches, the troops transferred down cargo nets into smaller Higgins boats. The smaller boats had flat bottoms, which could land more easily on a beach. A Higgins boat, also known as a LCVP (Landing Craft, Vehicle, Personnel), carried 30 to 36 men.

Dad told me, "I stayed low and in da back, but dat was not good." I imagined him as being cramped and trapped in a corner as he waited to go ashore, sort of seasick and nauseated. Dad described a more detailed account to his son-in-law Ron Ziegler. Dad had actually almost suffocated in a backward crush when soldiers attempted to protect themselves from bullets as the boat landed on the beach. Some soldiers were shot as they jumped over the side of the boat. Dad told Don May that bullets came into the boat as soon as the ramp opened. Dad quietly said to me once, "I knew it was going to be bad, but not dat bad."

Veteran James Stevenson of Milwaukee spoke with the *Milwaukee Journal Sentinel.* He had served with the 1st Division and was a machine gunner like Dad. He said, "Being a machine gunner, I was one of the last guys off [the boat]…When you get off the boat, the boat keeps going. You jump to the side, and you hope you don't go in over your head." He also remembered that at times soldiers were chopped up as boats unintentionally backed over them.

Higgins boats, also LVCP, used in amphibious landings in WWII. public domain photo

Alfred

Most of the time Dad spoke with few, if any, details. His comments were soft, isolated, and pained, and I had to decide where to place them in context. I suspect very early in his war experience, he was reluctant to abandon a severely injured soldier. Dad was basically told to move on through the chaos. His superior had said, "A lot of them are going to die."

* * *

Dad was never drawn to water or boats for the rest of his life. On a drive 57 years later, he looked down on scenic Lake Wisconsin from a bluff on Highway 113, north of Lodi, Wisconsin. He commented, "Some people like dat, but it holds not'ing for me." On a family outing with a boat, Dad asked to be taken back to shore after a couple of minutes on the water. We simply accommodated his request and never questioned why.

* * *

Leonard Huskey of Missouri served with the 9th Regiment of the 2nd Infantry Division, and he boarded a boat at Swansea, Wales. He landed on Omaha Beach under enemy shellfire on D-Day+1 near St. Laurent-sur-Mer. Leonard was never awarded a Bronze Arrowhead for an assault landing, and his descriptions were very similar to Dad's.

I spoke with Leonard on the phone. He had difficulty hearing me although he clearly heard my question, "Were Germans still there when you landed?"

"Gull darn right," he said. "The water was bloody way back."

After we struggled to communicate on the phone, I sent questions to Leonard, and he returned his answers to me in the mail.

"Were there bodies in the water?" I asked.

He wrote, "There were so many you could not count them. The water was bloodied. Boats and planes were shot down and sank."

Leonard described that the Germans shot with all kinds of weapons as soon as the doors opened on the landing craft. He landed "about 9 or 10 in the morning," and he added, "It is hard to remember. It was a bad time."

I wrote, "Where did you spend your first night?"

In shaky cursive, Leonard replied, "Small distance on shore. Fighting. No sleeping for days to come."

Almost 88 years old, he concluded, "I have service-connected problems. Hard of hearing. Metal still in my foot bone. And nerves."

* * *

Many accounts imply the beaches were basically under Allied control after D-Day. Stephen Ambrose wrote about the Germans after the first day of the assault. In his book *D-Day*, he described "...their fixed fortifications on the invasion front, their pillboxes and bunkers...were with only a few exceptions kaput." Yet Richard H. Rohmer wrote in *Patton's Gap* that Lieutenant General Bradley was aboard the *USS Augusta* off the beaches the following day. Rohmer wrote, "At that point Bradley was deeply concerned about the operational situation on Omaha Beach where his troops were suffering severe losses."

June 7 was described within a story in *LIFE* magazine, June 19, 1944:

> **By the afternoon of D-Day+1, the battle of this beachhead was already the most desperate of the invasion. The**

> **Germans had set up machine-gun positions atop the bluffs; and these, with ingeniously concealed batteries, had raked landing parties. Casualties of some of the assault forces had been high. Now most of the beach was still under shellfire.**

Even if there is some truth to Ambrose's description, his account definitely minimizes the efforts of the soldiers on Omaha Beach during the second day of the assault.

* * *

As I tried to document Dad's involvement in D-Day+1, researchers, historians, and veterans frequently inferred Dad was old and confused, or I was mistaken and guilty of exaggeration. Some assumed there were contradictions between his words and his records. There were none. Very early on, I made a major error. I extrapolated in both directions from Dad's assignment with the 35th Division. I assumed he had trained, traveled to Europe, served, and returned, all with the 35th.

Instead, he had trained with the 44th Division, transferred to Replacement Depot #1, was shipped to Europe as a replacement, was difficult to track in June, joined the 35th Division in July, and was eventually discharged from the 63rd Division:

- March 1943 to April 1944: 44th Infantry Division
- April 29: Replacement Depot #1 at Fort Meade, Maryland
- May 21 to June 2: Transported to ETO
- June 3: 11th Replacement depot APO 131
- No Date: Secret Embarcation Personnel Roster 16th Repl
- June 12 to July 9: received rations through APO 15325

ALFRED JOINS COMPANY D OF 320TH INFANTRY REGIMENT OF
35TH DIVISION ALONG WITH SEVERAL SOLDIERS FROM HIS
AUTOGRAPH PAGE OF STORY OF 320TH INFANTRY.

- July 13 Morning Report: D/320/35 from 41st Repl Bn APO 873
- Oct 1945 Discharge papers: 254th Regiment of the 63th Division

He would never have known all these attachments. Don May said, "We did not have a tour guide, so your dad would not

Alfred

know what outfit he was with." In addition, Dad did not care. For the war in general, he resolved, "I tried not to remember."

* * *

I have no doubt that Dad did exactly what he said he did. The man was honest, with a sort of childlike honesty that was blunt, but never malicious. If more complete records ever existed for him, there was a fire at the St. Louis Military Personnel Records Center on July 12, 1973. The fire destroyed 80 percent of the records for army personnel discharged between 1912 and 1960.

* * *

During the week of D-Day from June 5 to 12, 1944, Dad did not receive any rations of cigarettes, cigars, pipe tobacco, matches, candy, cookies, soap, blades, gum, or roll candy. Having a vertical line drawn though the week of D-Day on the ration card made perfect sense to Don May, "There was no one to distribute anything. They were clinging to the beaches."

ARMY EXCHANGE RATION CARD				
Pfc June 5th to July 30th 44				
NAME AND RANK Alfred N Endress				
A.S.N. 36237118 A.P.O. 15325				
ARTICLE	5th–11th	12th–18th	19th–25th	26th–2nd
CIGARETTES	·			
— or — CIGARS				
PIPE TOBACCO				
MATCHES				
CANDY				
GUM — or — ROLL CANDY				
COOKIES				
SOAP				
BLADES				

ALFRED'S RATION CARD FOR JUNE 1944 WITHIN REPLACEMENT GROUP APO 15325. NO RATIONS GIVEN JUNE 5-11, WEEK OF D-DAY.

* * *

A personnel roster was buried for years among my papers. I had received it from retired Lieutenant Colonel Philip Grinton of California. It did not seem significant at the time because it was undated, and I received it before I knew anything about replacements or D-Day+1. The names of Alfred Endres and Louis Gogal are listed on that undated document. Two words from that document finally slapped me in the face: *SECRET* and *EMBARCATION.*

SECRET EMBARCATION PERSONNEL ROSTER
Repl Detachment
X23C UNIT
16 Repl Depot

The assault landings were delayed a day because of bad weather, so possibly this undated list of soldiers was created to be used as needed.

I looked for distinctive names on the roster, names that would make an online search easier. I spoke with the son of one of the listed veterans, who told me his father was in headquarters (HQ), never fired a shot, and learned electronics during the war. He later used that skill to start his post-war business. I continued with other names on the list.

"Beach invasion on D-Day" is included on Benjamin Antal's (Rifle 504) page for the World War II Memorial. He called me after I wrote to him, and he used the words "horrible" and "devastating" to describe war. He ended up in the 30th Infantry Division, which was accidentally bombed by our own planes. When he returned home, he told his wife, "I do not remember."

Alfred

He pretended his lack of memory was the result of concussions he received in battle.

Joseph S. Sudarsky's (2nd Lt) obituary included his "participating in the Normandy invasion, landing on Omaha Beach."

George Chehanske's (HW/Heavy Weapons 607) obituary mentioned he was a member of the 38th Regiment of the 2nd Division and was part of the "second wave to land on Omaha Beach during the Normandy Invasion."

I continued to search names on that secret list for embarcation. I spoke with the grandson of John Carpino (AT/Anti-tank 504), also named John. He shared that his grandfather landed on the beaches on D-Day+1 and then served with the 30th Infantry Division. On August 8, he was wounded at Mortain, his intestines hanging outside his body. The veteran spent two years in the hospital and was covered in scars and welts. John asked his grandfather what he thought of the movie *Saving Private Ryan*. Grandpa said, "They made it look pretty easy."

* * *

When I told historians all that I had discovered from my research and from Dad's words, they accepted my conclusions about his experiences.

One said, "My guess is that your father was assigned to the 10 to 25 percent overage."

Museum Technician Rafael Alvarez suggested, "There were tens of thousands of replacements on the beach the first few days, and with all those unaccounted replacements with no assigned unit, it is possible that some did not get Bronze Arrowhead credit."

It seems Dad was part of the overstrength of an unknown group for the assault landing. The overstrength system was sort of a no-man's land of first being assigned and then passing through a pool to be assigned to another unit as needed to replace casualties. When Dad survived the beach landing, he reverted to being a replacement, unassigned but earmarked for the specific task that had been decided prior to his being sent overseas.

It took about four and a half months for a letter written by Dad's mother-in-law, my Grandma Miller, to find him in France after he was shipped overseas. I would never have understood Dad's possible involvement in D-Day+1 without my speech at the French Legion of Honor ceremony fueling Dad's comments about "dead bodies floating in water." Then my Grandma Miller's rerouted envelope, covered front and back with addresses, indicated his being "lost" in the replacement system. Finally, Albert Simon's discharge papers confirmed the likelihood of what Dad had said all along.

The envelope sent by Dad's mother-in-law from Lodi, Wisconsin, included the following path of addresses with APO meaning Army Post Office and IBPO, probably International Base Post Office:

- May 4, 1944: CO. H 174 Infantry, Camp Chaffee, Arkansas

- May 17: Directory Service Given, Camp Patrick Henry, VA

- June 15: Directory Searched 1st BPO (written on brown tape), INF 325 GLDR INF RGT, 1628 CO U

- June 21: No Record Co. C, 325th Gl. Inf.

- July 20: No Record PO 67 Army Directory Service

- No date: A.P.O. #15 (rest is hidden)
  c/o POSTMASTER, NEW YORK N.Y.
  BRANCH Inf, UNIT PP

- July 24: U.S. Army IBPO stamp, CONTROL
  SECTION 15th Replac Depot

- July 29: Directory Searched B.P.O.

- No date: 320 INF REGT (written on brown tape)

- September 14: NO RECORD, CO. C 320

- Finally, a large red "D" (delivered to Company D)

Probably upon his arrival in Europe, Albert Simon wrote his address on a 3.5-inch square piece of paper that we discovered in Dad's army trunk. Albert's address of APO 15032 Co P handled the overflow for the 10th Replacement Depot. It seems Albert was assigned to the 29th Division for D-Day and remained there for the duration of the war. Dad's APO 15325 Co U was a temporary address set up to handle the overflow for D-Day for the 1st Post Office. Companies A through M were traditional, whereas P through Z were used for replacements. Dad's "Co U" and Albert's "Co P" were consistent within this system.

During June 1944, the same address continued to be used for Dad, although "CAS DET" had been added to his purchase order for war savings bonds to begin in July. "CAS DET" indicates casual detachment, a group of men detached to operate separately from their group for a specific duty.

Dad authorized the purchase of war savings bonds with a rather shaky signature. The bonds were sent to Mom in care of

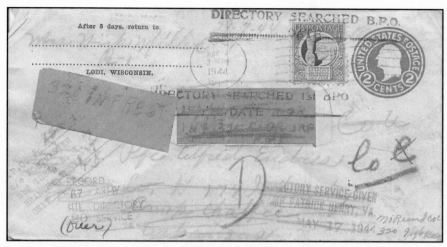

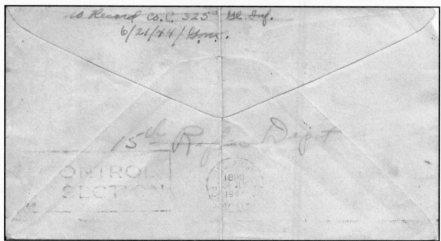

REPEATEDLY REROUTED ENVELOPE THAT TOOK FROM MAY TO SEPTEMBER 1944 TO FIND ALFRED.

her mother, my grandmother, Mrs. Nick Miller in Lodi, Wisconsin, where Mom was living. Plan 3 was designated as $18.75 Allotment / $25 Bond.

On June 16, 1944, still with APO 15325, Dad wrote to Mom, "Well, Honey, how are you? I hope fine because I am but miss you very much." He was alive, but I doubt he was fine.

SAVINGS BOND AUTHORIZATION TO BEGIN JULY 1944. ALFRED'S ADDRESS: Co U. CAS DET. APO #15325.

18. THE BOX UNLOCKED

On a Saturday about two months after the French ceremony, Dad spoke of "dead bodies floating in water." That following Monday, he and I had a phone conversation about D-Day+1, and by Wednesday, he was not well. His behavior had changed dramatically, and we focused on his medications and the possible need for lab work.

Dad phoned Jerry, Bob, Bev, and Yvonne on Thursday and told them Frenchmen were at the nursing home, along with his former boss, who was not able to return the following day, although his son could. This all seemed to revert back to the ceremony two months earlier. Dad asked for his children and wanted them near, and he thought Eileen and Del, who lived out of state, should be around. The nurses checked more frequently on his general orientation and on his blood sugar.

When Bob stopped at the nursing home that evening, he was surprised to find Dad sitting in a gathering area rather than in his room. The staff was keeping a closer eye on him because he was behaving so differently than he had during his previous five years. According to Dad's perception, the lettering on Bob's Wisconsin sweatshirt was backward and upside down. He wanted Bob to stay overnight. Later Bob described his visit in an email and reassured us, "Dad is in good hands."

Alfred

When I visited two days later, Dad ate ravenously, which he never had done before. After lunch, I wheeled him down the hall toward his room, and just as we approached the threshold of his door, he shouted out, "Anyone in here? Get out!"

I sent an email to my siblings that night:

> Dad was in the dining room. He wanted help cutting his cauliflower and asked me to feed him because his hands were not working. I helped with everything on his plate, the raisin cookie, then the buttered bun. He was sort of ravenous, asking me to give him another bite in quick succession. I fed him more slowly than he wanted. Is there a problem with his blood sugar? When we were about to enter his room, he shouted, "Anyone in here? Get out!"
>
> He did not feel well, sort of dizzy. He wanted a blanket, and he seemed a bit different, so I did not leave him to go to Bohlmans while he napped, as I had planned. He coughed and grimaced while he dozed. He seems to have a sore throat, but he did not identify the pain. I tried to do the 1 to 10 range of pain test, but it did not work. He definitely had pain in his face.
>
> Once he clenched his teeth, and I asked why he did that. He said, "Because I wanted to." He also thought the neck of his T-shirt was tight when it was not. An RN said she would keep an eye on him. Then Dad alternately opened and closed each eye. I thought he may have an eye issue because one was "weeping" at lunch, but he was being funny...as in him "keeping an eye" on someone.
>
> He was different...but sort of okay?

When Yvonne visited with her girls on that Wednesday, she called me because Dad wanted to know where his good clothes were for some gathering. She even considered asking whether he wanted to talk to a priest in case he felt he was dying.

Then, while I continued to talk, I heard Yvonne's daughters laughing with him in the background, which made everything seem relatively normal.

In just over two months since the French Legion of Honor ceremony, Yvonne's mother-in-law, who had seemed perfectly fine at the ceremony, was now in a Florida hospital, awaiting surgery for two brain tumors.

A tablemate had passed away.

Our family dentist, who had not felt well on the day of the ceremony, was diagnosed with pancreatic cancer and was on hospice care.

Also within those previous two months, Dad's brother Edward fell down a flight of stairs in his church and hit his head. The excessive loss of blood resulted in cognitive changes. He was in critical condition in the hospital for several weeks, and when he entered an extended care facility, a nurse gave him a pen and paper to occupy himself. He wrote rambling thoughts, which may have reverted to more than six decades earlier when Dad had made the choice between the two of them to go to war. Edward wrote a cluster of words, "Everyone thank you everyone to Alfred."

Each bit of bad news may have been a disruption for Dad, but over the course of about two weeks, Dad returned to his normal self. He never again ate ravenously or shouted when he entered his room. The staff never again felt the need to watch him in the gathering area of the nursing home.

Alfred

We still considered his behavior from a purely medical perspective and passed information on to Del, our doctor in the family. Bev, however, wondered whether his unusual flow of words about war could have caused his behavioral changes. Maybe Dad had accidentally unlocked the war vault, but we were fortunate because he was able to get the war demons back into the box. We never found a medical reason for his abrupt change of behavior from normal to abnormal and back again, all within a two week span of time.

Several weeks later, after more than five years in the nursing home, Dad changed his farewell to me after I had kissed him on the cheek and walked to the door. Casually I called, "See you next week."

He said, "Good luck," as I left the room.

I walked down the hall, a bit confused by his words. It was deliberate. "Good luck."

Bev shared that Dad's typical farewell to her on Thursday night had also been different. She and I talked about the changes we saw, subtle changes, maybe interpreted incorrectly, but we both noticed them. Dad was fully aware that I was researching and organizing his World War II experiences.

"Good luck." It was sincere. It was love and support. He knew he did not offer me much in details, but he wanted me to achieve whatever it was that I wanted.

Dad had been back to his old self for over six weeks when Bob and I were both at the nursing home one Saturday. Bob had brought an old brown camera from Dad's army trunk and asked about a letter from a buddy. In turn, I decided to ask a few questions.

"So you were involved in D-Day+1?" I asked.

He was a bit offended and answered, "Dey said I wasn't." He emphasized the first word.

My response was a mix of a sigh and a laugh, "Oh, Dad, that was me. You know, I thought I knew everything."

Then I asked, "Were you in Europe for several days or a month before D-Day?"

"Several days."

I showed him a photo of a Higgins boat. He took it in his hands and asked, "Where did you get dis?"

"Off the computer," I answered.

Dad responded to a different photo with soldiers holding a rope in choppy waters, "Dey are pulling in some guys."

I had been asking gentle questions for over five years, and I was always observant of Dad's reaction, careful to keep questions simple and objective. Each week I accumulated questions in my "Lodi bag," only asking them if conditions were right, hoping they would trigger some painless recollection and allow Dad the option to carry the discussion as far as he wanted.

One week I asked about fruit cocktail because I had read about a veteran who could never eat it again after the war. Dad had no particular aversion to fruit cocktail, so the conversation went nowhere, lasting seconds.

Twice I accidentally pushed the envelope on Dad's emotions. At the very beginning of my research, I read a brief chapter of my writings when I thought he might be interested in confirming what I had written. Before I finished my chapter, Dad said, "Dat is enough for today," but I explained there was only one more paragraph, and I finished reading. There was minimal

visible reaction, but there also was no reason for me to complete the chapter. I learned that day he was never going to verify what I had written anyway.

Another time, I asked Dad, "Do you remember a barn that burned in Gardelegen toward the end of the war?"

He quickly shrugged, raising and lowering his shoulders. His reaction was too fast for a man who typically reacted slowly. I held up a large photo that Robert Phillips had sent to me. Dad did not lean forward or really even look at it. His shrug was again too fast. The entire situation lasted seconds, but it was too long for Dad, and it was unnecessary. Again I had learned what was most acceptable for discussion. Fruit cocktail and Spam were acceptable. The burning barn was not.

I asked Dad a few more questions. "Did you go to the beaches with tanks or just men?"

"Just men," he answered.

I was always cautious, but at one point, Dad closed his eyes. His lower jaw locked. His brow furrowed. His face grimaced, and he clenched his teeth as he had done after telling me about the dead bodies floating in the water. Bob was facing the television, so I motioned for him to look at our father's face. Dad wiped both eyes, one after the other, with the back of his large stiff hands, fingers extended.

"It happened. It's over," he softly reminded himself.

He must have said that frequently during his life.

"Are you having bad images?" I asked.

"Oh, ya," he said, his eyes still closed.

I apologized, "I would never want that to happen."

I was finished, and I never spoke of World War II with him again.

* * *

As a teacher, I have learned that many of my frustrated math students are far more visual in their thinking than I am. My mental processes are more sequential; theirs are often more spatial. Some students see movies in their brains as they read, as if the words are in a real-time film. Some are baffled that I do not see my loved ones inside my forehead, wearing specific clothing and jewelry. One student asked me, "You mean you don't see music?"

I suspect Dad was more visual and three-dimensional than I am. He did not necessarily have a verbal entry of a Higgins boat in his mind. In his recollection, he had a vivid photograph or a video, carefully tucked away in a locked album or movie collection of war's atrocities. And it was not just images. Emotions were still firmly attached because they had never been separated by conversation. Robert Phillips told me it took 20-some reunions with the 35th Division to help him talk about his memories.

On the day after Dad's flashback to Omaha Beach, my cousin called to ask me a few questions about her upcoming trip to Germany. Within that phone conversation, I told her about my previous day with Dad and his flashback and his earlier comments about war and killing. She suggested I find someone to absolve him of guilt, something that brought peace to her during her cancer treatments. I decided to write the following letter to Monsignor Daniel Ganshert, whom I had seen the previous day at a funeral:

Dear Monsignor Ganshert,

Hello. I am the daughter of Good Samaritan resident Alfred Endres, and I have done research on his involvement in World War II.

When I first found out that Dad would receive the French Legion of Honor, I verbalized my possible goal all along ... to allow my father to die without the guilt of having killed. I thought recognition from the French would justify his experiences in World War II. He once asked a visitor from the Luxembourg Embassy about the citizens of that country, "They remember?" It seemed very important to him.

I have learned in the past five years that the primary issue lies not in what Dad saw...but in what he did. When Mom's gravestone was designed, Dad said of the praying hands for her and the flag for himself, "Hers is for praying. Mine is for killing."

When Dad received his Bronze Star, he neither touched it nor looked at it. When my sister from Colorado called him and congratulated him, he said, "I don't really want to talk about it. I don't know why you should get medals for killing."

In talking today with a cousin who has cancer, she suggested that I try to find someone who might be able to bless Dad in a way that he will feel cleansed of his violations of "Thou shalt not kill". Dad recounted his role in war to my oldest brother, "I got a lot of them, but I didn't like it."

*My father would most likely not respond to
Biblical verses, and when it comes to religion, he
is a very pragmatic person. Conversation has to be
gentle. I am always very careful in asking questions. Yet yesterday, Dad had flashbacks and
wept.*

*I just want to give some background which might
be helpful. Absolution is not something my father
can take from me. Not only are you a priest, I
believe you are the right priest for my father. (I
was at the funeral for Richard Williams yesterday.)*

*Thank you for whatever seems appropriate to
you. I do not need any sort of response.*

Sincerely,
Louise Endres Moore

Within days, I was aware that a priest had visited Dad at the
nursing home. He did not give the priest's name or elaborate on
the visit, but I knew that Dad was very content, possibly even
happy, with their conversation. Thank you, Monsignor Ganshert.

Less than four months later, Dad passed away, surrounded
by family members and after a two-night stay at Sauk Prairie
Hospital. I wrote a eulogy and read it at his funeral:

Alfred

Eulogy for Dad, Alfred N. Endres
January 31, 1918 – July 2, 2007

Dad was never much of a disciplinarian. He loved his kids, and he never thought we did much wrong…even when nine-year-old Jerry layered pepper within the tobacco of Dad's pipe. Dad's eyes filled with tears from the pepper, and he handed the pipe back to Jerry. In his most stern voice, Dad said, "Fill it and fill it right." After Virg died, Dad lamented having scolded Virg…once.

Dad did not worry about or put material posses-sions before people, and because we did not have many expensive things, he never needed to protect anything from his kids. He taught me to drive a stick shift the night before I was to drive the vehicle to work. I was a bit nervous and uncomfortable. I asked, "What if I wreck some-thing?" He simply reassured me, "You won't." If I complained about a broken antenna on a car, it was fixed immediately…but with a hanger.

We had a variety of animals...a horse, a spunky pony, a concrete pond for turtles, some with cracked shells, birds with broken wings and a drug-impaired dog named Nooker. When a child became allergic to cow milk, Dad acquired pesky goats that created total havoc on the farm, but if that was what his kids needed, he did it. Eileen was just in first grade when it was so cold the buses did not run. He made sure Eileen got to school, an empty school because no one else had ventured out of their homes.

Since Mom's death, we have had the opportunity to focus on Dad and the impact of World War II on his life. In late 2001, it seemed as if the pain of Mom's death caused the pain of World War II to resurface. We carefully went through his army trunk and then onto the Internet with snippets of names and addresses, finding a most gracious individual who told us he loved Dad as a brother. This man and Dad had spent Christmas '44 together in France, providing a French father with their own military rations of chocolate and fruit to give to his children as their only Christmas gifts that year. Dad received a ring in gratitude, which is a precious family heirloom.

He hated war, and in the late 60s, he responded to a radio announcement by saying, "I wish the people who got to decide would go fight their own wars." Multiple times, Dad said of the war, "I never expected to live through it." And so, in many ways, these past 62 years have been a gift, a gift of life and a gift of time.

Alfred

Even though Dad's relation with God was quite private, I believe he and God came to an understanding a long time ago in the foxholes of Normandy. Dad marveled at creation --- the uniqueness of every individual's face, an apple forming from a flower, a six-foot plant growing from a kernel of corn.

He loved math riddles. He would play cards and checkers with the grandkids, and he loved to tell stories. Some of his all-time favorites centered on the strength of Frankie Lambert and the creative comments of Meinrod Theis. If Dad was not telling a story, he was possibly an active participant in something that would become a future tale.

Once he devised a practical joke on me and directed Mom, "Do not tell Louise I had teeth pulled." Then as I read in the living room the day before Emily's baptism, he wiggled his new partial, complaining of the high costs of dentistry. I told him to leave well enough alone, and I continued reading. He repeated his comments about medical expenses, left the room, and returned with pliers in his hand, catsup on his chin, the dental appliance removed while matter-of-factly stating, "Well, that wasn't so bad." I was so shocked I didn't notice his delight. All I could say was, "Not today!"

Grandma Miller lived with us for 13 years, not necessarily an easy situation for Dad to have an extra adult female suggest how things could be done, but he never complained. He had an acceptance for how life evolved. About ten years ago, I asked whether Dad had gotten the hay in before it rained. He answered with a question. "You know what you do when it rains? — You let it rain."

Mom carefully followed doctors' orders; Dad created his own solutions. He would listen to a hospital doctor if the conversation occurred during a commercial break of a Packer game. And if a doctor asked for questions, Dad's question could be, "How old are you?" Following his second small stroke, Dad had to be restrained during physical therapy when he tried to demon-strate how he could do push-ups...from his toes... at the age of 83-and-a-half. The removal of a wart once involved varnish remover and the assistance of grandson Nick Waldow. I reprimanded Dad, "A doctor would not recommend that." Dad confirmed, "I do not recommend it." Yet he outlived Mom.

I suppose Dad may have fibbed or exaggerated in my lifetime, but I do not know when. However in a letter to his sister Catherine in February 1945, he wrote, "I hope that everybody is fine. I am, so til next time, Love, Alfred." I commented to him that the letter was written just after the Battle of the Bulge, and I questioned whether he could in truth have been fine. Almost apologetically, he asked, "What else could I say?" It was far more likely that Dad said things as he saw them...exactly as he saw them. After college, I took voice lessons for a short time. The teacher's first question was, "So

do you want me to be nice or do you want me to be honest?" I answered, "Honest." I am my father's daughter.

In the past couple of months, one new story emerged, first being told to a nurse at the nursing home and then credited to Eddie Meyer on Dad's final day before Monsignor Ganshert visited. Eddie Meyer had received the Last Rites from a priest, and as the priest was leaving, Eddie asked, "One more question, Father…any good restaurants between here and heaven?"

Dad left us with tidbits of humor and also peace of mind. In the hospital, he reassured us, "You have done everything you can." May he rest in peace.

19. THERE IS NOTHING NORMAL ABOUT WAR

During my research, I discovered the families of some veterans, while other families found me. They responded to my comments and questions on the 35th Infantry Division website. They told me stories about the honorable men they loved as those men approached the ends of their lives. There are stories that veterans do not want to tell and stories that people do not want to hear. Heroism, pride, and patriotism feel good, while the realities of war are disturbing.

Dad had said "Dere is not'ing normal about war."

Gordon Sorensen, a retired Methodist minister, lived two houses from me, and many people sought his advice. In writing this book, I was not confident how to handle the sensitive stories of veterans I did not know, along with the insensitive comments from people I knew. I asked Gordon, expecting a more complicated answer, but he simply said, "Truth is important."

These memories illustrate a comment from a veteran, "War brutalizes one's conscience."

And in Tom Brokaw's *Greatest Generation*, one of the veterans said, "War brings out the worst in everyone; no matter how honorable you are...things happen that make you feel ashamed later on."

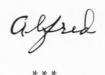

Alfred

* * *

I spoke on the phone with the grandson of a World War II veteran, and his love for his grandfather was evident. I saw a photo of his grandparents standing as straight and tall as the oak tree behind them. The couple had a proper appearance, almost regal, but not rigid.

When this veteran celebrated a birthday, I sent him a note, but I did not write about heroism. Instead I used the word, "incomprehensible." The grandson told me, "I could see relief in my grandpa's face as he read your card." I knew the following story before I wrote that note:

> *After Saint-Lô, our troops were taking prisoners of war. As this veteran moved in on a group of German troops, he saw that babies and children had been beaten to death, a sight that angered him to his core. He commanded his troops, "Do not waste your bullets and grenades." Therefore flame throwers were used to kill 15 German soldiers. Six decades after the war, the grandfather could still hear the screams of the Germans as they burned to death.*

He was ashamed. For him, there was no glory in war, and he did not want to be honored or recognized as a hero. Therefore, he turned down repeated requests to be a local parade marshal.

Nearing the end of his life, confident that he would not be judged by his grandson, this veteran confessed his story. The grandson treasured every moment he could spend with his grandfather, whose goal had always been to live in such a way so as to deserve the gift of life when so many others had not been given that chance.

* * *

Another veteran stared into space much of the time as he approached his death.

"What are you thinking about, Dad?" his son asked.

"Nothing good, Boy. Nothing good," the soldier replied.

The son told me, "I knew exactly what was on his mind. My father thought about the war a lot before he passed."

The son spoke lovingly of his father and described him as "honorable." The veteran told the following story exactly once, and before he finished, his eyes filled with tears, the only time the son ever saw his father cry.

The son shared the following story about his father and army buddies:

> *Approaching the edge of a small town, they heard an American soldier screaming loudly for someone to stop. They could also hear some German soldiers laughing. The American group was able to sneak up on the Krauts in a barn and see what was going on. There were three Krauts, and two of them were holding down the American soldier while the third Kraut was slowly and painfully castrating the American with a bayonet. The Krauts were outnumbered by the Americans, who were able to surprise them. To make a long story very short, they returned the treatment to the Krauts.*

Scores of years after the war, this honorable veteran was still coming to terms with that occurrence.

* * *

After the Battle of the Bulge, a group of soldiers slid down hills for amusement on make-shift sleds. The sleds were actually frozen German bodies. The men were light-hearted until the body of an American was discovered among their choice for "sleds." Then suddenly it became quiet, and the party was over.

* * *

Without these stories, I would never have completely understood Dad's simple words, "Dere is not'ing normal about war."

20. "SOME CAN TAKE IT, AND SOME CAN'T."

My writing cycles back to the statement that propelled it from the beginning…"Some can take it, and some can't."

This comment divides everyone into two distinct, mutually exclusive groups. It places a blame-like responsibility upon the veterans, who most likely gave the most and possibly lost the most in terms of the normalcy we take for granted. It disregards and dismisses what they have suffered, and it feels like judgment without respect.

Some civilians and veterans say the real heroes of war are those who never returned, those who died in combat. This definition again simply divides veterans into one of two distinct, mutually exclusive categories. If the real heroes are those who were killed, the inference is that veterans who survive the horror of combat did not do enough, or they would be dead.

Even Patton said, "…no bastard ever won a war by dying for his country. He won it by making the other poor dumb bastard die for his…"

Heroes are not so easily defined.

In addition, the families of veterans who never return from war are forever haunted by their loved one's absence. For them, the war never ends.

alfred

My brother Bob, a Vietnam veteran, spoke with an older gentleman who shared that his son had been awarded a military medal for action that took his life in Vietnam four decades earlier. While speaking with this man, Bob thought about how Dad would have liked him.

Following the soldier's death, his family received phone calls, "You probably think your son is a hero, but he is a murderer."

As Bob left the conversation, his words to this older gentleman were heartfelt, "Your son was a hero."

The father responded, "A lot of good that does me."

* * *

One definition of a hero is a person who does what has to be done when it needs to be done, regardless of the consequences.

I showed Tom Brokaw's book *The Greatest Generation* to Dad. I asked, "The author says that yours is the greatest generation ever. Do you think that is true?"

Dad answered, "No."

"Some people say you are a hero."

"Ach," he said.

Dad did not think of himself as a hero. He thought of himself as a survivor and a killer, nothing that brought him pride.

Robert Phillips (320/35th) said, "I am not a hero. That's for sure. I was just in the war and did what I had to do."

Another veteran said, "Most soldiers were nauseated with what they had to do to survive."

Heroism may be just showing up on the front line day after day for months on end, not knowing when luck may run out. The worst part of war may not be the actual terror of combat, but rather the eternal stretches of dread, not knowing what is happening, when enemies can sneak up from behind. Soldiers who suffer post-traumatic stress disorder (PTSD) lose trust in everything around them because of this everlasting heightened sense of alertness during war.

Orval Faubus (320/35th) wrote of the 35th Division, "It is not enough to say these men have walked through the Valley of the Shadow of Death. They have been through the Valley of Death itself."

* * *

Some speak of the horrible stare of soldiers with battle fatigue, those who have seen heavy action for too long. Their eyes are vacant and hopeless. One soldier broke down crying when he saw himself in a mirror for the first time after combat.

Within war, the ultimate loneliness is feeling expendable, and if one survives the war, the veteran feels alien when no one can relate to his experiences. The personal problems of others seem insignificant compared to what the veteran has witnessed. Many suffer though nightmares and question "What was it all for?" and "Who cares?" When a subsequent war starts, veterans may feel their efforts and suffering were in vain because there had not been enough benefit.

War correspondent Ernie Pyle spent the war among the ordinary foot soldiers. In his book *Brave Men,* he wrote, "I am sure that in the past two years I have heard soldiers say a thousand times, 'If only we could have created all this energy for something good.' But we rise above our normal powers only in times of destruction."

James Huston wrote in *Biography of a Battalion,* "The men felt very deeply the need for preventing the repetition of such a conflict as they had seen."

And Al Navarrette (320/35th) said, "There are no absolute winners. There are only varying degrees of losers; some lose more than others." (*Santa Fe Express,* April/May/June 2014)

* * *

As I researched, I considered the conditions that impact a soldier. The following list is just a casual starting point to understand a veteran's experience. Any given statistic is for the 60 American Infantry and Armored Divisions in the European Theatre during World War II. The first condition in the list is much more tolerable than the second.

Within a married couple from Cedarburg, Wisconsin, the father of one spouse served as a film projectionist for officers. His environment was more similar to the conditions given first in the comparisons, whereas the father of the second spouse was on the front lines, primarily living in the environment that was constantly more difficult. The war experience of one man had very little in common with the other.

Dad once said, "A lot of guys did not have to do much."

I asked, "You mean the ones who did not have to go?"

"No, da ones dat went. A lot of dem just got to run around."

Of the 16 million American soldiers in World War II, only 10 percent served in actual combat, while 90 percent served in support. A similar statistic is that for every one man in combat, there are ten who never saw action.

* * *

Just as the Finnish and Inuit languages have many words for types of snow, it seems the English language could benefit from multiple variations of the word "respect." I discovered that

Easier "To Take"		More Difficult "To Take"
Basic meals	vs	Rations/no food supplied
Sleeping in cots/beds	vs	Sleeping on the ground/foxholes
Shelter in buildings/structures	vs	Shelter in foxholes/outside
Hygiene regularly available	vs	Hygiene rarely available
Limited time in combat (least for a group: 3 days)	vs	Extended time in combat (longest for a group: 303 days)
Low casualty rate for unit (least: about 2 percent)	vs	High casualty rate for unit (highest: about 252 percent)
Cognitive knowledge of war	vs	Sensory knowledge of war (sight, smells, sounds)
Low number of battle (least: 12) casualties	vs	High number of battle (highest: 22,454) casualties
Serving in rear echelon	vs	Serving on front lines
Repairers of destruction	vs	Initiators of destruction
Minimal risk to one's life	vs	Constant threat to one's life
Saving lives (medical staff)	vs	Causing injury and death
Ability to defend oneself	vs	Defenseless (Medics)
Leaving scenes of destruction (Air Force)	vs	Living within the destruction (Infantry)
Never firing a weapon	vs	Survival based on weapons
Killing from a distance	vs	Proximity/close range killing
Killing enemy soldiers	vs	Killing children/civilians/own troops

respect for one's father may include a significant amount of fear. Some people respect their fathers for their accomplishments, acquired possessions, or accolades from others. My respect for my father includes no fear, and he never attained worldly possessions or awards. I respect his humility, honesty, his conscience, and his humanness. I respect him for his life experiences, of which he never boasted, those which he almost took to his grave had it not been for the timing of Mom's death and his broken hip.

Dad was gentle and kind. He enjoyed unique personalities and appreciated nature. He talked too softly and chewed too loudly. He was neither afraid nor impressed by much. He elected to go to war so that his brother would not have to. His patriotism was neither proud nor boastful. Instead, he was humbly grateful because he understood the true costs of war, and there was no simple way for him to explain it in words to the rest of us.

Before I knew anything about Dad's war experiences, I overheard someone say to a child about an adult, "He is going to kill you." That child had broken something insignificant. I was about 40 years old, and I pondered whether I had ever heard my father's name in the same sentence as the word, "kill." At that time, it was unimaginable for me, and sometimes it still is.

After Dad's death, he was described to us as a character, a legend, and an extraordinary ordinary man.

I will never classify soldiers as to whether they could take it or not because I do not know where they have been. In addition, I do not claim my father to be a hero. I only know whom I respect, and I hold my father and other veterans like him in my very highest regard.

SOME WORLD WAR II STORIES

MY BROTHER, RALPH WIPPERFURTH
(1924-1944)

By Jean Wipperfurth Lenling
Alfred's first cousin

As I write this biography of my only sibling, I still feel terribly sad when I think about his death almost 60 years ago at the age of twenty in the Battle of Saint-Lô. I feel cheated for myself and for my children. They never had an aunt, uncle, or cousins on my side of the family.

Ralph grew up near a lake, where he loved to fish with his father and swim with his friends. His activities were typical of a "city kid" in Madison…paper routes, Boy Scouts, and he entered contests with his model airplanes. He attended St. Bernard's Catholic Grade School and was proud of being first chair saxophone in the Madison East High School band.

When he graduated in 1942, he could not make many plans for his future because it was just a matter of time until he would be called to duty. He worked at Gisholt Machine Company and enrolled in some vocational classes before being drafted. He trained with the 106th Infantry Division and was transferred to the 330th Regiment of the 83th Division.

Ralph was in England on D-Day and wrote home shortly thereafter, "I suppose you heard the news. We are excited about it." That was the only letter we ever received because he was killed on July 16 in the Battle of Saint-Lô.

My mother answered the door on a summer day when a 16-year-old came with a telegram. Alone, she said, "No, I do not want it." She knew exactly what it was. To my parents' dying day, they mourned the loss of Ralph and never got over his death, sometimes calling my children by his name.

Endres relatives remember that Alfred saw Ralph shortly before his death, but they protected Alfred from the news of Ralph's death until Alfred returned home 15 months later. At the time of my brother's death, my mother sadly said to her sister, Alfred's mother, "Your boy could be next."

Recently I learned the specifics of Ralph's death, and I actually wish I had never found out. All I can say is that he probably died instantly. I think war is a terrible thing, and many people today are spoiled by not knowing the reality of it.

I still miss my brother.

CAPTAIN "BUDDY" (SYLVESTER) HOFFMAN (1920-1944)

By the author

Sixty-three years of accumulated memorabilia filled the tiny upstairs bedroom of our farmhouse. As my sister Bev and I separated items into bags for each of us eight siblings, I uncovered an 8x10-inch photo of Buddy Hoffman in his World War II sheepskin-lined leather bomber jacket and three-zippered pants. The jacket's tall, furry collar was double strapped to keep it snug at cold altitudes. Dad knew Buddy through his connection to Mom's family, and the two veterans had been inducted into the military the same month.

I was not enthusiastic about taking anything home with me, but I studied Buddy's face under the clouded glass within the simple gold frame. We all knew he had died in war, and he was our Grandma Miller's favorite of the nine Hoffman brothers. He had already completed his final required missions in war and then died on the flight he did not have to take. Buddy deserved respect, so his photo went home with me, where I cleaned the glass, polished the frame, and studied the photo again. I decided to find out the rest of the story.

Hoffman House restaurants, owned by the same Hoffman family, had been popular for years in Madison and the Midwest. I wrote a note on the website of the remaining Rockford location, and within 24 hours, I received a phone call from 93-year-old Bob Hoffman, Buddy's slightly younger brother. I could have easily talked with him for more than 47 minutes, but I had to watch the clock in order to teach my evening class.

Bob Hoffman told me that he and some of his brothers had spent their childhood summers on farms in the area of Roxbury, Wisconsin, rather than in the city of Madison. Louis and Kuni Wearnisch were Buddy's godparents, but the Hoffman brothers were not interested in working so hard on a farm where there were only girls. They would rather create adventures among the boys just two miles down the road on the farm of Nick and Louisa Miller, Dad's future in-laws.

Bob explained his brother's death, "Bud was a B-25 bombardier in the Pacific. He had completed his last mission and was scheduled to go home, but another bombardier came drunk for duty. Bud said he would take his place."

Two relatively low-flying planes set out to bomb a Japanese fuel site, with Buddy among five men in the second plane. The bombs in the first plane had accidentally been set with instantaneous fuses rather than delayed ones, and

"BUDDY" (SYLVESTER) HOFFMAN, 1920-1944, B-25 BOMBARDIER IN THE PACIFIC.

Buddy's plane could not avoid the immediate explosion of all the fuel blowing up from below.

Bob said, "Our brother Cos was on a ship. He got a call, and that is how we found out."

Eight out of nine Hoffman brothers served in WWII, and they had made a plan to open a restaurant upon getting out of service, something that would keep them all together.

The bodies of Buddy and the other four crew members were found in a jungle in the Pacific Theatre and eventually buried in Louisville, Kentucky. Upon their return from World War II, the other Hoffman brothers opened a restaurant as they had planned.

ALFRED COLUCCI

By the author

V ery early in my research, my sister Yvonne sent me the following article from a newspaper in Madison, Wisconsin. Mr. Colucci felt familiar to both Yvonne and me because, just as with our father, he was unable to talk about the war. Some people, even veterans, have suggested that Dad did not actually remember the war; he was just trying to be helpful to me with his brief and fragmented comments. Instead, I believe Dad and Mr. Colucci would have fully understood each other.

Former Student Recalls Colucci's Memorable Two Minutes of Silence
By Kurt Meyer
Wisconsin State Journal
December 14, 2002

Alfred Colucci, who passed away this week—"Big Al" as we students called him with something like affection— was principal at Madison West High School when I was there in the mid-1970s. I remember that he was respected and even liked by the students, no small achievement for a high school principal.

I remember his distinctively nasal voice on our homeroom loudspeaker reading the daily announcement with wry formality, always ending with his signature tagline "… and have a nice day."

But my most powerful memory of Mr. Colucci is of the only time I ever saw him at a loss for words. One day the history department at West assembled a group of faculty who had experienced World War II. Several classes

gathered in the school library for a special session of oral history with this group.

We heard Mr. Bach, the art teacher, who had flown cargo planes in Africa, describe his experiences.

Mrs. Kelly, the German teacher, gave her compelling and painful account of life as a teenager, a story already well known to her students. Allied bombers passed over her city of Freiburg on a nightly basis on their way to targets deeper in Germany. She described the awful choice that families faced—to shelter at the lowest levels of Freiburg's three-and four-level deep medieval basements and risk being buried alive, or to remain at higher levels and risk being killed directly by a bomb. She spoke of her brother, who never returned from the Eastern front.

A couple of other people spoke but I don't remember what they said. Then it was Mr. Colucci's turn.

He spoke in an uncharacteristically quiet voice, slowly, looking down at the table. He said he had been a soldier in the infantry, in constant combat for several months, along the front of the advance toward Germany in 1944 and 1945. He said he was one of six or seven survivors from a group that originally numbered around 200.

I forget the exact numbers and details 27 years after the event, but I very clearly remember how Mr. Colucci then stopped talking, in mid-sentence. In that room of maybe 75 kids and teachers, there was absolute silence for what had to be one or two full minutes.

Just silence. Nobody moved. Finally, after an eternity, with a small shake of his head and a brush across his eyes, he just quietly said, "I can't." Everybody breathed again and that was it. If there was any more in the program, I don't remember it. But I will never forget how, with two minutes of silence, Alfred Colucci told me more about war than all the history books I have ever read, or speeches I have ever heard.

Rest in peace, Mr. Colucci.

Alfred

JACQUELINE MARIE BERTHE PANAK
1927-2007

By the author

I met Suzanne Stone in a certification course for Milwaukee Area Technical College instructors, and somehow we shared our fathers' World War II experiences. She also spoke of her mother's deep respect for the veterans of D-Day.

Suzanne's mother, Jacqueline Marie Berthe Panak, was a French war bride, who met her American husband in France when he returned from duty in Africa on his way home to the United States. With him, Jacqueline left France to eventually raise nine children in Milwaukee, Wisconsin. She made one final request of her children upon her death. She asked that her ashes be returned to France and scattered among the rolling waves at the beaches of Normandy to join in spirit with those soldiers who had died there. Her wish was honored 63 years after the liberation of her homeland.

FAMILY AND FRIENDS REMEMBER ALFRED

***Alfred and Louise with their first twelve grandchildren, about
forty years after his return. Back: Cyndee Gordon, Aila Waldow,
Michael Endres. Center: Matt Endres, Alfred Endres, Louise Endres
holding Meg Moore, Tina Waldow, Nick Endres. Front: Amy
Gordon, Nick Waldow, Tony Endres, Greg Gordon, Emily Endres.***

***Alfred sledding on a farm hill at the age of 82 with
Louise, a couple of grandkids, their friend, and the
author.***

P ossibly before I even started school, Alfred taught me the song, "Jesus Loves Me, This I Know," and later he taught me how to drive, using an old truck. He was always very patient.

On the day he left for basic training, Eddie, Louise, and I took him to Portage, and when the bus took off, we followed it as long as we could. Louise was quite brave and did not cry too much. And of course, I remember Alfred coming home on furlough. With his time on leave running short, he finally decided to marry Louise after dating for almost six years. He was never in a big hurry.

When Alfred was in the nursing home, Eddie, Rita and I enjoyed our visits, but we just wished he would have talked louder.

~ Alfred's sister, Celia Endres Coyle

Alfred

My family's relationship with Alfred began during World War II when my sister Dolores was in Sr. Luana's fourth grade class at St. Benedict School in Chicago. Sr. Luana assigned each student to write letters to a soldier, saving her brother Alfred for Dolores.

During that school year, Dolores wrote letters to Alfred and eventually exchanged letters with his wife, Louise. She and baby Eileen even visited my family during Alfred's absence, and when Alfred returned home through Chicago, he may have met me before he met his own daughter. Within days of Alfred's return, my family's visit to the farm is documented with a photograph of my father holding me as an infant in front of a tractor in October 1945.

As a young boy, I spent a week or two during my summer vacation at the farm. Alfred and his sons tried to make a farmer out of the Chicago "city boy," but they never succeeded. I helped with chores, ate huge lunches and dinners, tried to keep the barn clean for the inspectors, and sold corn off the back of the pickup truck in Madison. Once I had to hang on for dear life as I rode a calf that took off on me, and I always suspected Alfred created that type of situation because he always had an amused look on his face.

I visited the farm a couple of weeks after Louise's death, and at that time, Alfred looked through his old army trunk with all the items from his time overseas. I can only imagine what he experienced, and I am glad he finally shared some of it.

I will always remember Alfred's big smile and how he made everyone feel welcome. It certainly was a good time in my life.

~Family friend Matt Engels

I wish I had spoken to my own father about the war, but he, like Uncle Alfred, did not talk about it. On the bottom of my dad's pewter replica of the flag raising, *Victory at Iwo Jima*, is his writing, "Simon Miller, Feb 19-45 to Mar 16-45. I was there during the whole operation, including the raising of the flag on Mt. Suribachi. There were 6,821 killed and a total of 25,851 casualties. I was one of the lucky ones."

I spent many summer days with Uncle Alfred on his farm, and somehow he made the work fun. One sunny day, Uncle Alfred and I went to Leo Statz's farm to set up the thrash machine, test grain bundles, and verify everything was operating properly for the following day when all the neighbors would come to help.

Everything was going well, so Uncle Alfred sent me to Leo's farmhouse for some beer. He warned me that Leo's wife was napping and did not like beer drinking, so I should be very quiet. I went onto the porch, carefully opened a potentially squeaky screen door, and tip-toed to the old ice box. I got the beers and made my way back out.

"Did Leo's wife hear you?" Uncle Alfred asked. I assured them they did not have to worry. They enjoyed their beers with big smiles on their faces, even offering me a sip for a job well done. Uncle Alfred asked me again, "Are you sure she did not hear you?" Then they began to laugh. Leo Statz was never married.

That is how things went when I visited Uncle Alfred.

~ Nephew James Simon Miller

Alfred

My family moved down the road from the Endres farm when I was in grade school, and we lived there for only about two years. We worked back and forth between our farms, helping each other with hay and other crops and even building a swing set.

I became part of the family when I spent one summer with the Endreses from Monday morning until Alfred returned me back home after chores were completed on Saturday night. There are so many memories. One involves the first time I cut hay on a nice, flat, rectangular field, clearly visible from the kitchen window. By the time I had cut half of the field, it looked like I was chasing snakes. Alfred looked out the window and simply said, "Well, nobody got hurt."

One night at dinner, Jerry and I had a corn-eating contest. Jerry said he won, but I said my cobs were longer, so we lined up our empty cobs end to end for Alfred to decide the winner, which is still being contested to this day.

I learned a lot from Alfred and will always cherish my memories.

~Family friend Alfred "Fritz" Frey

A s the oldest son on a farm, I spent a lot of time with Dad when the pace of life was so much slower than now. Sometimes when milking was finished, men came to our milk house from the neighborhood, which included a significant number of bachelors and widowers. Dad gave haircuts upon request or played his harmonica, always stored in the barn, while the rest sang and maybe had a beer.

We never had much money, and once I asked whether we could get some new forks while we threw silage from the silo with broken ones. Dad answered, "Wit' what? We don't have any money." However, the next day, he took the forks to our neighbor Matt Benzmiller, who welded them for free.

Dad was always strong emotionally, and he knew when to get mad and when to keep quiet. At times, he probably escaped to the barn when we had visitors almost every Sunday for thirteen years while Grandma Miller, his mother-in-law, lived with us. He had his own way of doing things and did not particularly appreciate suggestions.

Once Davie Hewitt, Kenny Statz, and I went sledding and sneaked some wine and cigarettes into the woods. Mrs. Hewitt was really mad and told Dad about it when he later picked me up. On the way home, the truck was very quiet. Finally Dad said, "I won't tell Mom, but don't do it again." I never heard any more about it.

He seemed to know when to get mad, and it was not very often.

~Son Jerry Endres

Alfred

My father, Adolph Endres, was more of a Type-A person, a cutting-edge farmer, and I remember him saying that Uncle Alfred was slow as molasses in January. He could not believe they were brothers, but there is a story about how my dad went to Uncle Alfred's to fill the silo when nothing was fully ready to get the job underway. My dad was impatient, but the longer he stayed, the more he discovered he was enjoying himself. That was just Uncle Alfred's pace, not so much on a mission and possibly just appreciating life more. He was soft-spoken and slow to speak, hard-working and gentle.

~Niece Joyce Endres Riedner

Before Louise researched this book, I would have said World War II was a small part of my dad's life, but now with an understanding of all he experienced, I would say it played a bigger part of who he was. His decisions in life were probably all affected by what he saw, felt, and knew from that experience.

At the dinner table, with possibly 11 of us gathered around, I was seated next to my dad. He dished up my plate, not with big helpings, but I knew I had to finish it all, and occasionally there may have been a comment about kids going hungry during the war.

Dad was always my hero, and maybe his personality would have been different had he not served in the war. I loved taking naps on the couch, me lying on top of my dad with his big round chest as my pillow. His quiet, calm demeanor was so comforting to me. He may have had that quality earlier in life than most people because he knew how short life can be and how suddenly it could have ended in war. Somehow he raised eight kids in a very gentle way.

~Daughter Bev Endres Gordon

Alfred

Going to a farm was always a bit of an adventure for us city kids. My siblings and I remember Alfred on his tractor, pulling a bunch of kids on a big, old, flatbed hay wagon for a long, bumpy ride through the fields. The story improved if we said there was manure on the fields, but it was probably just mud. It would fly up, and of course, we would scream and holler, everyone thinking it was so hilarious, which was Alfred's plan all along.

Another time we were squished together in our car, ready to return to Madison, when someone led Danny, the horse, over to our car to bid farewell to the city kids. That rickety, old horse stuck its head in the car and blew snot all over us. We laughed about that for years, and we still have not forgotten our Endres farm adventures.

~*Niece Janet Miller Toner*

U ncle Alfred said "ya" more than any other person on earth, and he always had time to talk to all of us kids when we descended like locusts on the farm because Grandma Miller lived there. Once he walked us down to the barn while he was milking, and when one of the cows pooped, he used toilet paper on the cow as if that was normal practice. He was just messing with us city kids.

My brother Tom remembers the harmonica being stored in the barn and also how everyone worried that Alfred planted his corn too late. When it came around to fall, he was harvesting just like everyone else.

Alfred was a quiet man, but he always had a smile for everyone, and thinking of him makes me smile now.

~Niece Diane Miller Ruppert

Alfred

I worked at the Lodi Canning Company during harvest season from seven at night until about seven in the morning on a clean-up crew with Uncle Alfred as the foreman. To this day, I am not fond of cream-style corn after I was coated in it each night while cleaning the canning area. We tried to stay dry while wearing rain gear and working with water hoses.

Late on one particular shift, I was spraying in one direction of the husking room while at the same time, I was being rained upon from behind. I discovered the mist was coming from the opposite end of the building, up over the huskers to the inspection tables below. There was some laughter, and I discovered Uncle Alfred and Irv Wildt to be the culprits.

As an eighteen-year-old, I got within 25 to 30 feet with my hose before the older men could get away, and I placed a steady stream on Uncle Alfred. The water hit in such a way that it was trapped under his waterproof jacket as it sprayed up from his hip. He was drenched, and it still brings a smile to my face when I think of one of Uncle Alfred's jokes that did not go as planned.

~Nephew Herm Miller

When I was young, I recall going to the Endres farm on Sundays for family get-togethers when Grandma Miller lived there. It seemed Uncle Alfred was always doing farm chores when we arrived, but we were welcomed with his smile as he took a break to greet us. Despite being a "grown up," he struck me as very approachable, warm, and personable. He was slow to speak and willing to listen with direct eye contact. This was not typical from my experiences with adults and farmers.

Once he asked whether I was interested in milking a cow. Reluctant but curious, I accepted the offer. After repeated failures on my part and with much patience and persistence on Uncle Alfred's part, I managed to extract a small cup of milk. I asked if I could drink it, and he responded, "Sure, but you may not like it." Now, being the son of a city milkman, I was certain I liked milk, but I was completely unaware that the raw milk needed processing and chilling to make it palatable to me. After taking a gulp of the warm raw milk that I earned from Bessie, a look of horror and disgust must have appeared on my face because I clearly recall my uncle's reaction of amusement and laughter.

He will always be a fond memory in this nephew's noggin.

~Nephew Daniel Miller

Alfred

When we said the Rosary as kids, we always prayed for Uncle Alfred in the army, and when he got married, we were able to go to the wedding and afterward, to the reception at a big white house on a hill. All the kids hung out at a windmill where there was a water tank filled with ice and lots of soda pop. Uncle Alfred was in his army uniform with lots of ribbons, and Aunt Louise looked beautiful in her white dress.

Much later in my life, when I was on the Madison Police Department, we had intense riots and protests against the Vietnam War. Alfred told me he almost joined the protesters but did not. He hated war. It was the most terrible thing a person could experience. I, having been in terrifying situations as a policeman, could understand his feelings. It is difficult to comprehend the terror a person would experience in war, not for a moment, but for days and months on end.

~*Nephew Dan Kalscheur*

I recall a photo of my brother Virg wearing a helmet, his ROTC uniform, and holding a set of binoculars, the same pose as George C. Scott in an ad for the 1970 movie, *Patton*. I find it remarkable that I recall the likeness of that pose of my brother and the Patton actor, yet none of us remembers a single comment about Patton from our father at any time during 57 years following the war.

At a surprise 70th birthday party, Virg toasted our father with words that brought tears to the eyes of some of our guests. I do not remember the words, just the emotion they brought forth.

Then shortly before Virg's death, he wrote to his parents, "Everything good that ever happened to me I owe to you and love you very much." After Virg's death, Dad verbalized his remorse for having scolded Virg…once.

I cannot create words for my brother as a tribute to his father, so these recollections will have to suffice.

On behalf of my brother.
Virg Endres
(1949-1989)
(by the author)

Cadet Virgil T. Endres, 20, son of Mr. and Mrs. Alfred N. Endres, Route 2, Lodi, uses field binoculars during a terrain observation exercise at the Army Reserve Officer Training Corps' advanced summer camp at Ft. Riley, Kan. Endres is a student at the University of Wisconsin at Madison.

Alfred

As I consider the impact of war on my father, I remember the movie *Bridge over River Kwai* on television when I was in junior high. I thought Dad would enjoy watching it, but he never set foot in the living room that night. Instead he spent the entire evening upstairs, something which I never recall him doing at any other time. I realize now he was just avoiding the war movie.

He never seemed to get mad at me, a little disgusted perhaps, but not mad. When I was sixteen and just learning to drive, I put gas into our car from the farm pump. Instead of driving forward, I put the car in reverse and backed into the pump as he watched. His reaction was simply, "*Ach!*"

When I was in high school, two square potholders somehow burned in the oven, resulting in what looked like two overdone pork chips. Mom served them on Dad's plate, and since it was a Lenten Friday, we explained pork chops were made by mistake instead of fish. Instead of wasting the chops, it was best to eat them. Then Mom and I watched with great anticipation until we could not control our laughter as Dad tried to cut into the "pork chops." He appreciated the prank, although not as much as we did.

On another occasion, we were skeptical about a pizza delivered by Uncle Pete from his salvage store. Even Dad was reluctant to eat it, considering its appearance or how it may have been frozen, thawed, and refrozen again. There was no way I would try that pizza if Dad did not.

A lot of my memories of my dad are about food, but avoiding waste was a strong lesson that he shared from his war experiences.

~Daughter Yvonne Endres Ziegler

Aunt Louise and Uncle Alfred came to so, so many of my activities. I don't think he ever said, "I love you," but his actions spoke louder than his words.

My memories of the Endres farm at Christmas are more vivid than at any other time of the year. There is a tiny bridge before getting to the farm. My mother would touch Dad's arm and say, "Harold, honk!" as a warning that the city slickers had arrived. As we piled out of the car into the cold, the house windows were always steamed. There were hugs at the door as smiling Aunt Louise dried her hands on her apron and Uncle Alfred, with his wavy hair and beautiful dark eyes, stood behind her to take our coats. Norman Rockwell would have loved to paint such a scene even if it was much louder than his typical settings.

The meal was a feast with all the trimmings. After dinner, while Uncle Alfred was still seated at the table, one of my eight cousins would magically appear with his harmonica. We then adjourned to the living room, where my mother played *O' Tannenbaum* on the piano. Even my Irish father seemed to enjoy this German moment. Uncle Alfred seemed pleased, and although he was very quiet, I know how proud he was of his family. His smile could melt ice, and I felt he was content with his life.

Over the years, I have spent Christmas in many different places, from serving food to the poor and homeless to a "Christmas Card Christmas" in Nuremberg, Germany, but of all my memories, I am most grateful for those at the Endres farm on Christmas Day.

~Niece Anne Grady

Alfred

I enlisted in the Navy during the Vietnam War, and shortly after I returned from boot camp, I ran into Uncle Simon Miller at the Okee Snack Bar. He talked about World War II, Iwo Jima, and "all those young boys who died there," and then he cried. The next day, when I told Dad of the conversation, he quietly said, "Simon has reason to cry." With my being just 18 years old, Dad knew I did not fully understand.

When I actually left for Vietnam, Dad said, "Don't volunteer for anything. Don't be a hero. It's not worth it." He told me a story how his group has been walking for days when an officer asked for drivers. Everybody volunteered, but Dad was suspicious, and in the end, the officer just wanted "drivers" for wheelbarrows.

Forty years after Dad's military training days, friends Rollie and Alice Keegan of Ohio visited us in Wisconsin. Rollie recalled how a guy in their unit had asked for a tape measure to show how he could expand his chest by two inches. With encouragement from Rollie and others, Dad measured his chest for an expansion of five inches. Rollie loved that story because the other guy was cocky and boastful, and Dad, without a word, had put him in his place.

Many times Dad did things in very quiet ways. On the painful morning of Virg's funeral, a bachelor neighbor, who obviously had not heard the news, asked for help to deliver a lamb. Dad looked at me and said, "We better go and see what we can do." We were not successful, and even though we were so justified not to help that day, we went, and Dad never said a word about the funeral.

~Son Bob Endres

ALFRED AND LOUISE ENDRES WITH ALICE AND ROLLIE KEEGAN DURING TRAINING.

Vision:

Right eye 20/ 20

Left eye 20/ 20

Hearing:

Right ear 20 / 20

Left ear 20 / 20

Height 67½ in.

Weight 149 lb.

Girth (at nipples): 37

Inspiration 42 in.

Expiration 35 in.

Girth (at umbilicus) 31 in.

MEDICAL RECORD OF ALFRED'S ABILITY TO EXPAND HIS CHEST BY FIVE INCHES.

Alfred

Alfred was a quiet-spoken man, while my husband Bob was the loud one. For Christmas one year, some of the Endres grandkids received gifts of walky-talkies, and Alfred was curious how far a voice would carry. He came to our house and asked Bob to talk to the Endres household, about three quarters of a mile away. After the little experiment, Alfred said to Bob, "You're so loud they can hear you without a walky-talky."

~Neighbor Mary Lou Karls

I will never forget the rise and fall of Uncle Alfred's voice as he spoke. He could be saying something profound or just an observation, but there was always a warm roll in his voice that I have never heard duplicated. He was quite succinct in his thinking, and no one told Alfred what to think. He had a quiet and wise sense of how everything stacked up.

~Niece Shirley Brabender Mattox

On the day Alfred broke his hip, he called our house about 2:30 in the afternoon and asked for help.

"Maybe you should bring Vic along," he said.

Alfred had fallen in the kitchen, while his Lifeline was on his walker in the laundry room. He had a choice between lying on the kitchen floor for several hours before he would be found or pulling himself up on the drawers of the kitchen cupboards and getting to the phone on a wheeled kitchen chair.

After we arrived, we called Alfred's home health nurse, who kindly came to the farm, evaluated him, and called 911 for a transport to the emergency room. The Emergency Medical Service thought that Alfred looked so good he did not need them, but as it turned out, his hip was severely shattered. We never expected a break, he never complained about pain, and he never lived at the farm as our neighbor again.

~ Neighbor Shirley Hellenbrand

I remember a soft voice coming from the "big man" in my life. If Dad raised his voice, we knew he was upset, and it did not happen very often. He worked hard but had time for us. Among many other things, he watched my Danette softball games, where he was proud when I played well and never seemed disappointed when I did not. He encouraged me to ride our horse and especially appreciated when I rode fast with the horse's tail flying in the wind as well as my own pony tail.

Dad did not love to travel, but he found Albuquerque and Taos interesting, and even though he never fully appreciated the music of Native Americans, he joined them with his harmonica while they played their guitars.

In some ways, I got to know Dad better when he was no longer able to farm. He then lived at Good Samaritan Nursing Home, a place he never wanted to be, but he adjusted better than any of us expected. I traveled to Wisconsin more often during those years, taking him to his grandkids' sporting events and just spending time with him. Occasionally I would stay overnight at the nursing home, he, in his recliner, and I, in the bed he never used. I never slept well, but it was definitely worth the effort because he liked having someone around, and those times are very special memories for me.

~Daughter Del Endres

Dad's philosophy was to make do and be happy with whatever we had. If someone had more money or material possessions than we had, his response was, "But dey are not as happy as we are." And he was basically right.

Dad never initiated the trips to visit his two out-of-state daughters. He asked, "Why don't you come home instead?" I love the beautiful Rockies, but Dad was not enthused, "If you see one mountain, you have seen dem all." Of the red soils of New Mexico, he asked, "What will grow in dat?" Anything other than fertile, black soil was a bit of wasted earth's surface for my dad, the farmer.

When I was young, Dad rarely used the telephone. He called me for the first time when my boyfriend was lost in the waters of Lake Superior. He was thinking of me and loved me. When I moved to Colorado, we talked weekly, and he was the person who called me with the news of our brother Virg's death. The day before Dad died, he called. "I want to say hello; we don't say hello often enough." The following day, I was the last person to speak to him on the phone. I hope it is true that hearing is our last sense to function. As I said that summer morning, "Good-bye, Dad. I love you."

~Daughter Eileen Endres Waldow

ALFRED'S GENERAL
TOUR OF DUTY

from *Story of the 320th Infantry* and personal documentation

March 6, 1942	Inducted into the army to eventually train in the states of Washington, Oregon, and California
April 1944	Fort Smith, Arkansas
May 21	Departed U.S. for European Theatre of Operations
June 2	Arrived in Europe as a replacement
June 7	Unconfirmed D-Day+1 involvement
July 13	Joined Company D of the 320th Regiment of the 35th Division
	Relieved 175th Regiment of the 29th Division
July 19	Liberated Saint-Lô, France
July 25	Carpet bombing breakthrough by 2,500 bombers
July 31	Liberated Torigni-sur-Vire
August 2 to 5	Crossed the Vire River and fought beyond it, day and night
August 7 to 12	Entire 35th Division fought at Mortain
August 10 to 12	1st Battalion/320th assigned to capture Hill 317
	Rescued "Lost Battalion" of 120/30th
August 16 to 17	Liberated Chateaudon
August 19	Liberated Janville
August 21	Liberated Pithiviers

alfred

August 24	Liberated Montargis with 134th Regiment
August 25	Liberated Courtenay
August 28	Liberated Troyes
August 30	Reached Seine River, seized bridge, and liberated Bar-sur-Seine
September 3	Liberated Joinville
September 13	Entire 35th Division established bridge head on Moselle River
	Attacked across Moselle River
	Patton watched troops from observation post of 1st Battalion/320th
	Daughter Eileen was born in U.S.
September 15	Fought at Dombasle
	Crossing of Rhine-Marne Canal and Le Sanon and Meurthe rivers
September 16	Liberated Haraucourt
September 17	Liberated Mazurelles and cut main highway leading east from Nancy to Berlin, closing western escape route for Germans
September 19 to 26	Repelled German counterattacks near Fresnes-en-Saulnois
Last days of September	Entire 35th Division ordered to clear Gremecey Forest of enemy
September 27	1st/320th attacked/captured high ground south of Gremecey
September 28	Received news of Eileen's birth
September 30	1st Battalion Commanding Officer Major Gillis killed in action

October 1	Finished clearing Gremecey Forest with 6th Armored
Month of October	Occupied defensive positions
	Endured unprecedented rains in Gremecey Forest
	Took first shower in Nancy since joining the 35th Division in July
November 8 to 12	Entire 35th Division began offensive in rain and mud
	320th assaulted western edge of Chateau-Salins Forest and Fresnes
November 17	Continued drive in the vicinity of Morhange in rain, mud, and sleet
By November 25	Liberated Bermering, Virming, Linstroff, Francaltroff and ten other small towns in rain, mud, and sleet
December 1 to 2	Continued drive toward German border
December 4	Captured Didefing and Bettring
December 5 to 6	Crossed Maderbach River
	Liberated Halving, Ballering, and six small towns on west bank of Saar River
December 8	Crossed the Saar River in assault boats
Next few days	Liberated Bliesbruck, France
December 12	Crossed Blies River into Germany
December 13 to 20	Captured Nieder Gailbach, Gersheim, and Renheim
December 21 to 22	Moved to Metz, France
December 23 to 25	Christmas in Metz
	Received replacements
December 26 to 27	Moved through France, Belgium, Luxembourg to Arlon area, south of Bastogne, for Battle of the Bulge

Alfred

December 27	Liberated Boulaide, Baschleiden, and Flebour in Luxembourg
December 31	1st Battalion/320th entered Villers-la-Bonne-Eau with 137th (Joe Demler had been captured there on January 29)
January 5, 1945	1st Battalion/320th reverted back to control of the 320th Infantry
January 9 to 18	Attached to 6th Armored Division for nine long, bitter-cold days
January 15	Liberated Oubourcy, four miles northeast of Bastogne, Belgium
January 18	Liberated Michamps and cut through Bourcy-Longvilly highway
January 19 to 22	Returned to Metz, France, for rest and rehab
January 24 to 29	Took defensive position in Vosges Mountains with 7th Army
January 30 to February 2	Moved to Holland into position with 9th Army
February 4	Took defensive positions to clear west bank of Roer River
After February 23	Captured Oberbuck, Kranzes, Schanz, and Kuppen in Germany
February 28	Crossed the Roer River at Hilfarth, Germany
March 1 to 2	Crossed Siegfried Line, liberated Venlo, Holland
	Captured 16 sizeable German towns
March 3	Captured Straelen and Nieukirk, entered Sevelen

March 4	Pushed 2.5 miles through hardened resistance in Germany
March 10	Reached Rhine River at Wesel, Germany
	Captured Kamperbruck, Kamp, Drupt, and six more German towns
March 26	Crossed Rhine River at Wesel, Germany
March 28 to 30	Captured a section of Autobahn Highway
	Captured Bottrop and Sterkrade
April 1	Crossed Emscher and Rhein-Herne Canals near Dortmund
Early April	Reached Ruhr River and cleared Prosper coal mine
April 11 to 12	Cleared Holthausen, Germany, while attached to 75th Division
April 12	Ordered to move 250 miles further into Germany to Elbe River
April 14	Probable witness to aftermath of massacre at Gardelegen, Germany
April 15	Crossed Germany's Saale River while attached to 83rd Division
	Captured Grosse Rosenberg, Kleine Rosenberg, Trabitz, Gottesgnaden, Breitenhagen, and Schmitz in Germany
April 18 to 19	Crossed Truman Bridge over Elbe River with 83rd Division
April 19 to 21	Occupied defensive positions east of Elbe River near Zerbst
	German Naval swimmers attempted to blow up Truman Bridge
April 23	Orval Faubus wrote of "wonderful rumors about peace"

Alfred

April 25	Assigned to occupational duties in vicinity of Hanover, Germany
May 8	Official end of war in European Theatre
Until May 29	Occupational duties in areas of Hanover and Munster, Germany
May 29 to June 14	Rest and recuperation in London
June to August	Assigned to 654th Tank Destroyer Battalion
August to Sept.	Assigned to 254th Regiment of the 63rd Division
September 23	Departed European Theatre of Operations on *Queen Mary*
September 28	Arrived in U.S. at Camp Kilmer, New Brunswick, New Jersey
October 13, 1945	Discharged at Camp Sheridan, Illinois

SOME MEMORIAL SITES
FOR THE 35TH DIVISION

LaMeauffe, France (Normandy Campaign)

- North of Saint-Lô in the LaMeauffe cemetery

- LaMeauffe was the first town liberated by the 35th Division after relieving elements of the 29th and 30th Divisions and entering combat in July 1944.

- "Gratitude from the inhabitants of La Meauffe to their liberators, the 35th American Division. This stone commemorates the visit of the delegation of that prestigious unit."

Chapelle of la Madelaine, Saint-Lô, France
(Normandy Campaign)

- East of the city of Saint-Lô toward Bayeux

- A chapel, which dates from the 14th century, contains artifacts and is dedicated as a memorial to the 29th and 35th Divisions, liberators in July 1944 of Saint-Lô, which was 95 percent destroyed during the war.

Torigni sur Vire, France (Normandy Campaign)

- At the entrance of the town on the road from Saint-Lô (D974)

- "In homage to the American 35th Infantry Division of which the 1st battalion from the 320th Regiment led by the Major W. Waring liberated the town on the 31st of July 1944"

Alfred

Mortain, France (Northern France Campaign)

- Situated near the Chapelle at the top of the hill where the 35th Division rescued the lost battalion of the 30th Division and for which the 1st Battalion of the 320th Regiment received the Presidential Unit Citation

- "In homage to the soldiers of the 35th Infantry "Santa Fe" Division, who from 10 to 13 August 1944 succeeded in saving the survivors of the "lost battalion" at the price of heavy losses of men"

Flavigny, France (Northern France Campaign)

- South of Nancy, adjacent to the Government Bridge across the Moselle River

- A monument bears the insignia of the 35th Division (and specifically the 2nd Battalion of the 134th Regiment).

- "For those who fought in this area and died for our Peace and Freedom, September 1944"

Francaltroff, France (Rheinland I Campaign)

- On a bunker on outskirts of Francaltroff

- "In honor of Colonel Bernard Byrne, commander of 320th Infantry Regiment of the U.S. 35th Division and the soldiers, in the liberation of the city Francaltroff on 20 November, 1944"

Boulaide, Luxembourg (Ardennes Campaign)

- The township (which includes Boulaide, Baschleiden, and Surre) erected a monument to assure the sacrifices of the 35th Division on December 27, 1944 will never be forgotten.

Lutremange, Belgium (Ardennes Campaign)

- Five miles south of Bastogne, in an area called Triangle of Devastation, which is bounded by Lutremange, Lutrebois, and Villers-La-Bonne-Eau

- A park-like setting surrounds a memorial, a display of photos and historical accounts, and a German thick-walled, reinforced steel rod, concrete pillbox.

- "This plaque is dedicated to the soldiers and officers of the American Third Army and the Commander General Patton and particularly to the 35th Infantry Division who fought the terrible war of this region during the winter 1944-1945 in order to push back the German invaders. We will never forget your sacrifices."

Villers-La-Bonne-Eau, Belgium (Ardennes Campaign)

- Less than one mile from Lutremange, Belgium

- Near the church, there is a display board of general information concerning the war's impact on Villers-La-Bonne-Eau, which is on the Circuit Historique (Historical Route). The 35th was in combat here at the turn of the year, 1944-45.

Schumann's Eck, Luxembourg (Ardennes Campaign)

- Crossroads area near Wiltz, Luxembourg

- A memorial trail leads along foxholes in the woods, where craters still exist more than six decades after the war.

- The 35th Division was part of Patton's Third Army during the Ardennes Campaign.

- Arrows on a map depict the Allied divisions that were engaged in Luxembourg and southern Belgium. At first

glance the arrows for the 35th Division seem less significant, but the 35th could not move far or fast due to the strength of the German opposition in its area.

Luxembourg American Cemetery, Hamm, Luxembourg (Ardennes Campaign)

- Three miles east of downtown Luxembourg City

- 5076 American servicemen are buried here along with General Patton, who was buried on Christmas Eve, one year after the Battle of the Bulge, following a car accident.

- One of two large granite maps portrays the Ardennes (Battle of the Bulge) and Rhineland campaigns with arrows for the divisions involved. Again it is important to remember that a relatively short arrow depicts the intensity rather than the scope of the contribution of the 35th Division.

- Less than one mile away from the American cemetery is the Sandweiler German War Cemetery.

35th Division Museum, Topeka, Kansas

- Within the Museum of the Kansas National Guard at Forbes Field, Topeka, Kansas

- Includes weapons, uniforms and artifacts of the 35th Division

- Includes memorial brick for Alfred N. Endres

Interstate 35

- A portion traversing Kansas and Missouri is a memorial to the men of the 35th Infantry Division. The history of the division is recorded on a bronze plaque and placed within the rest areas along that section.

INDEX OF NAMES

(Names mentioned in photo captions are italicized.)

Alamalema, Christophe, Vice-Consul, French Consulate in Chicago, 222
 -223, *226*

Alvarez, Rafael, Fort Bragg, 200, 274, 360

Anderson, Glen, 35th Inf Div, 5

Antal, Benjamin, 30th Inf Div, 273, 358

Barnett, Lloyd, 35th Inf Div, 203

Bohlman, Lyle, DDS, WWII Veteran, 68, 208-209

Brauntuch, Jack, 35th Inf Div, 74, 358

Briere, Pierre, French citizen during WWII, 216-218, 226, 359

Bullock, Keith, 35th Inf Div, 46, 122, 158

Byrne, Bernard A., Col. 35th Inf Div, 91, 344

Carpino, John, Anti-Tank 504, 274

Carey, Norman, 35th Inf Div, 53, 131-132

Chehanske, George, 2nd Inf Div, 274

Cline, John, 106th Inf Reg, 73, 352

Colucci, Alfred, 82nd Airborne Div, 310-311

Demler, Joseph, 35th Inf Div, 120, *121,* 122-124, *125,* 144, 244, 340,358

Duckett, James, trained with 44th Inf Div, 31-32

Ebey, Frank W., Lt. Col., 551st AAA Battalion, 101

Alfred

Esser, H. Robert, 30th Inf Div, 62, 68-69, 71-73, 184, 256

Faubus, Orval, 35th Inf Div, 37, 55, 75, 77, 82, 86-90, 95, 100, 107, 109, 125, 132, 138, 147, 149, 154, 157, 163-165, 172-173, 177, 179-180, 191, 198, 209, 299, 341, 352, 360

Foy, Jack, 35th Inf Div, 130

Ganshert, Daniel, Reverend, 285-287, 292

Gibeau, Albert, 35th Inf Div, 131-132

Gogal, Louis, 35th Inf Div, 5, 42, _94_, 95, 181, _182_, 273

Goralewski, Chester, 35th Inf Div, 40

Graff, James, 35th Inf Div, 197

Grecsek, Edward ("Eddie"), trained with 44th Inf Div, 31, 231-234, 238

Grinton, Philip, Lt. Col. (Ret), 273, 358

"Griffiths," 35th Inf Div, _86, 87,_ 88, 134

Hager, Fred, 35th Inf Div, 5, 155-156

Harrington, Walter "Hank," 35th Inf Div, 259

Haskett, Charles, 8th Air Force, 113

Helmer, Clelaon Arthur, 35th Inf Div, _87_

Hinson, Herman ("Stud"), 35th Inf Div, 44, 60-61, 95, 132-136, 154-156

Hoffman, Robert, 359

Hoffman, Sylvester, "Buddy," WWII Air Force, 307, _308_

Honeycutt, John C., 35th Inf Div, 4, 42, 74

Huckaby, Raymond, 35th Inf Div, 102-103, 105-106, 117, 205-206, 244, 358

Huskey, Leonard, 2nd Inf Div, 118, 127, 244, 268-269, 358

Huston, James, 35th Inf Div, 47, 56, 95, 100, 109, 114, 116, 126-127, 138, 161, 163, 166, 173, 184, 299, 352, 360

Irwin, Frederick, trained with 44th Inf Div, 31

Jeffalone, Jack, trained with 44th Inf Div, 31

Johns, Ronald, 35th Inf Div, 5, 42

Johnson, Ned D. Jr., 35th Inf Div, 5, 42

Keating, Frank, 102nd Inf Div, 170

Keegan, Roland, trained with 44th Inf Div, 31, 330, *331*

Keller, Eugene, 35th Inf Div, 5

Koontz, Merle, 35th Inf Div, 127

Kruchten, Joseph, WWII Veteran, *198,* 199

Lane, Benjamin, 35th Inf Div, 3, 5, 7, 11, 15, 42, 54, 94, 95, 103, 105, 136, 147, *149,* 155-157, 193, 207, 209, 244, 255, 358

Leatherberry, Bonard, trained with 44th Inf Div, *21,* 219

Leff, Murray, 35th Inf Div, 92, 201, 352, 357

Linquata, Michael, 35th Inf Div, 44, 54

Lochner, Leo, WWII Veteran, 183

Majerczyk, Johnnie, 35th Inf Div, 5, 42

Maleck, LeRoy, 35th Inf Div, 128-129, 353

May, Donald, Military Police, 13-17, 18, 46, 66, 110, 136, 166, 175, 196, 215, 225, 245, 252, 256, 265, 267, 271-272, 358

Melnikoff, Steven, 29th Inf Div, 200, 358

Miller, Donald A., 35th Inf Div, 249

Miller, Simon, WWII Veteran, 317, 330

Mitchell, W. C., 35th Inf Div, 5, 42, *43, 148,* 234

Morse, John, 106th Inf Div, 110-111, 353

Navarette, Al, 35th Inf Div, 300

Newman, Art, 35th Inf Div, 70

Notley, William, 35th Inf Div, 105, *149*

Overstreet, Charles, 252nd FA BN, 169

Panak, Jacqueline Marie Berthe, French citizen during WWII, 312

Phillips, Robert, 35th Inf Div, 13, *41*, 42-46, 48-50, 52-53, 55, 63-64, 67, 70-73, 77, 83, 88-89, 102, 116, 127, 131-132, 136, 150, 164, 169, 174, 177, 181-182, 187, 197, 202, 228-229, 243-244, 265, 284-285, 298, 358

Poelluci, Frank, trained with 44th Inf Div, 31-33, *34*, 37, 176-177, 234-236

Rosenberry, Sara, U.S. Embassy in Luxembourg, 140, 143, 207, 358-359

Rowe, Carl E., 35th Inf Div, 44

Ruzek, Frank, trained with 44th Inf Div, 31

Schaal, Alvin, anti-tank unit attached to 36th Inf Div, 187, 189, 358

Schoo Donald, 633rd Anti-Aircraft Artillery Battalion, 202

Schuster, Andrew, Brigadier General, 219

Scocos, John, Col., Sec. Wisconsin Dept. of Veteran Affairs, 222

Simon, Albert, 29th Inf Div, *249*, 250-251, 255, *257*, 258-259, *260*, 262, 264-265, 275-276

Stevenson, James, WWII Veteran, 267

Stockell, Charles, WWII Veteran, 255

Sudarsky, Joseph, WWII Veteran, 274

Torkelson, George, 45th Inf Div, 18-19, 356

Walsh, John, 35th Inf Div, 223, 358

White, Howard S., 35th Inf Div, 148, 150, 355

Wiedenhoeft, Glen, 35th Inf Div, 259

Wintemburg, Harry, 87th Inf Div, 54

Wipperfurth, Ralph, 83rd Inf Div, 247, 305-306

WORKS CITED

Arendt, Laurie (editor). *Back from Duty: Ozaukee Country's Veterans Share Their Stories*. Washington DC: Veterans History Project, 2002.

Ambrose, Stephen E. *Citizen Soldiers: The U.S. Army from the Normandy Beaches to the Bulge to the Surrender of Germany June 7, 1944 - May 7, 1945*. New York, NY: Touchstone, 1997.

Ambrose, Stephen E. *D-Day, June 6, 1944: The Climactic Battle of World War II*. New York, NY: Simon & Schuster, 1994.

Bradley, Omar N. *A General's Life: An Autobiography*. New York, NY: Simon & Schuster, 1983

Brokaw, Tom. *The Greatest Generation*. New York, NY: Random House, 1998.

Bulge Bugle. Official Publication of Battle of Bulge Association, Inc., Philadelphia, PA.

"The Bulge" Remembered: 60ᵉ Anniversaire de la Battaille des Ardennes. Le Gouvernement du Grand-Duche' de Luxembourg, 2004.

Cole, Hugh M., editor, "The Ardennes: Battle of the Bulge, 1944-1945." *The U.S. Army in WWII, European Theater of Operations*, Office of the Chief of Military History, Department of the Army, 1965.

Cline, John. *The Service Diary of a German War Prisoner #315136.* [Online] Available http://www.indianamilitary.org, 2 November 2017.

D'Este, Carlo. *Eisenhower: A Soldier's Life.* New York, NY: Henry Holt & Co., 2002.

Eisenhower, Dwight D. *Crusade in Europe.* New York, NY: Doubleday, 1990.

Faubus, Orval Eugene. *In This Faraway Land: A Personal Journal of Infantry Combat in World War II.* Little Rock, AK: Pioneer Press, 1993.

Fussel, Paul. *The Boys' Crusade: The American Infantry in Northwestern Europe, 1944-1945.* New York, NY: Modern Library, 2003.

Hatch, Alden. *General George Patton: Old Blood and Guts.* New York, NY: Sterling Publishing Co. Inc., 2006.

Huston, James A. *Biography of a Battalion: The Life and Times of an Infantry Battalion in Europe in World War II.* Mechanicsburg, PA: Stackpole Books, 2003.

"Gardelegen Massacre: 13 April 1945." [Online] Available www.scrapbookpages.com/Gardelegen/Massacre.html, 1 November 2017.

Leff, Murray. *Lens of an Infantryman: A World War II Memoir with Photographs from a Hidden Camera.* Jefferson, NC, and London: McFarland & Company, Inc., 2007.

Lerwill, Leonard L. *The Personnel Replacement System in the United States Army.* Washington DC: Department of the Army, 1954.

Linderman, Gerald F. *The World within War: America's Combat Experience in World War II*. New York, NY: The Free Press, 1997.

Maleck O.D., LeRoy R. *What Am I Doing Here?* Bloomington, IN: Author House, 2009.

Mauldin, Bill. *Up Front*. New York, NY and London: W.W. Norton & Company, 2000.

Meyer, Kurt. "Former student recalls Colucci's memorable 2 minutes of silence," Madison, WI, *Wisconsin State Journal*. December 14, 2002.

Milwaukee Sentinel, "Queen Mary Brings Badger Home." September 28, 1945.

Morse, John W. *The Sitting Duck Division: Attacked from the Rear*. Lincoln, NE: Writers Club Press, 2001.

"Mud." [Online] Available. http://www.wwiireels.com, October 28, 2017.

134th Infantry Regiment. [Online} Available http://www.coulthart.com/134/, 1 November 2017.

O'Neill, James H. "The True Story of the Patton Prayer," *Review of the News*, October 6, 1971, first appearing as government document in 1950, http://www.pattonhq.com/prayer.html. (accessed October 28, 2017)

"Over There. Over There. Over There…" [Online] Available http://475thmpeg.memorieshop.com/CHAPTERS/FOUR/Chapter4.html, 1 November 2017.

Patton, George S. *War as I Knew It*. Boston, MA and New York, NY: Houghton Mifflin Company, 1947.

Phillips, Michael M., "The Lobotomy Files." *Wall Street Journal*. December 11, 2013 [Online] Available http://projects.wsj.com/lobotomyfiles/. (accessed 1 November 2017)

Pyle, Ernie. *Brave Men*. Lincoln, NE: University of Nebraska Press, [2001]

Pyle, Ernie. *Here is Your War: Story of G.I. Joe*. Lincoln, NE. University of Nebraska Press, 2004.

Reardon, Mark J. *Victory at Mortain: Stopping Hitler's Panzer Counteroffensive*. Lawrence, KS: University Press of Kansas, 2002.

Rickard, John N. *Patton at Bay: The Lorraine Campaign, 1944*. Washington DC: Brassey's Inc., 2004.

Robbins, William C. (executive editor). *Front Page 1839-1988*: *Wisconsin State Journal*. 1988.

Rohmer, Richard. *Patton's Gap: An Account of the Battle of Normandy 1944*. New York, NY and Toronto: Beaufort Books, Inc., 1981.

Rooney, Andy. *My War* [sound recording (cassette)]. New York, NY: Random House Audio, [1995].

Ryan, Cornelius. *Longest Day: June 6, 1944*. New York, NY: Simon & Schuster, 1994.

Santa Fe Express: The 35th Divisionnaire. Horton, KS.

6th Armored Division. [Online] Available http://www.super6th.org/tank68/tank68_6.htm, 1 November 2017.

Toland, John. *Rising Sun: The Decline and Fall of the Japanese Empire Volume 2, 1936-1945*. New York, NY: Random House, [1970]

29th Infantry Division Historical Society. [Online] Available http://www.29infantrydivision.org/, 1 November 2017.

320th Public Relations Office. *Story of the 320th Infantry.* Hameln, Germany: 1945.

35th Infantry: Trail of the Santa Fe Division. Kentucky: Turner Publishing Company, 1994.

35th Division Website [Online] Available http://www.35thinfdivassoc.com, 1 November 2017.

Wertenbaker, Charles C., "Sudden Storms and Sudden Death Shook History's Greatest Armada," *LIFE Magazine*, 19 June 1944.

Wisconsin Veterans Museum. [Online] Available www.wisvetsmuseum.com/oral-histories/transcripts/, 1 November 2017.

White, Howard S. "The Eyes Have It!" (unpublished memoir) Havana, IL. 18 May, 1988.

ACKNOWLEDGMENTS

There are so many people who offered their knowledge and encouragement that I fear I will forget someone, not because of my lack of appreciation, but because of my blurred memories over so many years of organizing these materials.

Most importantly, I acknowledge my husband and daughters, who have lived within my obsession and my stacks of paper. They supported me in my search and never questioned my need to finish what I started. Meg and Kate were always willing to help me with artistic suggestions and technical help.

Additionally, a long list of family members and family friends wrote memories, read my writings, offered advice, fed me stories, and looked forward to an end product. For almost two decades, they listened to my words, "I am working on my book."

When I found Kira Henschel, I was no longer alone on the very solitary process of writing a book. From our first conversation, I felt trust; I felt respect. She made all the difference in my sense of hope and security that I would actually finish my project.

A variety of people read early copies of this book and offered helpful suggestions for its structure and terminology, especially military terminology. Murray Leff, Kurt Meyer, Fr.

Brendan McKeough, Allen Buchholz, Sara Rosenberry, Roberta Russo, Ray Crary, Col. Roger Aeschliman, Mike Ven, and Tom Martinelli guided me from their different perspectives and areas of expertise.

Mike Martin gave advice on a very early draft when I believed a math instructor like me could not improve upon anything that had already been published. My first draft included huge paragraphs of quotes because I was so delighted just to find information that related to my father.

Most likely I connected with Lt. Col. Philip Grinton through an online document, originally from a Station List located in the National Archives in College Park, Maryland, which Britain's D-Day Museum in Portsmouth had received from Lt. Col. Grinton. In addition to the online information, he also sent me a critical document that led me to my father's status as a replacement soldier.

Laurie Arendt has been knowledgeable and encouraging with nothing to gain. I contacted her early in this project and near its completion about interviewing and logistics.

Marge Bullock offered me addresses, maps, and newspaper clippings in addition to immediate replies to all my questions about the 35th Division. She also led me to Robert Phillips.

How I wish Robert Phillips and Don May could have seen the end result of all our phone conversations and all of the education they provided me. I am consoled at least that I was able to send them passages that contained their own words.

Ray Huckaby, Leonard Huskey, Joe Demler, Alvin Schall, Ben Lane, Steven Melnikoff, Benjamin Antal, Jack Brauntuch, John Walsh, George Torkelson, Willie Lambert, Richard O'Brien, all World War II veterans, gave me more than I ever requested when they chose to call and speak with me.

Margaret Poelluci, Leona Duckett, Shirley Hinsen Bragg, Jane Esser Brewer, Todd Wiedenhoft, John Carpino, Lanny North, Jean Lenling, Bob Hoffman, David Juergens, Jim Evers, Jay Collins, Landon Lawson, Jerry Grecsek and Roberta Russo answered questions, or searched for long-lost letters, or told me stories about their loved ones who served in World War II. A few more people, whose names I wish to keep private, trusted me with unpleasant yet important stories included near the end of the book.

Who would invite a family to spend three nights at one's home in Europe with very little knowledge of those four guests? Sara Rosenberry would. She also was a very important liaison from the citizens of Luxembourg to my father.

One day, I read a poem and thought, "I can do that." I wanted to condense my father's story into a page. However, I needed Suzanne Stone, my daughter Meg, and Marianne Szabo to make suggestions on what I had first written.

Ernest Ndzebet and the Quebec son-in-law of George Lajoie, along with Tom and Corinne Barany and Gisele Verrisimo, provided translation between French and English, so I could communicate with people in France, understand memorials in Luxembourg, and learn from foreign books.

Pierre Briere ensured that a French citizen would present the French Legion of Honor Medal to my father. He also graciously answered my emailed questions and expressed his gratitude to my father by inviting him each year to the D-Day dinner at his restaurant, Elliot's Bistro in Milwaukee.

Alfred

Susan Retzer kindly "grabbed a frame" from the National Archive video when she was a referral of a referral from a referral at Milwaukee Area Technical College. We have never met.

John Aarsen and Rafael Alvarez from Fort Bragg's 82nd Airborne Division Museum tried to make sense of my questions and find documents from simple markings on a very old envelope.

Multiple people from the Wisconsin Veterans Museum have helped me to understand discharge papers and gain a general understanding of military terminology.

Geoff Gentilini from Golden Arrow Research became my requested gift for a couple of birthdays. He was able to be my "boots on the ground" at the National Personnel Records Center in St. Louis.

Orval Faubus and James Huston felt familiar to me because of their respective journals of *In This Faraway Land* and *Biography of a Battalion*. I could never have understood my father's experience without their detailed histories.

Making the book into an audible form was more involved than I expected. During one session, I spoke into the microphone to Chris, "At least you won't shoot me if I stutter." Very quietly from the next room, I heard, "Not yet." Thank you, Chris Kringel, for your patience.

I am truly grateful for the efforts of all these people to help me complete my father's journey.

ABOUT THE
AUTHOR

R aised with seven siblings on a farm in Lodi, Wisconsin, Louise Endres Moore graduated from St. Norbert College in Psychology with minors in Mathematics and Education. She taught in the Waukesha and Wauwatosa school districts until the births of her two daughters, Meg and Kate, and later completed a Master of Science in Computer Science Education from Cardinal Stritch University as an adjunct instructor at Milwaukee Area Technical College.

Her interest in psychology sustained her through the years of researching her father's path in World War II and his reluctance to speak of it.

Louise lives with her husband, Kelly, in Cedarburg, Wisconsin. Their two grown daughters, Meg and Kate, both live in Kansas City.

For more information, please visit www.AlfredtheBook.com